The Principles
of
Earned Value Management

A Cost and Schedule Control System

James Kudzal

Published by Brook-Anthony Corporation

Waldorf, Maryland

Cover by James Kudzal

Tables and Figures by James Kudzal

ISBN: -13: 978-1535222235

DEDICATION

To Tara,

The love of my life.

Thanks for your patience during the preparation of this book.

Contents

xi

INTRODUCTION

Believe it or not, every project doesn't go exactly as planned. In fact, you may have agreed to fund a project, only to see it come in over budget. Maybe you were a project manager and weren't happy when you had to deliver it behind schedule. How did you feel at that moment when you realized there was going to be a problem? If you found that it was then too late to turn things around, your experience is not uncommon.

This book is designed for anyone who would like to get advanced notice that their project is about to go out of control with respect to cost or schedule. It describes a simple, yet powerful tool known as Earned Value Management (also known as EVM or simply *Earned Value*). Earned Value will tell you, in no uncertain terms, how your project is unfolding with respect to

- ➲ the rate at which you are spending your money,

- ➲ the value you are getting for the cost you are incurring,

- ➲ the rate at which you are accomplishing work,

- ➲ and whether you are on track to meet your planned targets.

Not only will these tools be helpful for you in understanding your project, but they can also be used to communicate progress and expected outcomes with your management, customers, and other stakeholders. You will be more productive in meetings when you can share objective information relating to project status and forecasts.

Whether you are an EVM novice and want to get a better understanding of the subject, or an experienced user who wants to have a handy reference, this book was written for you. The material is intended to be understood by, and useful for, everyone from an executive sponsor, to a project/program manager, to a cost and schedule analyst.

If you are new to the subject, consider reading the chapters in sequence. The topics are developed step-by-step in a manner that makes the concepts easy to comprehend. The sections build on each other and often make reference to subject matter presented in earlier chapters. If you already have a good understanding of Earned Value and just want a refresher on a particular topic, you will find it easy to navigate among the chapters in any order that you wish.

Most of what you need for good EVM planning is already available in any well-developed project plan. Earned Value planning incorporates basic principles of project management such as task identification, cost budgeting, and scheduling. Chapter 2 is a review of those topics that are important to proper Earned Value planning.

The remaining chapters deal with the application of EVM while in the project implementation phase. We will develop the Earned Value concepts and indicators that you'll use in your analysis of project status, addressing issues like

➲ What data do we need to collect?

➲ How frequently should we do an analysis?

➲ What are the different measures of progress?

➲ When are these measures relevant?

➲ How do we interpret the results?

We'll also address the issue of forecasting, or making predictions about the future outcome of the project.

In addition to the standard indicators, you'll find some new ones that are being introduced here. We hope you'll find them useful and maybe they'll eventually be incorporated into the mainstream of EVM. These include Fiscal Variance, Cost Efficiency Improvement Factor, Schedule Efficiency Improvement Factor, Percent Concluded, and others. Also included is a discussion of Earned Schedule.

Each chapter has a set of exercises that are designed to enhance and reinforce the material presented there. There are many "learning moments" contained within the exercises so you are encouraged to do as many of these as you can.

So, let's get started.

Chapter 1

WHY USE EARNED VALUE?

What is Earned Value Management? Why has it become so popular? In this chapter we'll gain an appreciation for Earned Value as a cost and schedule control tool. Here we will see the many benefits the system has to offer before exploring the details of the process.

1-1 SIMPLE AND POWERFUL

As mentioned in the Introduction, Earned Value is the popular term used to refer to Earned Value Management, or EVM. It is a system of simple, but very powerful, indicators which allows us to determine the condition of our project with respect to the cost and progress of its work. While EVM refers to the entire collection of gauges and results that is the subject of this book, its name is derived from one of the key indicators that comprise the system.

Earned Value Management can assist us in understanding project status and in making forecasts about project outcomes. In addition, it can be used as an aid in communicating status and forecasts to others such as project sponsors or clients. We will be able to determine exactly how much our project varies from the planned budget or schedule. The specific indicators are relatively simple to calculate and easy to understand.

Earned Value is becoming more and more common as a standard project management evaluation and reporting tool. It is complementary to, and designed to be used in combination with, other project management performance indicators, such as product quality and critical path analysis, in order to give us a more complete understanding of project status. Let's see what makes EVM so popular.

1-2 OBJECTIVE MEASURE

The Earned Value Management system is comprised of a set of objective indicators. These provide us with hard numbers that allow us to understand

- ➲ how much our project is over budget or under budget for the work performed,

- ➲ how much work was actually performed vs. what was planned,

- ➲ how much value we received for each dollar spent,

- ➲ how much the project is ahead or behind schedule,

- ➲ how much the project is actually going to cost when it is completed,

- ➲ when we expect the project to actually be completed,

- ➲ and more.

We all know that figures can be misused, and that we can mislead others through the improper use of statistics. For instance, if we were told that 75% of all criminals drink coffee, would we conclude that coffee promotes bad behavior? If a report revealed to us that over 90% of drug addicts drank milk when they were children, would that be reason enough to ban dairy products?

Obviously, most of us are not fooled by these relationships, because we have a good understanding of the context in which they are applied. All the more reason it is important that we have a good understanding of EVM and what the numbers actually mean. Like any other system of figures, Earned Value numbers can be misused.

Figures can be provided in both relative and absolute terms, as well as incrementally and cumulatively. They each have their uses and care must be taken not to use them inappropriately.

The material that we will be exploring will give us an appreciation of how to properly obtain and use Earned Value data to evaluate our project. We will also understand how the figures can be misrepresented, and to guard ourselves against common misuse and misinterpretations.

1-3 GIVES US EARLY WARNING

Fluctuations in a project's cost or schedule are natural and inevitable, and most projects can accept some minor variation. When the difference between what was planned and what is actually occurring is very small, we're not too concerned. However, as the difference begins to grow, there comes a point at which it is no longer acceptable. The boundary between acceptable performance and unacceptable performance is known as the acceptable *tolerance limit*. If our project actuals go beyond the acceptable tolerance limit we say that the project is out of control.

For instance, suppose we have a one year project with a budget of $500,000, where the acceptable tolerance limits for cost are identified to be plus or minus five percent. This means that this project will be considered a success with respect to cost if it is completed within five percent ($25,000) of

$500,000.

Now we certainly don't want to wait until we get near the end of the project in order to determine whether we'll make it or not. By then it'll be too late to do anything about it if we are significantly off track. With Earned Value we'll be able to objectively understand the status of our project very near to its beginning.

The trick in successful project control is to monitor and evaluate on a regular and frequent basis. This will allow us to discover divergences before they become unacceptable and irreversible. Just like driving a car, it's a lot easier to stay in control by making frequent minor adjustments than having to rely on wild swings.

With EVM, we will know at the end of the very first reporting period whether or not we are operating at a pace to deliver the project within budget and schedule.

1-4 FLEXIBLE

Earned Value can be used for many types of projects. Whether we are developing software, designing the next generation of jet aircraft, or just building a doghouse in our back yard, we can utilize the tools of EVM. Once we learn the system and put it into practice, we will find that, while EVM may be applied differently for different needs and situations, the principles are the same.

EVM was originally conceived as a tool to assist the US Government in managing large scale acquisition programs. Because of this, it had a reputation in some circles as an overly bureaucratic measurement system requiring lots of overhead and support, and as such is not appropriate for smaller projects. Nothing could be further from the truth. EVM is appropriate for any size project, and for smaller ones it can be applied rather inexpensively.

Earned Value can also be applied at a variety of levels. While many focus on EVM indicators at the project level, EVM is also valid, appropriate, and indispensable when used at the subproject level, task level or anything in between. Most of the software packages will give us Earned Value data down to the individual task level.

As we will see, care must be taken to not rely only on the project-level indicators when analyzing the status of a project. Many times problems under the surface can be masked at the project level.

1-5 FACILITATES FORECASTING

EVM utilizes point-in-time analysis. We can find different sets of Earned Value data for different specific dates. This means that any time we produce a set of Earned Value data, we must realize that there is a *data date* associated with it. So, obviously, the data is valid only for that specific date. We often say that the EVM indicators are functions of time. What this means is that if we look at Earned Value figures for a different data date, we will likely see different results.

When presenting a set of Earned Value data, we must indicate the date for which it is relevant. Similarly, if we are reviewing Earned Value data prepared by others, we must make sure we are aware of the data date associated with the figures.

Comparisons among the different sets of data over time will allow us to generate trends and facilitate forecasting. Of course we will want to get enough actual data behind us to have good statistical significance before we put too much weight into our predictions, but we will be able to make those predictions nonetheless.

Exactly what happens in the future is unknown today of course, but we will be able to make educated guesses about the project outcome by combining Earned Value data with reasonable assumptions about how the project will unfold.

To guide us through the process, there are several chapters devoted to forecasting.

1-6 CUMULATIVE AND INCREMENTAL ANALYSIS

Earned Value indicators can be computed on an incremental or a cumulative basis. *Incremental data* will indicate how the project performed in the last period, say the last week. We can use *cumulative data* to determine exactly where the project is today for all the work that has been done so far.

Cumulative representations smooth out fluctuations in the incremental, or short-term, data. Obviously, the ultimate measure of project success will depend on how the cumulative data look at the end of the project. Incremental data, however, will be more sensitive to trend changes. As we'll see it is important to utilize both in order take advantage of the full power of EVM.

1-7 SOFTWARE SUPPORT EXISTS

The major general project management software tools on the market will compute Earned Value data for us automatically. There are also many specialized software packages that are focused more narrowly on the use of EVM tools and the preparation of Earned Value reports.

In either case, the main requirements are that we establish a project baseline plan, and that we enter *actual data* to reflect what is really happening in the project. The baseline is simply a list of tasks that need to be performed, a budgeted cost for each task, and the scheduled dates for when each task is to be performed. This will serve as the standard by which we will measure project performance.

The actual data will be compared with the baseline standard. The difference between what we wanted to accomplish and what actually happened is called a variance. If the variances are too large, we say that the project or one of its components is out of control.

All of the relevant software packages will give us tabular reports of the variances and other indicators. Some will also offer graphing capability. We will see similar presentations of earned value data in this book, and we will have the opportunity to generate our own when we play with the exercises at the end of each chapter.

1-8 IN WIDE USE

EVM is understood by professional project managers world-wide. The concepts and terminology are well-known. Professional certification exams for project managers have Earned Value as an important component. Many U.S. Government contracts require that Earned Value data be provided by the performing activity as a measure of project progress and as a means of determining payments.

As the power and simplicity of Earned Value becomes more and more appreciated, and as more organizations come to understand that it is relatively inexpensive to implement, we will find that Earned Value will take a more prominent role in the project control process.

EXERCISES

1-1: What is Earned Value Management? Who uses it and for what purposes?

1-2: What are tolerance limits and how do they relate to project control?

1-3: What does it mean that EVM analysis results are functions of time?

1-4: What types of projects are appropriate for Earned Value Management? How can EVM be applied differently for different types of projects?

1-5: What must be developed in the project planning phase in order to utilize the tools of EVM during the project implementation phase?

1-6: What is the difference between incremental and cumulative data? Why should both be considered?

1-7: What is forecasting? What role does it play in project management?

1-8: Perform some independent research on the history of Earned Value Management. When was it first developed and by whom? In what document was it first promulgated? How has EVM evolved over time?

Chapter 2

PLANNING FOR EARNED VALUE

While EVM is a tool that we use to track project progress during the implementation phase of a project, a proper foundation needs to be set during the planning phase in order to get the most out of the system. This chapter provides an overview of the planning processes that are essential for the proper preparation of Earned Value assessments. We'll also review some terms and definitions which we will need to understand in order to fully appreciate Earned Value as well as to implement it properly.

2-1 PROJECTS

A *project* is a vehicle through which we meet a set of objectives for a supervisor, sponsor, customer, or client. We will use the term *customer* to indicate anyone on the receiving end of a project, whether internal or external to our organization. While we can satisfy customers in many ways that do not include projects, projects have some properties that distinguish them from other business operations.

Projects are unique—no two are exactly alike. Projects have well-defined objectives and success criteria. Projects are temporary, i.e. there are definite start and end dates. Also, projects are change agents. Something is different in the organization after the project is completed than what was there before.

The *project team* is the group of people performing the work of the project, and they are led by a person known as the *project manager*. The project manager is responsible for the proper planning and implementation of the project.

2-2 REQUIREMENTS

Projects have clearly defined *deliverables*. Deliverables are items that are produced by the project team and can include products, services, or information. They are explicitly identified in the agreement documents (e.g., contracts or statements of work). Deliverables have *specifications* associated with them which describe their properties and acceptance criteria.

Also associated with deliverables are the methods by which their satisfactory delivery will be measured. This usually includes some test or inspection to verify compliance. The *quality* of a deliverable refers to the degree to which the completed deliverable meets (not necessarily exceeds) the intended specification. It is usually at the deliverable level that customers will accept and formally approve the work performed on the project.

Normally, acceptable *tolerance limits* are associated with the different criteria and verification methods, and these too are part of the specifications. The tolerance limits describe an acceptable range for a particular property of the deliverable. Deliverables with criteria outside of the acceptable tolerance range are rejected, while those within tolerance are accepted.

For example, assume we are producing a piece of equipment that will be a component of a satellite and this component has a weight specification of 14.8 pounds, plus or minus 0.2 pounds. If our deliverable weighs 15.2 pounds, it will be rejected because it will be out of tolerance with respect to weight.

While Earned Value does not address measuring quality directly, it is important to know what constitutes the successful completion of an activity in order to perform a proper EVM analysis. A task cannot be declared 100% complete unless its output, or work product, meets the quality standards.

As we will see, tolerance limits will also be specified with respect to cost and schedule, and EVM can be used to measure how well our project is performing within defined cost and schedule tolerance limits.

The set of deliverables is one part of the project *requirements*. In addition to the deliverables, other requirements must be considered in the performance of the project activities. These can include

➚ schedule or budgetary constraints,

➚ restrictions on availability of resources,

➚ organizational policies and procedures,

➚ demands for reporting frequency and format,

➚ customer preferences,

➚ and others.

The number and types of requirements in a single project can be quite extensive.

The goal is to have a clear, consistent, and unambiguous set of the requirements that can be agreed upon by all the parties involved. Depending on the project, this could take an extensive period of time and may require some negotiation. While it can be later modified, a base set of requirements is necessary to begin the next stage of project planning.

2-3 WORK BREAKDOWN STRUCTURE

Work must be performed in order to produce the deliverables and meet the other requirements. The next step in the planning process is to identify that work. The most commonly used tool for this is known as the *Work Breakdown Structure* or *WBS*. Figure 2-1 depicts an example of a simple WBS in graphic form. It is not intended to be necessarily complete, but rather just to illustrate the tool.

The WBS is hierarchical and resembles a personnel organization chart in form, but is designed to display the organization of the work within a project. It shows how the work can be subdivided, or decomposed, into smaller and smaller pieces.

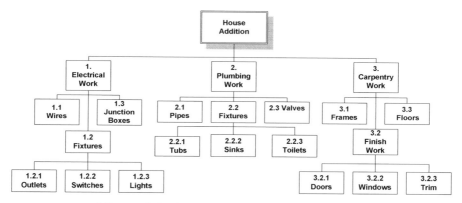

Figure 2-1: Graphical representation of a WBS

The top box represents the entire project. In this case, the project is to put an addition onto an existing house. The idea of the WBS is to decompose the work until we get to the level of detail to which we want to control.

Each box is labeled with a *WBS number*. The WBS number is used to help us easily differentiate among the separate boxes and serves as a handy reference. Notice that 1.2 and 2.2 are both entitled "Fixtures." They are obviously different because one is for electrical work and the other is for plumbing work. Using the WBS number will help us avoid confusion between the two items. All of the electrical work activities begin with "1," while all of the plumbing work activities begin with "2."

The WBS includes no information regarding the sequence in which the work must be performed. The WBS numbers have no meaning in terms of setting schedules. They are just unique identifiers like serial numbers. The purpose of the WBS is to identify **what** needs to be done, not the order in which it is done. That will come later when we do scheduling.

The activities at the finest level of detail in which we are interested are called *tasks* or *work packages*. It is at the task level that we will assign work to the project team members, distribute the budget, schedule the work, monitor progress, and control the project.

Each task produces an output called a *work product*. A work product could be a deliverable, a partial deliverable, a tool, verification results, or some other item required by the project. A work product is objective and measurable.

Think of the work product as the deliverable that the project team is producing for the project manager. The project manager will accept the team's output at the work package level. It's important to know what constitutes a successfully produced work product so it is clear to everyone when a task is fully complete.

Notice that the tasks in this example are expressed using nouns instead of verbs. They are being described in terms of their work products instead of the activities themselves. In this case the word "Install" was omitted from the name of each task in the interest of brevity. This is not a problem if the work is understood by all involved. However, sometimes the same item may have separate steps involved. For example, installing the valves and inspecting the valves may be two separate tasks. In this case, we may want to include the verbs in the task description for the sake of clarity.

The basic tasks or work packages are represented by the boxes at the lowest level of the WBS. Tasks do not all have to be on the same level, but none have more detail below them. In our example, the tasks are shown in Table 2-1. The other (higher level) boxes in the WBS represent *summary tasks*. Summary tasks are activities that are composed of other tasks.

WBS Number	Task Name
1.1	Wires
1.2.1	Outlets
1.2.2	Switches
1.2.3	Lights
1.3	Junction Boxes
2.1	Pipes
2.2.1	Tubs
2.2.2	Sinks
2.2.3	Toilets
2.3	Valves
3.1	Frames
3.2.1	Doors
3.2.2	Windows
3.2.3	Trim
3.3	Floors

Table 2-1: List of Project Tasks or Work Packages

There are no absolutes in determining the size of tasks. A rule of thumb is to make their duration appropriate to the level of control we feel we need to have over the work, i.e. how often we need to track progress. This can vary with factors such as the skill level of the people performing the work, the routineness of the work, and the frequency at which we can gather objective performance measurements.

Ideally, we'd like to have good objective measures at the end of every period at which we do our formal evaluations. For example, if we do a formal evaluation of project status on a weekly basis, we'd like to have something to report for every task in progress that week.

Task List: House Addition
1. Electrical Work
1.1 Wires
1.2 Fixtures
1.2.1 Outlets
1.2.2 Switches
1.2.3 Lights
1.3 Junction Boxes
2. Plumbing Work
2.1 Pipes
2.2 Fixtures
2.2.1 Tubs
2.2.2 Sinks
2.2.3 Toilets
2.3 Valves
3. Carpentry Work
3.1 Frames
3.2 Finish Work
3.2.1 Doors
3.2.2 Windows
3.2.3 Trim
3.3 Floors

Table 2-2: WBS in Outline Form

If our tasks are too small, the cost of tracking goes up and we'll be paying for reporting precision that we aren't using. If our tasks are too large, we'll be sacrificing objectivity in the measure of our task status. This can often be remedied, however, by identifying measurable milestones within the performance of a longer duration task. We will revisit this topic later when discussing how to determine the actual percent complete of a task in progress.

We must not forget to include any risk mitigation and project management activities that we need to support the project. These can include data gathering, report generation, organizing and developing resources, and communicating with stakeholders. They need to be planned, budgeted, and scheduled just like the technical tasks.

Using the graphic form of the WBS, like in Figure 2-1, is ideal for team brainstorming sessions and presentations because it is easy to see the relationships among the elements. Most software programs, however, do not have the ability to accept the data in this fashion. In this case we'll need to input the WBS in outline form. Table 2-2 shows the same WBS depicted in Figure 2-1, but expressed in outline form. The non-bold items are the basic tasks, and the bold items are summary tasks.

2-4 ESTIMATING AND BUDGETING

In order to perform our project tasks, we need to employ *resources*. Resources can be people, equipment, materials, facilities, tools, information, or anything else that we may need to produce the work products. We must identify the types of resources required, and then make the proper assignment of resources to the tasks in our WBS.

Every assignment will be followed by an *estimate*, or our best determination, of the amount of each resource to be used. This could be the number of labor hours, or the *effort*, for each person or the number of pounds of raw material that will go into a deliverable.

Since resources cost money we want to estimate the total cost for each resource and then the total cost of each task. This will be based on the charge rates and efforts of our human resources, and the unit costs and levels of usage of our material resources. For example, assume Task A requires 16 hours of a plumber's time, and the charge rate for the plumber is $70 per hour. The estimated cost is then $1120 (16 hours × $70/hour).

Our estimate for the cost of the entire project is simply the sum of costs for each individual task plus any reserve we'd like to add to cover risk. We refer to this as the *bottom-up* approach since we begin our estimating at the bottom level (work package level) of the WBS.

Sometimes we are able to estimate the cost of a project using a *top-down* approach. Instead of estimating the cost of each individual task and adding those up, we could estimate the cost at the project level. For example, many housing contractors have formulas that they use to estimate this way. For a given style house it may cost a certain number of dollars per square foot. Multiplying this by the area of the planned house the contractor can come up with a figure for the total project without first having to estimate at the work package level.

This method may work well for us too if we have a lot of historical data and confidence behind this approach.

Regardless of which estimating method is used, we will still need to budget our money at the task level. This way, during implementation, we can compare budgeted costs with actual costs task by task.

It's probably worthwhile spending a moment to discuss the difference between estimating and a budgeting. The cost estimate is our best assessment of what we believe the work will cost when we actually go to perform it. Our budget represents how much money we are planning to devote to the work. Since the budget is what we are planning to spend, we must be prepared to manage the work to that level. Obviously, our budget should nearly match our estimate.

Here we want to avoid a common pitfall. We do not want to generate our estimates from the budget. Even if we are given a budget to do the project ahead of time, we can't ignore the step of doing a credible estimate. If all we do is allocate the budget dollars among the tasks (i.e. perform a budgeting exercise), and don't do a proper estimate, we will have no idea if the work can be done for that amount of money or not. We'll be flying blind.

It's OK to get our budget first, but we must then validate that figure by doing a proper estimate. If our estimate is significantly higher than the budget, then we need to have discussions with the appropriate stakeholders. If we agree to a budget that we know is impossible to meet, we've just agreed to fail. In this case no system, not even EVM, will be able to help us be successful.

In addition to generating a budgeted cost for each task, we also need to determine each task's *duration*. The duration represents how much time, on the calendar, it will take to perform a task. This is different from the effort described earlier. As an example, consider a plan to have two people working simultaneously on a task devoting an effort of 32 hours each. The total effort, or work, will be 64 person-hours. If both workers are available 8 hours per day, the duration of the task will be four days.

We use the duration to schedule the work and to see how the cost is distributed over time. Having the duration of each task will be necessary in order for us to set up our schedule, which is another mandatory ingredient for proper Earned Value analysis.

2-5 SCHEDULING

Projects take time. The collection of planned start and finish dates for the performance of our project tasks is called the *schedule*. The difference in time between the start date of the first task and the end of the last task is the project duration.

It is more complicated to determine a project's duration than it is to determine its total cost. The cost of a project is one dimensional; it's simply the sum of the costs of the individual tasks. Since usually some of the tasks can be performed concurrently, the duration of the project is normally less than the sum of the durations of the individual tasks.

Certain tasks need to be performed in a particular sequence. Before we assemble our schedule, we need to gain an understanding of how our tasks depend on each other. For instance, we cannot begin product testing until the developed product is complete.

A *Precedence Diagram* is a convenient way to graphically depict the relationships between the tasks and their sequencing. It displays the flow of work throughout the project. Figure 2-2 is an example of a Precedence Diagram for a very simple project. Note that this is not the same project we used earlier in our WBS discussion.

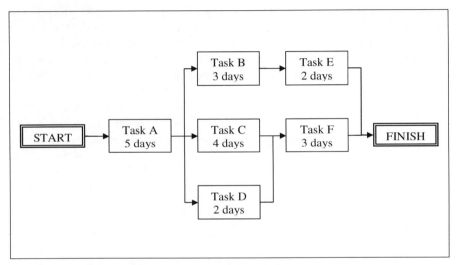

Figure 2-2: Precedence Diagram

The boxes represent the tasks and the arrows show the relationships (or dependencies) between the tasks. We also see a "Start" milestone and a "Finish" milestone. The work of the project originates at the Start, proceeds through the network in sequence in the direction of the arrows, and is complete when the Finish is reached.

The Precedence Diagram must contain all of the tasks in the WBS. These include the technical work, project management support work, and the risk mitigation activities. The only things we should omit at this stage are the contingency plans we've identified to address certain risks. This is because we don't know if we'll need to perform this work or not.

The dependencies between the tasks for a project will depend upon the approach that we decide to pursue in developing our project deliverables.

Even though there is a general flow of time from Start to Finish through the network, it is **not** on a time scale. That is, we cannot draw a horizontal axis, label it with dates, and determine when things occur based on the location of the box. The absolute position of the boxes has no meaning in terms of when the tasks are to be accomplished. Also note that the boxes are all the same size and independent of the task durations.

In this example we have six tasks to perform. Task A can start immediately when the project starts. Tasks B, C, and D cannot begin until Task A is completed. This is because they need the output, or work product, of Task A as an input to begin their efforts. Task E cannot begin until Task B is completed. Task F must wait until both Tasks C and D are completed before it can begin. And finally, the project cannot be finished until both Tasks E and F are completed.

If each task is scheduled to be performed as soon as possible (based on the durations and restrictions imposed by the dependencies), then the planned dates for each task are represented in Table 2-3. The First Day represents the earliest day of the project that the task can begin, assuming the task starts that morning. The Last Day represents the last day of activity of the task, assuming that the task is completed that evening. Note that these dates represent *work* days after the start of the project and not calendar days.

As we can see from the table, the duration of the project is 12 work days. This is, of course, because the project will end when the last task finishes. The sum of the task durations, however, is 19 days. There is a difference because we are planning to perform some tasks concurrently.

Notice that there are three paths through the network in Figure 2-2: A-B-E, A-C-F, and A-D-F. If we add up the durations along each of these paths, we get the data shown below.

➲   A-B-E   10 days

➲   A-C-F   12 days

➲   A-D-F   10 days

Task Name	Duration [days]	First Day [morning]	Last Day [evening]
A	5	1	5
B	3	6	8
C	4	6	9
D	2	6	7
E	2	9	10
F	3	10	12
Project	12	1	12

Table 2-3: Project Schedule

We can see that A-C-F is the longest path and its duration matches the project duration. The tasks A-C-F, performed in this order, require 12 work days to perform. The other paths require less time. There is no down time or days of inactivity along the path A-C-F, while the other two paths are shorter by two days, so they each have two days of inactivity available at some time during the project.

Since the project duration is defined by the duration of the path A-C-F, it is critical that Tasks A, C, and F are not delayed since this would impact the finish date of the project. Because of this, Tasks A, C, and F are known as *critical tasks*. This does not mean that they are inherently more important than the other tasks. It just means that the way this schedule is constructed, if any of these critical tasks is delayed, the project will be delayed day for day.

The critical tasks form a path called the *critical path*. It is important to identify the critical path because we want to pay special attention to it when we implement the project. We will find that the critical path will always be the longest path (in terms of cumulative duration) through the network. Also, the critical path defines the project duration.

Each other path through our network has a duration of 10 days. This means that there are 2 days of margin available on these other paths to absorb some delay without impacting the planned project completion date. These 2 days of margin are known as *slack* or *float*. For example, Tasks B and E can be up to two days late (together) without impacting the project. Task D can also be two days late.

Remember that the assumption in assembling our schedule in Table 2-3 was that each task would start as soon as possible based on the restrictions imposed by the dependencies. These dependencies are, however, only one set of constraints that we will need to consider. Other factors can affect how we structure our schedule as well. For example, if all of the resources won't be available on the dates we'd like to use them, we may need to reschedule some activities.

Before we can finalize the schedule, we must ensure that it is realistic, achievable, meets all of the constraints, and satisfies our customer's expectations. This isn't always easy, and sometimes it may take several iterations and trials before we get everything to come together.

It's beyond the scope here to discuss methods and strategies for creating the perfect schedule. In this case, we are going to assume that the dates represented in Table 2-3 are satisfactory.

The next step, in preparation for Earned Value Management planning, is to depict the task schedules on a time scale. The most common representation is known as a *Gantt Chart*. We can see the Gantt Chart for our project in Figure 2-3. Here the tasks are listed down the first column. We may choose any order we'd like. Here they are in alphabetical order by task identifier.

On the horizontal is a time scale. Normally these would be actual calendar dates, but here we are just looking at the number of work days after project initiation. Using relative dates like this is a common representation during planning, especially if the planned start date is as yet unknown.

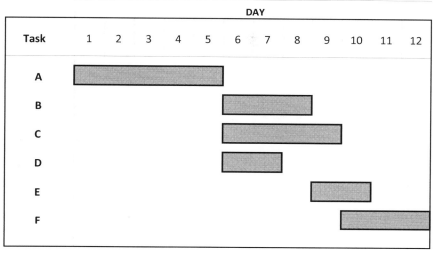

Figure 2-3: Gantt Chart

There is one horizontal bar representing each task. The length of the bar corresponds to the duration of the task. The position of the bar under the calendar indicates when the task is scheduled to be in progress. Gantt charts are very popular because they are intuitive and present snapshots of when the work is planned to take place.

2-6 SPENDING PLAN

Now that we know when the tasks are planned to be performed, we can combine this information with the task budgets in order to develop a spending plan. Let's assume that the budgeted cost for each task is as shown in Table 2-4. The budget for the entire project is $4000.

Task	Duration [days]	Budget [$]
A	5	1100
B	3	600
C	4	600
D	2	500
E	2	300
F	3	900
Project	**12**	**4000**

Table 2-4: Project Budget

The total project budget of $4000 is also known as the project BAC or *Budget at Completion*. The BAC is defined to be the total amount of money budgeted to do the work in question, in this case the entire project.

The total budget to perform each task is known as the task BAC. The task BACs add up to give us the project BAC.

We can see from this that the Budget column in Table 2-4 could have been labeled as the BAC column. In this case it's just another name for the same item. We will be using the term Budget at Completion extensively in later chapters.

Next we want to allocate these funds over time. For simplicity we'll assume that the budget for each task will be evenly distributed over the duration of the task (keeping in mind that this won't be true for every project). We can then determine the cost per day for each task. The result is in Table 2-5.

Task	Duration [days]	Budget [$]	Budget/Day [$]
A	5	1100	220
B	3	600	200
C	4	600	150
D	2	500	250
E	2	300	150
F	3	900	300
Project	**12**	**4000**	

Table 2-5: Cost Breakout

Now we can spread the daily budget for each task over the days that the task is scheduled to be in progress. This is shown in Table 2-6. In a situation where a task did not have its budget evenly distributed over time, the table should realistically reflect the distribution in the plan.

Notice that this is similar to the Gantt chart, with the bars replaced by numbers. The numbers in the body of the table represent the cost per day budgeted for each task. If we add horizontally for each task, we get the total cost for that task.

If we add vertically, we can see from the Total row near the bottom the amount of money we plan to spend for the entire project each individual day. The bottom row (Cum Total) displays how much money we are planning to spend on a cumulative basis from the beginning of the project through any given date. This data is important for several reasons.

	Day											
Task	1	2	3	4	5	6	7	8	9	10	11	12
A	220	220	220	220	220							
B						200	200	200				
C						150	150	150	150			
D						250	250					
E									150	150		
F										300	300	300
Total	220	220	220	220	220	600	600	350	300	450	300	300
Cum Total	220	440	660	880	1100	1700	2300	2650	2950	3400	3700	4000

Table 2-6: Project Cost Profile (all figures in dollars)

We need to have a good understanding of where the money is going and when we are planning to use it. It is also important that we share this information with the people who are funding the project. We need to make sure that they can provide the funds at least at this level since this is the rate we are planning to spend the money. If they can't, then our schedule may be a bit too ambitious and will need to be modified.

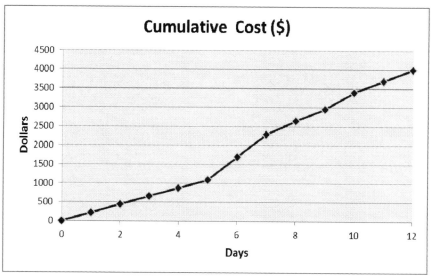

Figure 2-4: Cumulative Planned Cost

These funding requirements can be depicted graphically. If we plot the Cum Total in Table 2-6 vs. time, we get the curve in Figure 2-4. This represents the cumulative cost to be incurred by the project if all the work goes according to plan.

This information will also be used when we implement our plan. Once we begin performing the tasks and spending actual money, we'll be able to compare the actual spending with our plan to get a sense of how our plan is progressing. This factors into how we will judge the performance of the project. If we don't have a standard, we don't have a reference point from which to do this measurement.

2-7 BASELINE

When everything falls into place and there is mutual agreement between the parties involved, a baseline is created. The *baseline plan* refers to the formally approved plan that is acceptable to both the customer and the project team. This baseline will be the roadmap for how the project will be implemented, and will be the standard by which successful project performance will be judged.

Keep in mind that there are many other facets to project planning that we did not discuss here. Our focus was to develop the items necessary to support EVM during the implementation phase.

While the planning processes described here are presented in an idealized fashion, with sequential stages, real-world planning is an iterative process. Whenever we move to a new stage, we may develop additional information that would cause us to reconsider and adjust some of the results we developed in an earlier stage.

When the plan evolves to the point where both parties are willing to agree with its contents, they normally sign a document to that effect. This agreement document could be as formal as a contract between separate legal entities, or just a letter of understanding between two groups in the same organization.

The plan that is attached to that agreement document is now called the baseline plan. It documents the shared understanding of the project objectives, and will be the basis by which the project success will be measured. Once it becomes official, the only way a baseline plan can be modified is through a *change*.

A change is an intentional modification to the baseline. It usually includes a fair amount of documentation, and requires the formal approval of both parties. This signed document, which authorizes an amendment to the project baseline is called a *change order*.

There may be many changes over the life of a project, and, hence, many baselines. There is, however, only one baseline at a time. When we measure project status, we must compare the actual outcomes relative to the current official baseline.

After the baseline is set, we often refer to the cumulative Planned Cost curve as the cumulative Baseline Cost curve. It can be drawn with or without the individual data points. See Figure 2-5 for the graph without the data points.

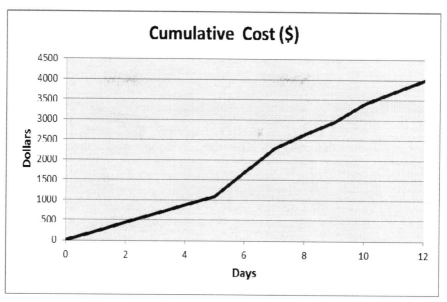

Figure 2-5: Cumulative Baseline Cost Curve

2-8 SUMMARY

The following parts of the baseline plan will be important in order to perform an Earned Value analysis:

- A complete list of tasks to be performed. These should include any risk mitigation and project management activities.

- A budgeted cost for each task.

- The planned start and finish dates for each task.

- The criteria to determine when a task is satisfactorily complete.

Now that we have a baseline plan, we are ready to begin the project implementation phase. Two sets of activities are taking place in that phase. The first is *project execution*. This is where we carry out the work described in the baseline plan. We verify that the project team is prepared, the tools and materials are available, and the path is clear for the work to be performed as planned.

The second component of implementation is *project control*. This is where we monitor actual performance and determine if the project is proceeding as planned. If we find ourselves over budget or behind schedule, we need to identify the root cause and then take the appropriate corrective action.

In the next chapter we will begin our discussion of project control and how Earned Value Management helps us to identify project status. In later chapters we'll look at forecasting and how we can use EVM to make predictions about the future.

EXERCISES

2-1: Identify the information necessary to be developed during the planning phase in order to properly utilize EVM during project implementation. Why are these needed? How will they be used?

2-2: What is the difference between an estimate and a budget?

2-3: Explain the purpose of the WBS. What is a work package?

2-4: What is a requirement? Explain how requirements fit into the project planning process.

2-5: Describe the difference between a work product and a deliverable.

2-6: What are the differences between a Precedence Diagram and a Gantt Chart? When would each be used?

2-7: What is the significance of the critical path? How can it be identified? Can a project have more than one? Why or why not?

2-8: Use the data in the table below for this exercise.

    a) Draw the Precedence Diagram and identify the critical path.

    b) If every task is planned to begin as soon as possible, what are the scheduled start and finish dates for each task?

    c) Determine the project duration.

    d) What is the project BAC?

    e) Draw the Gantt Chart depicting the soon-as-possible schedule.

    f) Determine the cumulative funding by day needed to support the schedule as planned, and plot these points on a graph to generate a cumulative Baseline Cost curve. Assume that the budget for each task can be applied evenly over the life of the task.

Task ID	Predecessor	Duration [days]	Budget [$]
A	–	4	480
B	–	2	130
C	A	3	420
D	A	6	900
E	A, B	3	510
F	C	2	180
G	E	1	100
H	D, F	3	420

Chapter 3

VARIANCE AND VALUE

3-1 BASELINE PLAN

At this point we are assuming that all of the planning activities we discussed in the last chapter have been completed. The tasks are identified, the budgeted cost and schedule for each of these tasks are known, and baseline plan has been prepared and approved.

A cumulative cost curve has been generated from the data in our baseline plan. A sample idealized cumulative Baseline Cost curve is shown in Figure 3-1. This represents the total amount of money that we are planning to spend from the beginning of the project through a given date. For example, if "Today" were the end of Week 25, we should have spent $500,000 if everything went according to plan.

In this example we can see that the project has a Budget at Completion, or BAC, of $1 million. The BAC is the total amount of money that we are planning to spend on the project to perform all the tasks in our schedule.

There may be additional funds incorporated into the project budget that are not part of the BAC. These would include any *reserves* set aside to address risks that we've chosen to handle by contingencies or for unidentified risks. Since we are not intending to spend these funds, we exclude them from the BAC. We can see the relationship among these items in the following equation.

$$\begin{matrix} Total \\ Project \\ Budget \end{matrix} = \begin{matrix} Budget \\ at \\ Completion \end{matrix} + Reserves$$

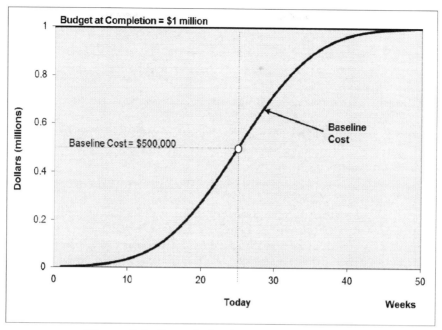

Figure 3-1: Cumulative Baseline Cost Curve

In a later chapter we will address how to incorporate any of the reserves we may need to use into our analysis.

We can see that the duration of this sample project is 50 weeks, at which time the entire BAC is planned to have been spent. We refer to this interval of time as the project *Planned Duration*, or PD.

3-2 VARIANCE

When the implementation phase of our project begins, and we actually start performing work, we will be able to collect data indicating what is actually happening in the project. We can then compare these actual figures with our baseline and make judgments about how well the project is progressing. The measured difference between the actual and the plan is called a *variance*.

If the project in Figure 3-1 were complete, and ended up with a total actual cost of $1,090,000, we would say that the project was delivered over budget with a variance of magnitude $90,000. We can measure variances in a number of variables such as cost, effort, time, amount of material used, etc. Of course we don't have to wait until the end of the project to begin measuring variances. In fact we can measure these at any point in time and we want to get started as soon as possible.

A certain amount of variance can be tolerated. If the variance grows to a particular level, however, it will be considered unacceptable. The boundary between the acceptable range and the unacceptable range is known as the *acceptable tolerance limit*. If the project in Figure 3-1 had an acceptable cost variance of plus or minus 10%, we would say that any total cost at the end of the project between $900,000 and $1,100,000 would be acceptable, i.e. within 10% of the BAC.

Indicators with variances that are on the acceptable side of the tolerance limit are said to be *within tolerance*. Those with variances outside of the acceptable limit are said to be *out of tolerance*. A project is deemed to be *out of control* when at least one major indicator is out of tolerance. Therefore, assuming an acceptable tolerance limit of plus or minus 10%, our earlier example of a $1,090,000 total project cost would be within tolerance, and thus be considered acceptable.

The acceptable tolerance limits for all the important indicators should be identified in the baseline plan. This will ensure that everyone is aware of how the success of the project will judged. As we will see, Earned Value Management makes extensive use of variances and tolerance limits.

If changes occur, they will be incorporated into the plan by providing a new set of baseline figures from which variances can then be measured. Variances are always measured from the current officially approved baseline plan.

3-3 ACTUAL COST (AC)

As the work in the project progresses, actual costs are being incurred. These can be compiled and tracked on an incremental and a cumulative basis. We can plot the cumulative data on a graph and generate a curve that we call the cumulative *Actual Cost* curve. In later chapters we'll discuss how we make use of the incremental data.

This Actual Cost, or AC, curve represents how much money was spent through today to perform the work that was actually accomplished. The information to generate this curve can come from time card data for internal labor, or invoices for procured materials or contract labor.

As we are compiling our actual cost data, we need to include *all* of the costs for the work actually performed whether or not we have actually yet paid for that work. The accounting should be on an accrual basis and not a cash basis.

For example, assume that we are using a subcontractor to install a heating unit in a building we are constructing. If the subcontractor has completed all of the work satisfactorily, but has not invoiced us yet for its effort, should we include the cost of that installation in our total Actual Cost figure for today?

The answer is yes! We need to include all costs which we are obligated to pay, **for the work performed**, whether or not we have actually paid for it yet. This may require us to contact the subcontractor to verify the cost so we will know what figure to include in our analysis. If that is not available, then the figure will need to be estimated.

This is a very important point. If the Actual Cost is not constructed properly, it would be easy for someone to misrepresent the status of the project by deferring cash payments or by making advanced payments. In the example above, if we took credit for work being performed, as we should, but indicated that it cost nothing, this would skew the results and indicate an unrealistically high cost efficiency.

The term *Actual Disbursement* is commonly used to describe the actual cash paid out of the project as of today regardless of actual work performed. The un-invoiced work completed by the subcontractor will yield no contribution to the Actual Disbursement. Similarly, if we prepaid for materials to be used in a future task, we will have a contribution toward Actual Disbursement, but no contribution to Actual Cost until the material is used.

We will not be working with Actual Disbursements here. It's not that tracking Actual Disbursements is not important. It does have its role in financial management, but it is not a part of Earned Value Management.

Figure 3-2 depicts the cumulative Actual Cost curve for our sample project. As we can see, the Actual Cost we have incurred through today is $300,000. The difference between the Actual Cost and the Baseline Cost is a variance. In this case, the magnitude of the variance is $200,000.

This is but one example of the many types of variances that we are likely to encounter. It is a very popular one however, and one we may see in many project status reports.

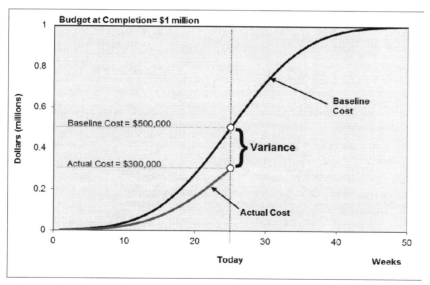

Figure 3-2: Variance between Actual Cost and Baseline Cost

3-4 FISCAL VARIANCE (FV)

The variance in Figure 3-2 goes by many names. Some **incorrectly** refer to this as the Cost Variance. This is **not** the Cost Variance! We will see in the next chapter that the Cost Variance is something different entirely.

The correct name for this is the *Spending Variance*. The Baseline Cost refers to the amount of money we had budgeted to spend if the project went according to plan. The Actual Cost refers to the amount of money that we actually spent to perform the work accomplished to date. The difference then is a spending variance.

While it is perfectly acceptable to use Spending Variance, we're not going to use it here in order to avoid the use of the initials SV, which we want to reserve for Schedule Variance to be introduced later.

Instead, we'll use the synonymous term *Fiscal Variance* to refer to the difference between the Actual Cost and the Baseline Cost. The term *fiscal* is already in wide use by governments and other organizations when referring to their spending. For example, the U.S. Congress commonly refers to their spending plan as their Fiscal Plan.

To be more precise, the Fiscal Variance, or FV, is calculated by subtracting the Actual Cost from the Baseline Cost as can be seen in the following equation.

$$\frac{Fiscal}{Variance} = \frac{Baseline}{Cost} - \frac{Actual}{Cost}$$

Going back to our sample project, we can see the Fiscal Variance identified in Figure 3-3. For today, the Fiscal Variance = $500,000 - 300,000 = $200,000, which means that as of Week 25, the project spent $200,000 less than had been planned.

This is obviously a very large variance (percentage-wise) and would be a major cause for concern in a real project. However, in this chart, the magnitude of the variance was made intentionally large in order to clearly illustrate the elements.

We could calculate FV on any earlier date as well. The date for which the variance is valid is known as the *data date*. Of course, different data dates generally give us different values for the Fiscal Variance. Any time we prepare variance data, it is important to include the date for which the figures are valid, otherwise the report is incomplete.

A positive Fiscal Variance indicates that we spent less money than we planned as of the data date, while a negative FV indicates that we spent more than planned. It is generally considered to be bad if the project requires more money than planned. The customer may be required to produce more funding than anticipated to support the project, resulting in a potential hardship. It is not normally a hardship to the customer to ask for less money than planned.

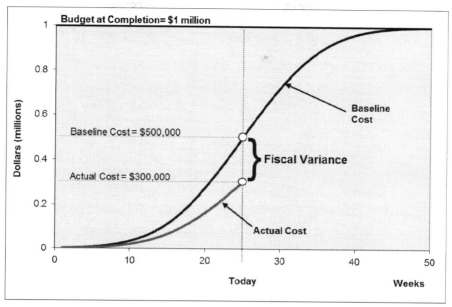

Figure 3-3: Fiscal Variance = Baseline Cost – Actual Cost

3-5 INTERPRETATION OF FISCAL VARIANCE

Let's see if we can interpret how the Fiscal Variance can aid us in our project performance analysis. Assume we have a project where the cumulative Baseline Cost to date is $20,000 and the cumulative Actual Cost is $19,000. How is this project doing so far?

a) Good

b) Bad

c) Not enough information to determine

First of all, we can compute the Fiscal Variance. FV = $1,000. A positive result indicates that we actually spent $1,000 less than we had planned to spend so far.

Many would say that the project is doing well. Our management may not be concerned. Our contacts in the finance department are surely pleased, because the project is not putting any pressure on them to come up with more money than what was indicated in the plan. With this reasoning we might choose "a" as our answer.

The correct answer, though, is "c." We don't have enough information to determine the status of the project. Why is this? First, let's consider some of the possible causes for a positive Fiscal Variance:

a) We could have estimated incorrectly when we put our plan together. It now turns out that the actual costs are less than planned. This could be good. It may allow us to free up funds and apply them to other tasks or projects.

b) Maybe the project is way behind schedule. We haven't spent the money because we haven't completed as much work as planned. This is bad, because our project could still fail if we miss our planned due date.

c) This could be a symptom of someone cutting corners on project deliverables. Maybe inferior quality materials are being used, or processes are not being performed as they should be. This is obviously bad and would need to be corrected.

d) There is some genuine cost savings due to the application of new technologies or a more efficient process than planned. This is certainly good, for it may allow us to deliver the project under budget.

Now consider if the situation were reversed, and the Fiscal Variance was calculated to be negative (the project spent more money than planned as of today). What could be some of the causes here?

a) We may have underestimated the cost of the work when the plan was put together. In this case, our budget is likely insufficient, which is manifested by the current overspending. Clearly, the situation is bad, and we may need to get more funding in order to complete the project.

b) Maybe we estimated correctly, but are having more than our typical share of problems in this particular project. Problems are occurring that are driving up the cost. This will also have a negative impact on our project.

c) Our tasks are costing what we budgeted, but the project is ahead of schedule. Doing some work earlier than planned will front load the spending, but maybe the total project will not cost any more than the total planned budget when it's over. While this could still be a problem in the short term if there are cash flow issues, some stakeholders may be very happy with an early delivery. So it's possible to be good in the long term.

As we can see, the results of a positive *or* negative Fiscal Variance do not give us the entire picture. FV tells us how much money we have spent vs. what we had planned to spend against the calendar. It does not tell us how the project is doing for work performed so far. It's possible that the project is over budget for each task performed, but if the project is far enough behind schedule, we will still calculate a positive FV.

Notice that with either a positive or negative Fiscal Variance, the situation could be good or bad. Also, the variance could be for a cost reason or for a schedule reason. It's just too difficult to tell what is going on based on the Fiscal Variance alone. This is because we have cost and schedule information co-mingled in a single figure.

This doesn't mean that the Fiscal Variance is unimportant. Senior management, finance departments, and customers may be focusing on this figure. If they do not understand EVM, this may be an important indicator for them, and we need to explain why it has the value it has.

For this reason alone, the Fiscal Variance is worth knowing. In fact, even for project managers, it is not entirely useless as an indicator, it's just rather limited in giving a good understanding of how well the project is progressing with respect to cost or schedule. It's even less valuable in helping forecast how the project will end.

This limitation in Fiscal Variance is the reason Earned Value Management was developed. As we will soon see, we can decouple the cost and schedule information and look at each of these components separately. The other variances and indicators that we will develop are a lot more indicative of the true status of our project. With these we will have a better understanding of how our project is actually performing.

3-6 VALUE

An important step in understanding EVM is to agree on a definition of the term *value*. Here it does not have the same use as in many other management disciplines such as salvage value, market value, appraised value, replacement value, or book value. This is our definition.

> *The value of any piece of work is defined*
> *to be the budgeted cost to do that work as*
> *expressed in the baseline plan.*

This applies to any piece of work, whether it is a task, a summary task, a subproject, or a full project. The value is independent of the actual cost of performing that work.

As an example, look at the data in Table 3-1, which is a project that we used in the previous chapter. At that time we said that the Budget column could be labeled as the BAC column. Well, we can give that column yet another name—we can call it the Value column.

Notice that the budget for Task A is $1100. That means that the value of Task A is $1100 by definition. Assuming that there will be no change orders affecting Task A, then the value of Task A will always be $1100, no matter what the actual cost will be to perform it.

Now, let's assume we have completed the task and that the Actual Cost turned out to be $1200. We'll further assume that this over-spending, or variance, was not due to anything that went wrong during implementation. Instead, our analysis revealed that we estimated the cost of this task incorrectly. We determined now that it really *does* cost $1200 to perform this task. In fact, if we plan to perform this task in any future project, we're going to budget $1200 to do the work, because that's the correct amount.

Task	Duration [days]	Budget [$]
A	5	1100
B	3	600
C	4	600
D	2	500
E	2	300
F	3	900
Project	**12**	**4000**

Table 3-1: Project Budget

For the balance of *this* project, however, the value of the task is still $1100, because that's what's in the baseline plan. The only way we can modify the value of a piece of work is to have a change order and officially amend the baseline plan.

The point of all this is to emphasize that the value of a piece of work is defined when we set our baseline plan, and is independent of the actual cost that we discover later when we perform the work, regardless of the reason.

Another way to think of *value* is as a measure of accomplishment. When we perform a piece of work, we deliver the value associated with that work. While we will be expressing value most commonly in units of dollars, value can also be expressed in hours, work products, or any other set of units.

So, from now on, any time we see the word "value" associated with any figure in the EVM system, it will indicate budgeted money (not actual money) by definition.

3-7 PLANNED VALUE (PV)

The value of a piece of work represents the cost of doing the work as expressed in budgeted dollars. If we determine how much value we plan to deliver, period by period, over the life of a project, we can draw a cumulative *Planned Value* curve. This Planned Value, or PV, curve represents the value of the work that we plan to deliver over time. An example of a Planned Value curve can be seen in Figure 3-4.

This looks suspiciously like our cumulative Baseline Cost curve, and numerically it is identical. Since our plan is to deliver the work on budget, i.e. for its planned cost, we of course find that the Planned Value curve equals the Baseline Cost curve.

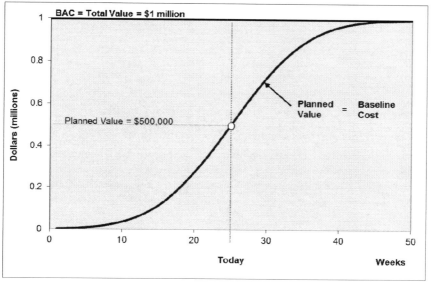

Figure 3-4: Cumulative Planned Value Curve

Planned Value is usually used when making reference to the *work* involved. Baseline Cost is used when referring to the planned *cost* to deliver that work. Practically speaking, though, the terms may be used interchangeably in calculations, because they will yield the same numerical results. We will never get in trouble if we mix them up.

Notice that Planned Value has the word "value" in its name. This means that, by definition, it is expressed in budgeted (or baseline) dollars and not actual dollars. The EVM system normally uses the term Planned Value for these curves, and we will follow that convention here. So for our purposes:

$$\frac{Planned}{Value} = \frac{Baseline}{Cost}$$

Just think of it as a different name for the same item. From this point onward, we'll begin using the term Planned Value in place of the Baseline Cost.

Later we will be introducing another term called Earned Value which will also be expressed in budgeted dollars. At that time the term Baseline Cost may be considered to be ambiguous, since we'll have two items expressed in baseline dollars. The Planned Value will then be a more precise term; it indicates how much value is planned to be delivered during a given period of time as well as the amount of money budgeted to do that work.

The Fiscal Variance can then be redefined as follows. This is the form we will be using from now on.

$$\frac{Fiscal}{Variance} = \frac{Planned}{Value} - \frac{Actual}{Cost}$$

3-8 SUMMARY

⮕ The reserves are not part of the Budget at Completion.

⮕ Variances are used to describe the differences between our plans and what actually occurred.

⮕ The Actual Cost must include all of the money that we are obligated to pay for the work actually accomplished, regardless of whether a payment was made or not.

⮕ The Fiscal Variance alone is not sufficient to give us a good understanding of how well the project is progressing.

⮕ In the EVM system, the word "value" will always indicate budgeted money and never actual money.

⮕ Planned Value will now be used in place of Baseline Cost to represent the spending plan.

The questions that were addressed in this chapter are summarized in Table 3-2. The formulas introduced in this chapter are summarized in Table 3-3.

Question	Answer
How much money was budgeted to perform all of the work?	BAC
What is the value of all the work to be performed?	BAC
How much time was planned to perform all of the work?	PD
How much money was actually spent through today?	AC
How much money was planned to be spent through today?	PV

Question	Answer
How much work was planned to be performed through today?	PV
How much less (or more) money was spent than planned through today?	FV

Table 3-2: Question Summary

Total Project Budget	=	Budget at Completion	+ Reserves
Fiscal Variance	=	Baseline Cost	− Actual Cost
Fiscal Variance	=	Planned Value	− Actual Cost

Table 3-3: Formula Summary

EXERCISES

3-1: What type of funds does the BAC include and exclude?

3-2: What is the definition of "value" as applied to EVM? How does it relate to Actual Cost?

3-3: Describe the differences between Actual Cost and Actual Disbursement.

3-4: What is the difference between a change and a variance? When are each of them used?

3-5: How do the cumulative Baseline Cost curve and the cumulative Planned Value curve differ? Why can they be used interchangeably in calculations?

3-6: Consider a project with a Fiscal Variance of −$20,000. What does this mean? What are some possible explanations for this?

3-7: As of today, the Actual Cost for a particular project is $10,000 while the Planned Value is $10,500. What is the Fiscal Variance? Is this good or bad? Why?

3-8: Fifteen percent of a $120,000 project was planned to be complete as of today, while $20,000 has been spent so far. What is the Fiscal Variance? What are some possible causes to explain this situation?

Chapter 4

COST VARIANCE AND SCHEDULE VARIANCE

In this chapter, we introduce Cost Variance and Schedule Variance, show how they relate to Fiscal Variance, and see how these can be used to interpret project performance.

4-1 BASELINE PLAN

Figure 4-1 is a Gantt chart of the baseline plan for a sample project we'll be working with in this chapter. To keep things simple, we'll assume that there will be no changes to the baseline over the life of this project. We are also not considering any reserves.

Task	Budget	Actual Cost	January	February	March
A	$10,000		▭		
B	$9,000		▭		
C	$16,000			▭	
D	$8,000			▭	
E	$7,000				▭
F	$19,000				▭
Monthly Planned Value			$19,000	$24,000	$26,000
Cumulative Planned Value			$19,000	$43,000	$69,000

Figure 4-1: Project Baseline Plan

Notice that the plan is to perform six tasks over a three-month period. Two tasks are planned for January, two in February, and finally the last two in March. Note that each task is planned to start and be complete within a single calendar month. Later we'll look at examples of projects where the activities span reporting periods.

The tasks are identified by the letters A through F. Next to each task name is the budgeted (or baseline) cost for performing the task. As we defined in

37

the last chapter, this budgeted cost is also the *value* of each task. We can see that the value of Task A is $10,000, the value of Task B is $9,000, and so forth.

Near the bottom of Figure 4-1 are the Monthly Planned Value totals. The Monthly Planned Value for January is simply the sum of the budgets for the tasks that we plan to perform in January, or the value of the work that we plan to deliver in January. Also, since we obviously plan to do this work on budget, the Planned Value reflects the amount of money in our budget that we plan to spend in January.

The cumulative Planned Value figures in the bottom row just reflect the sum of all the Monthly Planned Values from the beginning of the project through the end of the current month. For example, the cumulative Planned Value for February equals the Planned Values for January and February combined ($19,000 + $24,000 = $43,000).

The project Budget at Completion (BAC), is $69,000. This is the total amount of money we are planning to spend over the life of the project (as well as the total value that we are planning to deliver). The cumulative Planned Value curve for this project can be seen in Figure 4-2. This is identical to the cumulative Baseline Cost curve.

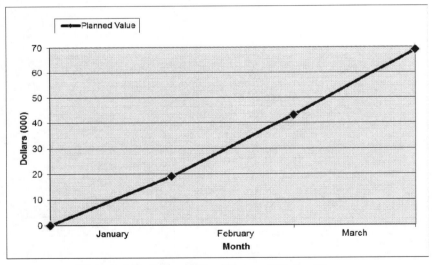

Figure 4-2: Cumulative Planned Value Curve

4-2 CURRENT PLAN

We normally track two different plans. The Baseline Plan reflects the costs and schedules of the tasks as they are officially agreed-to by the principal parties. The Baseline is the standard that we use to measure the project's performance and provides the basis from which we measure variances.

Ultimately, the success of the project is judged by how well it meets the baseline.

There is another plan that we track as well. We call this the *Current Plan*. For work already completed, the Current Plan reflects the actual costs as well as the actual start and finish dates of the tasks. For work not yet performed, it reflects the revised plan based on current expectations. The Current Plan may be different from the Baseline, and it is the difference between the two that generates the variances.

4-3 JANUARY STATUS REPORT

Let's fast forward to the future and assume it is now the end of January. We have some progress to report. A summary of January status can be seen in Figure 4-3. In this depiction of progress, a shaded bar reflects a completed task. Also, we are shifting the bars to reflect their newly scheduled dates in the Current Plan.

Task A was started and completed on time. Task B did not even start. It is being rescheduled to begin in February. Task A has some Actual Costs to report. Instead of the $10,000 that was budgeted in the plan it actually cost $11,000.

Task	Budget	Actual Cost	January	February	March
A	$10,000	$11,000	� bar		
B	$9,000		·········→	☐	
C	$16,000			☐	
D	$8,000			☐	
E	$7,000				☐
F	$19,000				☐
Monthly Planned Value			$19,000	$24,000	$26,000
Monthly Actual Cost			$11,000		
Monthly Earned Value			$10,000		

Figure 4-3: January Status and Current Plan

As of the end of January, how is our project doing with respect to schedule? The project is obviously behind schedule. Some of the work that we planned to perform in January was not completed. In fact the project is behind schedule by a whole task—Task B.

How is our project doing with respect to cost? It is obvious that we can only evaluate the cost performance for the work that has been performed so far. The only task performed was Task A. $10,000 was budgeted, but it actually cost $11,000. So *for the work performed* (which is an important qualifier), it cost $1000 more than planned. If all future work is performed with the same cost efficiency as Task A, the project will be delivered over budget.

We will use the commonly accepted convention that being under budget or ahead of schedule is generally good, while being over budget or behind schedule is generally bad. We can then summarize that the schedule and cost performance to date, is bad and bad since the project is behind schedule and over budget.

4-4 JANUARY MONTHLY TOTALS

Let's look at the monthly totals for January at the bottom of Figure 4-3.

First, the Monthly Planned Value is given as $19,000. Where did this come from? Why Figure 4-1 of course. This is our baseline plan, and the baseline never changes. That is, unless there is an official modification, which we indicated would not be the case in this sample project. Remember, this reflects the value of the work planned to be delivered in January, and the amount of money planned to have been spent in January, regardless of what actually happens.

Where did the figure for the Monthly Actual Cost of $11,000 come from? It reflects the Actual Cost of all the work performed in January. In this trivial case only one task was performed and it actually cost $11,000 to do the work.

The Actual Cost data can be added to the graph in Figure 4-2 to give us Figure 4-4. Notice that at the end of January the Actual Cost is less than the Planned Value (Baseline Cost). Using this graph alone, some people could easily be convinced that this project is performing well with respect to cost.

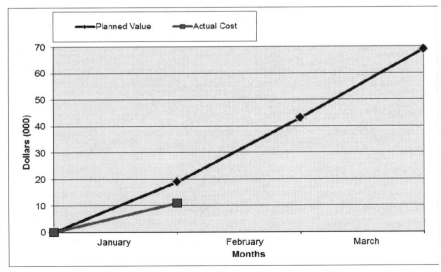

Figure 4-4: Baseline vs. Actual

The difference between the two curves in Figure 4-4 was introduced in Chapter 3 as the Fiscal Variance or FV. Also known as the Spending Variance, it gives us the difference between the money that was budgeted through today and what was actually needed. The formula for Fiscal Variance is repeated here.

$$\frac{Fiscal}{Variance} = \frac{Planned}{Value} - \frac{Actual}{Cost}$$

This can be expressed using the initials of the terms as Equation 4-1.

$$FV = PV - AC \qquad\qquad (4\text{-}1)$$

For the end of January, we can use the information from Figure 4-3 to compute a figure for the Fiscal Variance.

$$FV = \$19,000 - \$11,000 = +\$8,000$$

Here a positive Fiscal Variance indicates that less money was spent than had been planned *at this point in time*. In this case, we needed $8,000 less than was budgeted in our baseline plan as of the end of January. A negative number would have meant that more was spent than planned. Notice that even though we spent less money than planned, the project is still **over budget** and **behind schedule**!

While we did need more money to fund the work that was over budget (Task A), we did not need to fund the work that was not performed (Task B). The net result is that less was required overall because the project is far enough behind schedule. We also know that if past performance were to continue, the project would be delivered over budget.

We can now see that the graph in Figure 4-4 is not entirely adequate to help us determine the status of our project, or communicate it to our stakeholders. We realize too that we could take this chart and mislead certain individuals into thinking that we are doing a good job keeping our costs under control. As we discussed earlier, FV is misleading because we have cost and schedule information co-mingled in a single figure.

By decoupling cost and schedule, we can get a more accurate assessment of project status and be able to make better predictions about the future. The missing piece that will allow us to do this is the value that we earned in January, or January's *Earned Value*. As we'll see, by adding the cumulative Earned Value data to the chart, we will be able to see at a glance how our project is doing with respect to cost and schedule.

4-5 EARNED VALUE (EV)

Go back to Figure 4-3 and notice the last monthly figure for January, the Monthly *Earned Value* of $10,000. This represents the value that was earned for the work that was performed in January. In this simple project, only one task was performed in January—Task A. By completing that task, we can say that we have *earned the value* of that task. It is important to understand that we can't earn the value of a piece of work unless we perform the work.

By definition, the value of a task is the budgeted cost for that task. So, by performing Task A in January, we have an Earned Value, or EV, for the month totaling $10,000. Remember, the value of a task is independent of the actual cost to do the work, so the $11,000 actual cost doesn't even enter into it.

Question: Does a task need to be complete in order to earn any value? The answer is no. If a task is in progress, a portion of that task's value can be counted towards being earned. For example, if Task A were only 60% complete as of the end of January, we could say the earned value was $6,000 instead of $10,000.

It can get tricky to identify the Earned Value of a task in progress because determining the percent of work actually complete is not always easy. There will be more discussion of tasks in-progress in later chapters.

4-6 COST VARIANCE (CV)

Let's define the first of two new variances here. It is known as the *Cost Variance* or CV. This is distinct from the Fiscal Variance.

$$\frac{Cost}{Variance} = \frac{Earned}{Value} - \frac{Actual}{Cost}$$

This can be expressed using the initials as Equation 4-2.

$$CV = EV - AC \tag{4-2}$$

By substituting the numbers for the end of January, we get the following.

$$CV = \$10,000 - \$11,000 = -\$1,000$$

The convention with Cost Variance is very easy to remember: positive is good and negative is bad. A positive Cost Variance indicates that the work performed to date is under budget (generally considered to be good); a negative Cost Variance indicates that the work performed is over budget (generally bad). If the work is exactly on budget, the Cost Variance is zero.

In our sample project, a Cost Variance of −$1,000 means that our project is **over** budget by $1,000. In other words, it cost $1,000 more than planned to do the work accomplished so far. Remember that this was the same determination we made earlier with a simple assessment of Figure 4-3.

The nice thing about Cost Variance is that it gives us an absolute number reflecting how much the project is over or under budget *for the work performed,* not against the calendar. The Cost Variance is divorced from schedule considerations.

There may be any number of reasons why our project is over budget. We may have used more material or labor hours than planned. Maybe our unit costs were higher than planned. Maybe we just budgeted incorrectly or ran into unexpected problems.

One reason can be eliminated automatically, however. It cannot be due to a schedule reason. The CV gives a true indication of cost regardless of whether the project is ahead or behind schedule since we have taken schedule out of the equation, literally!

Both terms that make up the Cost Variance (Earned Value and Actual Cost) reflect the same work—the work that was actually performed. It doesn't matter if we are ahead or behind schedule since it ends up washing out. The Fiscal Variance, on the other hand, is comprised of two terms that reflect different amounts of work. The Actual Cost is derived from the work that was actually performed, while the Planned Value reflects the work that *should* have been performed. This is why the Fiscal Variance could be due to a cost reason, a schedule reason, or both.

4-7 SCHEDULE VARIANCE (SV)

Related to the Cost Variance is another variance that we'll define here as the *Schedule Variance* or SV.

$$\text{Schedule Variance} = \text{Earned Value} - \text{Planned Value}$$

This can be expressed using the initials as Equation 4-3.

$$SV = EV - PV \tag{4-3}$$

Using our example for the end of January we get the following.

$$SV = \$10,000 - \$19,000 = -\$9,000$$

The same convention applies here as to Cost Variance, i.e., positive is good and negative is bad. A positive Schedule Variance means that more work was performed than planned. A negative indicates that less was performed. If the same amount of work was performed as planned, the Schedule Variance would be zero.

In our example for the end of January, the Schedule Variance is negative which indicates that the project is behind schedule by $9,000. What does that mean? How can a project be behind schedule by a dollar amount?

The project is behind schedule by Task B, which should have been performed but wasn't. What is the value of Task B? Why $9,000 of course, its budgeted cost. The Schedule Variance indicates schedule status in terms of work delivered vs. work planned, expressed in units of value. Here we are looking at the amount of effort that was performed (or value delivered) **not** the status with respect to time. In later chapters we will investigate schedule status in terms of time units.

The Schedule Variance might be more correctly referred to as the Work Variance or Accomplishment Variance. It indicates how much work or activity the project is ahead or behind schedule, not how much time the project is ahead or behind schedule. The term Schedule Variance has been in long term use so we are probably going to have to live with it for a while.

We are not implying here that the Schedule Variance should be used as a substitute for our critical path analysis or other time-based analysis methods. Schedule Variance should be considered a complement to these not as a replacement.

For example, it is possible that a project could be behind schedule by a week, but if there were only a few hours worth of activity scheduled to be performed that week, it might be very easy to make up the slippage. This would be reflected in the Schedule Variance. On the other hand, a project may be behind schedule by only a day, but if there were a thousand hours of activity to be performed that day, this would certainly be a more challenging situation to make up. This too would be reflected in the Schedule Variance.

A word of caution is appropriate here. At the project level, the Schedule Variance does not indicate if the correct tasks were performed. For example, we could be behind schedule for tasks on the Critical Path but be ahead enough with tasks off of the Critical Path in order to give us an aggregate positive Schedule Variance.

If the tasks on the Critical Path are behind schedule, the project is still likely to be completed late regardless of the value of the project-level Schedule Variance. One simple approach to address this issue is to compute the Schedule Variance a second way—by only considering the critical tasks (i.e. the tasks on the critical path).

Many practitioners routinely calculate SV both ways to gain this added perspective of schedule performance. If either of the Schedule Variances (all tasks or critical tasks) is negative, then we are concerned that the project has schedule issues.

As we can see, analyzing schedule performance is more complicated than analyzing cost. Dealing with cost is relatively simple because cost is one-dimensional. If we add up the costs of all the tasks we get the project cost. This doesn't work with the schedule. If we add up the durations of all the tasks, we don't generally get the project duration.

Since our schedule is multi-dimensional, we need to look at it from a number of different perspectives in order to get the complete picture. Calculating the SV of the Critical Tasks is similar to the CV since the sum of the durations of the Critical Tasks does equal the project duration. We can't ignore the non-critical tasks, however, because if they are delayed enough they can turn critical.

This is a good time to note that there are actually two different types of Schedule Variance. The one that we defined here is officially known as the Value-Based Schedule Variance and is sometimes denoted as SV($) because we usually track value in monetary units. The other Schedule Variance is known as the Time-Based Schedule Variance and is denoted as SV(t). SV(t), which will be introduced in a later chapter, is expressed in units of time.

If we see SV used without any indication of whether it is value-based or time-based, it will always mean value-based. We will use the designation SV($) when it is used in conjunction with SV(t) for emphasis and to avoid confusion.

4-8 RELATIONSHIPS AMONG THE VARIANCES

The Planned Value, Actual Cost, and Earned Value figures that we determine in the course of our project evaluations are independent of each other. That is, knowing the values of any two of these gives us no hint of the value of the third. Each of these three variables must be determined separately.

This is not so for the variances, however. The three variances *are* related to each other. If we know the values of any two we can calculate the third. For example, the Fiscal Variance equals the Cost Variance less the Schedule Variance. See Equation 4-4.

$$FV = CV - SV \qquad (4\text{-}4)$$

How do we know this is true? Well, if we take the formulas for CV and SV and perform a substitution into Equation 4-4, we will find that, after combining terms, it reduces to Equation 4-1, which is our original definition for Fiscal Variance.

Let's take a look at the relationship in Equation 4-4. We can see that if CV increases, then so does FV. However, if SV increases, then FV decreases. To see how this works, assume we have a project that is on schedule (SV equals zero), but the work performed so far cost more than planned (CV is negative). If the work was over budget by $10,000, then CV equals −$10,000. Using Equation 4-4 we find that FV equals −$10,000 also. This makes sense. This means that if the tasks are costing more than planned, then we will spend more money to cover that cost overage.

Now assume that CV equals zero, so all tasks are on budget, and that the project is ahead of schedule (SV is positive). If SV were to equal $10,000, Equation 4-4 tells us that FV equals –$10,000. This also makes sense. If the work is ahead of schedule, even if the tasks are on-budget, we need to spend the money earlier than planned to cover this additional work.

So we can see that there are two ways that we can over spend resulting in a negative Fiscal Variance: 1) if the cost for the work performed is over budget, or 2) if the work is ahead of schedule. Being ahead of schedule is the more benign of the two because after the project is complete, the contribution of SV to the FV will disappear. The effect of the Cost Variance will be permanent, however, and would have to be offset by changes in the cost efficiency of other tasks.

We now know that if we determine the Fiscal Variance from Equation 4-4 it must always match the result when using Equation 4-1. Let's check it out for our sample project. Recall the variances that were generated for the end of January.

$$FV = +\$8,000$$

$$CV = -\$1,000$$

$$SV = -\$9,000$$

If we recalculate FV from Equation 4-4 we get the following.

$$FV = -\$1,000 - (-\$9,000)$$

$$FV = -\$1,000 + \$9,000$$

$$FV = +\$8,000$$

It's clear that Equation 4-4 does work. It also explains why the project spent $8,000 less than planned. While the work performed cost $1,000 more than planned, there was $9,000 worth of work that the project was behind schedule, which means that funds were not required for that work, *yet*. Notice that we have two bad situations (being over budget and behind schedule) adding up to something seemingly good (less overall spending vs. the calendar).

Remember what we said earlier about FV. It's not very helpful to us in understanding the situation because we have cost and schedule information co-mingled in a single figure. What we've done here by introducing CV and SV is to decouple FV into its separate cost and schedule components. Now we can look at each piece separately and get a better understanding of the situation.

For example, if we have overspent (FV is negative) we can explain how much is due to a cost reason (CV) and how much is due to a schedule reason (SV). This is a great tool for us to use for our own understanding as well as to explain status to other project stakeholders.

For the record, we can rewrite Equation 4-4 to express CV or SV in terms of FV. These forms are shown here as Equation 4-5 and Equation 4-6.

$$CV = SV + FV \qquad (4\text{-}5)$$

$$SV = CV - FV \qquad (4\text{-}6)$$

4-9 FEBRUARY STATUS REPORT

Let's get back to our sample project. Assume it is now the end of February. We can see from the current status, summarized in Figure 4-5, that February was a good month.

Task	Budget	Actual Cost	January	February	March
A	$10,000	$11,000	▨		
B	$9,000	$10,000		▨	
C	$16,000	$14,000		▨	
D	$8,000	$6,000		▨	
E	$7,000	$5,000		▨ ← ⃤	
F	$19,000				☐
Monthly Planned Value			$19,000	$24,000	$26,000
Monthly Actual Cost			$11,000	$35,000	
Monthly Earned Value			$10,000	$40,000	
Cumulative Planned Value			$19,000	$43,000	$69,000
Cumulative Actual Cost			$11,000	$46,000	
Cumulative Earned Value			$10,000	$50,000	

Figure 4-5: February Status and Current Plan

Tasks C and D, the two tasks originally planned for February, were started and completed on time. In addition, Task B, which was deferred from January, was also completed. Not only that, Task E (which was originally scheduled for March), was completed early. The third column of the figure shows the Actual Costs for each of the tasks performed.

How is the project doing with respect to schedule now? Good! The project is ahead of schedule. Everything that was scheduled to be performed is complete, and an additional task was completed.

How is the project doing with respect to cost? This month we have more data to take into consideration. In January we only had one task to consider, so we could eyeball it easily. Now we have five tasks to take into account.

Let us do it brute-force by taking the difference between the Baseline Cost and Actual Cost of each individual task and then netting it out. We'll also use the same convention as Cost Variance, where under budget is a positive difference and over budget is a negative difference. The results are shown in Table 4-1.

Task	Budget [$]	Actual Cost [$]	Difference [$]
A	10,000	11,000	−$1,000
B	9,000	10,000	−1,000
C	16,000	14,000	+2,000
D	8,000	6,000	+2,000
E	7,000	5,000	+2,000
		Total	+4,000

Table 4-1: Project to-date through the end of February

Notice that the net result is a positive $4,000. This means that for all the work performed so far, it cost $4,000 less than originally planned. So we were able to turn the project around from bad and bad in January with respect to both cost and schedule to good and good in February.

4-10 FEBRUARY MONTHLY TOTALS

Look at the monthly figures for the end of February toward the bottom of Figure 4-5. The Monthly Planned Value is $24,000. Where did this come from? Why the original plan depicted in Figure 4-1, of course. Remember, this is what was planned in the baseline and the baseline never changes.

How about the Monthly Actual Cost for February? Where did this come from? It is the Actual Cost of the four tasks that were performed in February. The actual costs of Tasks B through E add up to $35,000.

Finally, look at the Monthly Earned Value for February. Where did this come from? By now we realize it is the sum of values or budgets of the work performed in February. Since Tasks B through E were performed in February, the total value earned is the sum of the Baseline Costs for tasks B, C, D, and E or $40,000 ($9,000+16,000+8,000+7,000).

If we wish, we can use these monthly totals for February to determine the monthly variances. This will give us useful information, but at this point we want to concentrate just on the variances between the cumulative values for the project to-date.

The bottom of Figure 4-5 shows the cumulative figures for the Planned Value, Actual Cost, and Earned Value through the end of February. They are determined by adding the monthly figures for January and February.

$$Cum\ PV = \$19,000 + \$24,000 = \$43,000$$

$$Cum\ AC = \$11,000 + \$35,000 = \$46,000$$

$$Cum\ EV = \$10,000 + \$40,000 = \$50,000$$

These cumulative values can be added to the graph in Figure 4-4 to produce Figure 4-6. We can evaluate the status of the project by looking at the graph with the three curves. A trained eye can look at Figure 4-6 and immediately determine that the project is under budget and ahead of schedule. This can be determined from the relative positions of the curves to each other. How to interpret Earned Value curves will be a topic of discussion in the next chapter.

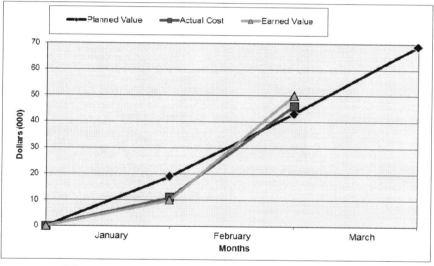

Figure 4-6: Cumulative Curves through February

4-11 COMPARING THE VARIANCES

Let us begin by calculating the Fiscal Variance using Equation 4-1 above. Using the cumulative values we get

$$FV = \$43,000 - \$46,000 = -\$3,000$$

This negative variance indicates that as of the end of February, the project has spent $3,000 more than planned. At first glance this seems like an undesirable situation (and may well be for funding reasons), but it does not tell the whole story.

As we saw earlier, the project is good and good with respect to both schedule and cost. We are ahead of schedule by Task E, and under budget by $4,000. This won't stop our senior management or customer from being concerned, because the Fiscal Variance could be a key indicator for them.

Now let's calculate the Cost Variance for the project to-date through the end of February. Using the cumulative values in Equation 4-2 we get the following.

$$CV = \$50,000 - \$46,000 = +\$4,000$$

This indicates that the project is under budget. More precisely, the work performed so far cost $4,000 less than planned. This agrees with the result of our brute force approach exhibited in Table 4-1.

We'll now calculate the Schedule Variance for the project to-date through the end of February. Using the cumulative values in Equation 4-3 we get the following.

$$SV = \$50,000 - \$43,000 = +\$7,000$$

This means that we are ahead of schedule by $7,000 worth of work. We know that we are ahead of schedule by Task E. What's the value of Task E? Why, $7,000 of course.

So the indicators tell us that a project that was in bad shape at the end of January was turned around to be in good shape by the end of February. The variances that we introduced here are tools that we can use to help us better understand the status of our project. They can also be used to help us convey this status to others in presentations or written reports.

In summary for the end of February, we get the following.

$$FV = -\$3,000$$

$$CV = +\$4,000$$

$$SV = +\$7,000$$

We can also use Equation 4-4 here to compute the Fiscal Variance by the alternate method.

$$FV = CV - SV$$

$$FV = \$4,000 - \$7,000 = -\$3,000$$

If we spent $3,000 more than planned, our management and finance departments will surely be interested in having us explain this increased need for money. As we can see, the additional $3,000 required was a result of the project being ahead of schedule by $7,000 worth of work, with this being partially offset by $4,000 in cost savings for the work performed so far.

So here we have two good things (being under budget and ahead of schedule) adding up to something seemingly bad (more overall spending vs. the calendar). Now we shouldn't be complacent with a negative Fiscal Variance. If we are so far ahead of schedule that it actually impacts our funding situation, we could have a real problem.

Of course, being ahead of schedule and under budget won't always result in a negative Fiscal Variance, nor will being behind schedule and over budget (as in January) always result in a positive Fiscal Variance. These examples were intentionally chosen here to make a point.

We should determine all three variances every evaluation cycle. How concerned we will be depends on how the results compare with the acceptable tolerance limits that were established in the baseline plan. We'll see more on how to work with tolerance limits in coming chapters.

4-12 SUMMARY

The Fiscal Variance, while being a very common indicator, can be misleading because it combines the cost and schedule data together in a single figure. By decoupling the FV into its cost and schedule components, we can determine how much of the variance is due to a cost reason and how much is due to a schedule reason. CV and SV allow us to do this, which results in us getting a better understanding of the true status of our project.

The questions that were addressed in this chapter are summarized in Table 4-2, and the formulas that were introduced in this chapter appear in Table 4-3.

Question	Answer
How much work was actually performed through today?	EV
How much money was budgeted to perform the work accomplished so far?	EV
How much under (or over) budget was the work that was actually performed?	CV
How much more (or less) work was performed than what was planned?	SV

Table 4-2: Question Summary

$CV = EV - AC$	$FV = CV - SV$
$SV = EV - PV$	$CV = SV + FV$
$FV = PV - AC$	$SV = CV - FV$

Table 4-3: Formula Summary

EXERCISES

4-1: Identify some possible reasons for a positive CV. For a negative CV.

4-2: Identify some possible reasons for a positive SV. For a negative SV.

4-3: What impact does a project's being behind schedule have on the project CV? Explain.

4-4: Prove that Equation 4-4 is true given Equations 4-1, 4-2, and 4-3.

4-5: Fill in the six empty cells in the following table with either the word "planned" or "actual" in order to properly describe the properties of each variable.

	Cost	Work Performed
Planned Value		
Earned Value		
Actual Cost		

4-6: Based upon cumulative figures, a project has a Cost Variance of $5,000 and a Schedule Variance of –$3,000.

a) What is the Fiscal Variance?

b) What is the status of this project? Include effect of FV in the answer.

4-7: Start with the project depicted in Figure 4-5 of the text. Assume it is now the end of March, and Task F is 80% complete with an actual cost so far of $25,000.

a) Calculate the monthly and cumulative figures for March.

b) Determine the values for CV, SV, and FV. What is the status of the project?

c) Draw the graph with the cumulative cost curves for Planned Value, Earned Value, and Actual Cost through the end of March.

4-8: A $3600 task was scheduled to be completed three days ago. It is currently 2/3 complete, and $2250 has been spent on this task so far.

a) Determine the task BAC, PV, EV, and AC.

b) What are the CV, SV, and FV for the task?

c) Summarize the task status

d) If the rest of the task is performed with the same cost efficiency as in the past, what will be the total actual cost of the task when it is completed?

Chapter 5

UNDERSTANDING CUMULATIVE CURVES

In addition to helping us evaluate the health of the project, EVM is a great tool to help us communicate status with stakeholders. A graphic display is an especially useful way to depict status and trends. In the previous chapters we looked at cumulative curves, but didn't discuss how to interpret the graph. This is the subject of the current chapter.

5-1 EXAMPLE #1

Let's begin by reviewing a point we made in the last chapter. Here in Figure 5-1 we have a graph with the Planned Value and Actual Cost curves. The Budget at Completion (BAC) is $1 million and the Planned Duration is 50 weeks. Consider the following two questions based upon the information in the graph.

Question: What is the status of this project's cost for the work performed so far?

    a) Over budget

    b) Under budget

    c) On budget

    d) Not enough information to determine

Question: What is the status of this project's schedule for the time elapsed so far?

    a) Ahead of schedule

    b) Behind budget

    c) On schedule

    d) Not enough information to determine

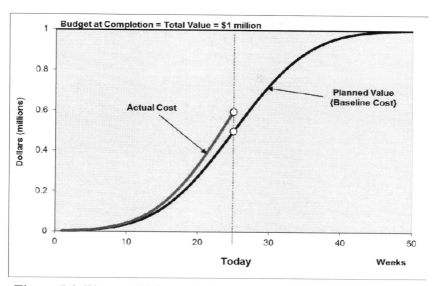

Figure 5-1: Planned Value and Actual Cost curves for Example #1

We can tell that the Fiscal Variance is negative since the Actual Cost exceeds the Planned Value. However, as we have learned, the Fiscal Variance is not an indicator of how the cost compares to the plan for the work that has been performed. In this case, the answer to both of these questions is "d" (not enough information to determine).

Since we don't have the Earned Value data available to us, we have no way to determine the Cost Variance or the Schedule Variance, so the graph is limited in its usefulness. We must also be careful not to make assumptions about the cost or schedule status.

By adding the cumulative Earned Value curve to the graph, we'll have more complete information on the status and health of the project. It will need to be provided independently since there is no way of inferring the Earned Value from the other two indicators—it is a totally independent variable.

5-2 EXAMPLE #2

Figure 5-2 is an example of a graph with all three curves. If we are familiar with interpreting this type of graph we can get an overall feel of the project health with respect to both cost and schedule.

Question: Based on the project depicted in Figure 5-2, what is the status of the cost for the work performed so far?

    a) Over budget

    b) Under budget

c) On budget

d) Not enough information to determine

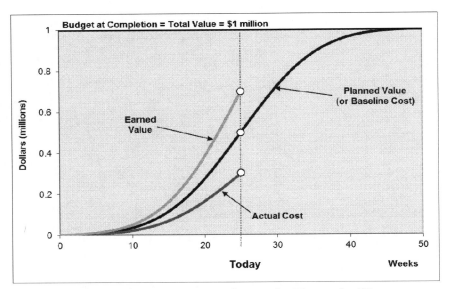

Figure 5-2: Cumulative Curves for Example #2

We know now that "b" (under budget), is the correct answer. The cumulative Earned Value and Actual Cost curves both reflect the same work, i.e. the work that was actually performed. The Earned Value is what we planned to spend to get the work done. The Actual Cost reflects what we actually spent. If we actually spent less than planned, which is the case in Figure 5-2, this means the project is under budget. The project will always be under budget any time we see the Earned Value curve above the Actual Cost curve.

If the Earned Value curve were to be below the Actual Cost curve, it would mean that the work cost more money than planned. In other words the project would be over budget. Once we get familiar with these charts we will quickly be able to get a good understanding of the overall status of the project.

Another way of looking at it can be seen in Figure 5-3. The upper horizontal line indicates the cumulative Earned Value as of today. The lower horizontal line indicates the Actual Cost as of today. From the last chapter we learned that this difference is the Cost Variance. If the Earned Value is greater than the Actual Cost, the Cost Variance is positive and the project is under budget.

Question: Based on the project depicted in Figure 5-2, what is the status of this project's schedule for the time elapsed so far?

a) Ahead of schedule

b) Behind budget

c) On schedule

d) Not enough information to determine

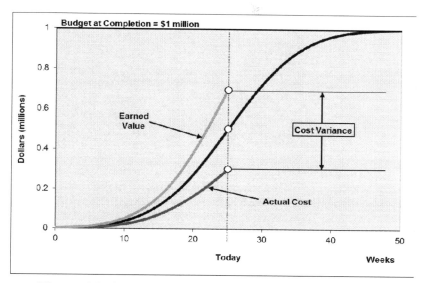

Figure 5-3: Cost Variance = Earned Value – Actual Cost

Of course "a" (ahead of schedule), is the correct answer. The cumulative Earned Value and Planned Value curves are both expressed in terms of budgeted dollars or value. The Earned Value curve reflects the value of the work that was actually performed as of today. The Planned Value curve reflects the value of the work that was planned to be performed.

If the Earned Value is greater than the Planned Value, as in our example, it means that the project delivered more value (performed more work) than had been planned through today. In other words, the project is ahead of schedule, or doing well (provided, of course, it includes the correct work).

We can see the same thing by looking at Figure 5-4. The upper horizontal line indicates the cumulative Earned Value as of today. The lower horizontal line indicates the Planned Value as of today. From the last chapter we learned that this difference is the Schedule Variance. If the Earned Value is greater than the Planned Value, the Schedule Variance is positive and the project is ahead of schedule.

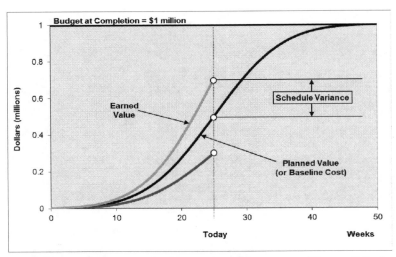

Figure 5-4: Schedule Variance = Earned Value – Planned Value

5-3 EXAMPLE #3

Consider the following two questions based upon the information in Figure 5-5.

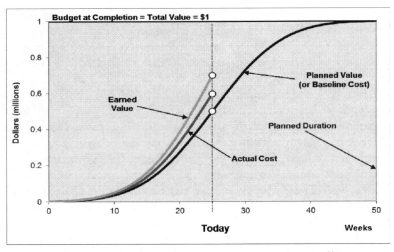

Figure 5-5: Cumulative curves for Example #3

Question: What is the status of this project's cost for the work performed so far?

    a) Over budget

b) Under budget

c) On budget

d) Not enough information to determine

Question: What is the status of this project's schedule for the time elapsed so far?

a) Ahead of schedule

b) Behind budget

c) On schedule

d) Not enough information to determine

In this case, the answers are "b" (under budget), and "a" (ahead of schedule). In fact this is the same result as in Example #2 above. Compare the graphs in Figures 5-2 and 5-5. Even though the curves are in different positions, they result in the same assessment of cost and schedule status.

5-4 GRAPH ANALYSIS SUMMARY

If Earned Value is the top curve of the three on the graph, then the project status is always good-good (under budget and ahead of schedule). If Earned Value is the bottom curve, then the project status is always bad-bad (over budget and behind schedule). In each of these cases, the relative position of the other two curves is irrelevant for determining overall cost and schedule status. Yes, by switching the other two curves, we would change the magnitude of the variances, but not the overall status.

If Earned Value is the middle curve then one variance is good and the other is bad. Which is which, *will* now depend on the relative positions of the other two curves.

Here are some more specific guidelines.

➲ If all three curves are identical, i.e. lie right on top of each other, it means that the project is on budget and the *amount* of work performed equals the amount of work that was planned to be delivered. Keep in mind that it may not be the same work as planned.

➲ If the Earned Value curve is above the Actual Cost curve, the project is under budget for the work that was performed. This means that if this trend continues, the project is on track to be delivered under budget when it is completed.

➲ If the Earned Value curve is below the Actual Cost curve, the project is over budget for the work performed so far. If this trend continues, the project is on track to be delivered over budget when it is completed.

➲ If the Earned Value curve is above the Planned Value curve, the project is ahead of schedule. That is, more work was performed than planned. If this includes the correct work, and the trend continues, the project is on track to be delivered before its planned completion date.

➲ If the Earned Value curve is below the Planned Value curve, the project is behind schedule. Less work was performed than planned. If this trend continues, the project is on track to be delivered behind schedule.

As we can see, the only thing that matters in determining overall cost and schedule status is where the Earned Value curve is with respect to each of the other two curves. *It is totally irrelevant where the Actual Cost curve is with respect to the Planned Value curve.* If the Actual Cost curve is greater than the Planned Value curve, but the Earned Value curve is greater than both, then the project is still under budget and ahead of schedule!

One word of warning. So far, we've only been considering data representing the overall status of the project. It is possible that this may lead us to an incorrect conclusion.

Consider a situation where the Planned Value, Earned Value, and Actual Cost curves are identical. This would suggest that everything is going exactly as planned. While this would be true on average, this is not necessarily true at the task level. Half of the tasks could be out of tolerance over budget while the other half are out of tolerance under budget in a way that they balance exactly. In this case, all of the tasks are out of tolerance yet the project-level indicators are signifying that everything is going according to plan.

We need to be careful and not look only at the project-level results. The task-level figures will give us a more complete and accurate picture of project status. This we will address in a later chapter.

A similar case can be made for the schedule, i.e. some tasks can be ahead of schedule while others are behind. An additional device introduced in the last chapter, which is helpful for understanding the schedule status, is to repeat the analysis looking only at the critical tasks. Since it is the set of critical tasks that defines the project duration, we want to make sure that the critical path is still on track. Even if the aggregate Schedule Variance is positive, if the Schedule Variance of the critical tasks is negative, the project is still likely to finish late.

5-5 CURVE PROPERTIES

Let's investigate some of the properties of these curves. As we can see from Figure 5-2, all three curves have their first data point at the origin, i.e. cost equals zero and time equals the project start date.

The Planned Value curve can be drawn completely at the beginning of the implementation phase of the project. It is how we plan to do our work and spend our money over time. Since the Earned Value and Actual Cost curves reflect the work actually performed, they can only be drawn out through today. We obviously can't have any real data for anything in the future, although we could make projections.

Question: Where does the Planned Value curve terminate on the dollar (vertical) axis? Answer: At the project BAC (Budget at Completion). Using Figure 5-2 as an example, the Planned Value curve will terminate at $1 million on the dollar axis. This will occur at the planned completion date (Planned Duration) of the project. Remember that the cumulative Planned Value curve indicates the money we are *planning* to spend (or the work we are planning to perform) through a given date.

Think of the Planned Value as representing the portion of the BAC that is planned to be delivered as of a given date. It is a function of time and it will vary by date according to the following relationship.

$$PV = BAC \times (Planned \% \ Complete) \tag{5-1}$$

Notice that the BAC is not a function of time, i.e. its value will not vary by date. The Planned % Complete, however, is a function of time and *will* vary by date. So, for example, if the project is planned to be 50% complete as of today, then the Planned Value will be 50% of the BAC.

Question: Where does the Earned Value curve terminate on the dollar axis? Answer: Also at the BAC since the Earned Value is expressed in baseline or budgeted dollars. Using Figure 5-2 again, the Earned Value curve will eventually terminate at the $1 million level. When the project is actually complete, all of the value will have been delivered. This will occur at the actual completion date of the project instead of the planned completion date.

The Earned Value represents the portion of the BAC that has actually been delivered as of a given date. It is a function of time and will vary according to the following relationship.

$$EV = BAC \times (Actual \% \ Complete) \tag{5-2}$$

For example, if 60% of the work of the project is actually complete, then the Earned Value will be 60% of the BAC.

Note that neither the Planned Value nor the Earned Value can exceed the BAC. When the Planned Value reaches the BAC the project is planned to be done. When the Earned Value reaches the BAC the project is actually done.

Question: Where does the Actual Cost curve terminate on the dollar axis? Answer: Anywhere! As we know, actual costs at the end of the project can be less than, equal to, or greater that the planned budget. However, the Actual Cost will stop growing at the same time that the Earned Value curve reaches its maximum, i.e. the actual completion date of the project.

Note that there is no way to determine Actual Cost in terms of BAC. This is because the Actual Cost is not expressed in units of value. The data for AC must be independently obtained.

The properties of the three curves are summarized in Table 5-1.

Curve	Terminus	
	Cost-Axis	Time-Axis
Planned Value	Budget at Completion	Planned Duration
Earned Value	Budget at Completion	Actual Finish Date
Actual Cost	Actual Total Cost	Actual Finish Date

Table 5-1: Cumulative Curve Termination Points

Now that we know how to read the graph, we can get a quick snapshot of overall project performance. As we said, we don't want to rely on this graph alone. As powerful as it is, there are certain circumstances where considering only project level (high-level) data can be misleading. Nevertheless, we can appreciate how the different indicators average out at the project level.

5-6 SUMMARY

In this chapter we learned how to interpret the Earned Value graph and look at some of the properties of the three curves.

The formulas that were introduced in this chapter appear in Table 5-2.

$$PV = BAC \times (\text{Planned \% Complete})$$

$$EV = BAC \times (\text{Actual \% Complete})$$

Table 5-2: Formula Summary

EXERCISES

5-1: What can be determined if we have a graph that contains only the Planned Value and Earned Value curves?

5-2: If the PV, EV, and AC curves are identical, does this mean that the project is going exactly as planned? Why, or why not?

5-3: A piece of work has a total budget (BAC) of $60,000. As of today it is

40% complete, although only 35% was planned to have been complete. What are the values of the variances that can be computed? What does this say about the status of the effort?

5-4: Explain why the Actual Cost cannot be determined from the BAC in the same way that the Planned Value and the Earned Value can.

5-5: Why does the Schedule Variance always go to zero at some point after the end of a project? At what date does it go to zero? Why is this not the case for Cost Variance?

5-6: For each of the six graphs depicted below (a through f), identify the status of the project at the end of Week 3 with respect to cost (over budget or under budget), schedule (ahead of schedule or behind schedule), and spending (over spent or under spent). Explain possible causes of each situation. What other information would be helpful in order to have a more complete assessment of project status?

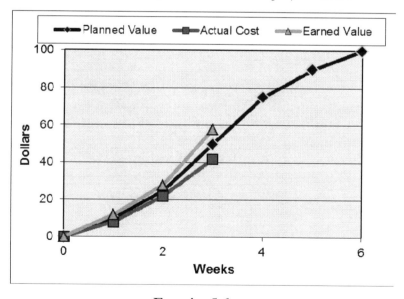

Exercise 5-6a

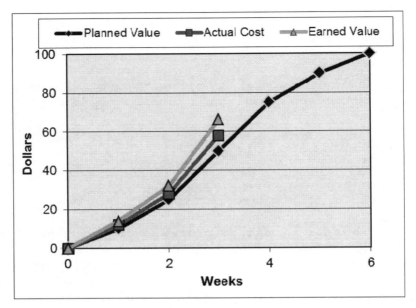

Exercise 5-6b

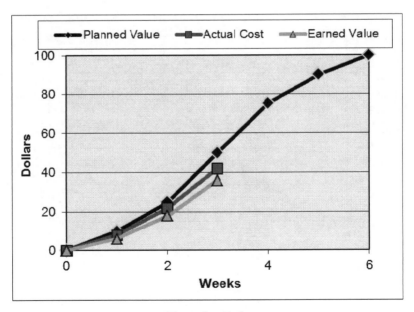

Exercise 5-6c

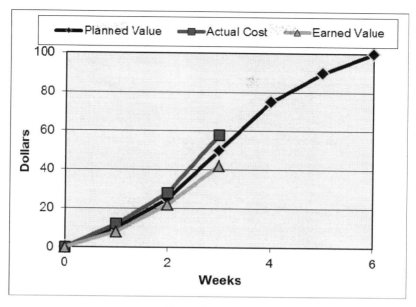

Exercise 5-6d

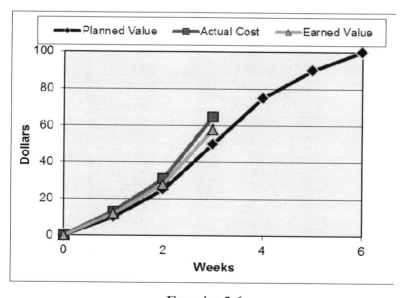

Exercise 5-6e

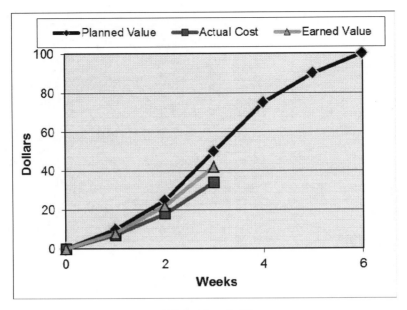

Exercise 5-6f

Chapter 6

MODERN AND TRADITIONAL CONVENTIONS

6-1 INTRODUCTION

Until now we've been using the terms Planned Value, Actual Cost, and Earned Value in discussions of concepts and in the formulas. In this chapter we'll introduce another convention commonly used to describe EVM, but using different names for these three main variables. Both conventions are equivalent—only the names are different.

The *Modern Convention* is the one we've been working with so far and is the more recently developed of the two. Its attraction is that it can be more compactly written using two-letter initials for the variables.

The *Traditional Convention* was used when EVM was initially developed. Here the names of the terms are more descriptive of the values they represent, and four-letter initials are used for the variables.

Since each convention has its own set of pros and cons, each has its own set of advocates among EVM practitioners as well. It is not our intent here to promote one over the other. We should be familiar with both, however, since we may likely see either convention in the working world.

6-2 MODERN CONVENTION

In the Modern Convention, the three main variables are expressed just the way we've learned them so far. Specifically, we have Planned Value (or PV), Earned Value (EV), and Actual Cost (AC).

Now let's take a look at the formula for Cost Variance. Equation 6-1a is using the full name, while Equation 6-1b is using the initials.

$$\frac{Cost}{Variance} = \frac{Earned}{Value} - \frac{Actual}{Cost} \tag{6-1a}$$

$$CV = EV - AC \tag{6-1b}$$

The Schedule Variance is shown in Equations 6-2a and 6-2b.

$$\frac{Schedule}{Variance} = \frac{Earned}{Value} - \frac{Planned}{Value} \qquad (6\text{-}2a)$$

$$SV = EV - PV \qquad (6\text{-}2b)$$

To complete the set, the Fiscal Variance is given in Equations 6-3a and 6-3b.

$$\frac{Fiscal}{Variance} = \frac{Planned}{Value} - \frac{Actual}{Cost} \qquad (6\text{-}3a)$$

$$FV = PV - AC \qquad (6\text{-}2b)$$

The terms and their initials are summarized in Table 6-1.

Initials	Term
PV	Planned Value
AC	Actual Cost
EV	Earned Value
FV	Fiscal Variance
CV	Cost Variance
SV	Schedule Variance

Table 6-1: Modern Convention Terms

While it is simple to refer to an item by its initials, it has been known to cause some confusion with novices. The primary culprit is that most of these two-letter initials end in the letter "V." Sometimes the "V" is used for "value" and other times it is used for "variance." A common comment is that "there are too many Vs floating around." Naturally, with regular use, we will become accustomed to working with the initials, and they become second nature.

Another potential area of confusion is often voiced from those who work in areas such as financial or risk analysis. There, the initials PV and EV are used for Present Value and Expected Value, respectively. Those items are outside of the EVM system. Multiple uses for the same initials in proximity to each other will require care and an understanding of context in order to avoid confusion. While this may be a consideration when adopting conventions, with regular use and care this too can be successfully handled.

6-3 TRADITIONAL CONVENTION

When Earned Value Management was originally developed, the Traditional Convention was the only one in existence. The Modern Convention was not developed until later and only came into widespread use around the turn of the twenty-first century. Even though the Modern Convention is growing in popularity, the Traditional Convention is still in common use today.

The attraction of the Traditional Convention is that the terms used are more descriptive of the variables that they represent, and some of the potential confusions just mentioned with the Modern Convention are avoided. On the other hand, the Traditional Convention uses four-letter initials, which some think to be more cumbersome and less user friendly.

Even if we choose to work with the Modern Convention, it is still important to be familiar with the Traditional Convention. Currently, much of the literature in existence uses the Traditional. Also, many software packages out there use Traditional as well.

All of the variances still keep their same names and same two-initial designations in the Traditional Convention. Here we still use CV to represent Cost Variance, SV for Schedule Variance, and FV for Fiscal Variance. BAC is also used to represent Budget at Completion. Nothing is different with these.

In the Traditional Convention, Earned Value is known as *Budgeted Cost of Work Performed* (or BCWP). Earned Value and Budgeted Cost of Work Performed mean the same thing—they're synonymous. If you think about it, it makes sense. The words themselves describe the term.

Earned Value = Budgeted Cost of Work Performed

Earned Value is expressed in budgeted (or baseline) dollars. Also Earned Value represents the work that has been performed, i.e. the work actually done. Remember, we can't earn the value unless we actually do the work. Here the equivalence is expressed using initials.

$$EV = BCWP$$

The Traditional term for Actual Cost is *Actual Cost of Work Performed* (or ACWP). Notice that ACWP represents the same work as Earned Value, i.e. the work performed. The difference is the cost. ACWP represents the actual cost of that work instead of the budgeted cost.

Actual Cost = Actual Cost of Work Performed

Using the initials we have the following.

$$AC = ACWP$$

We can begin to see a pattern here. Notice that the first two letters refer to the cost component of the item, while the last two letters refer to its work component.

Equations 6-1a and 6-1b can now be rewritten in the Traditional Convention as Equations 6-4a and 6-4b.

$$\begin{array}{c}\text{Cost}\\\text{Variance}\end{array} = \begin{array}{c}\text{Budgeted Cost}\\\text{of Work}\\\text{Performed}\end{array} - \begin{array}{c}\text{Actual Cost}\\\text{of Work}\\\text{Performed}\end{array} \qquad \text{(6-4a)}$$

$$CV = BCWP - ACWP \qquad \text{(6-4b)}$$

As we'll soon see, there is some merit in using the four-letter initials instead of the more concise two letter versions. We'll discuss that later in this chapter, but first let's take a look at the other variances.

The Schedule Variance uses Earned Value and Planned Value. We already did Earned Value when we looked at Cost Variance. It is still BCWP. The Traditional term for Planned Value is *Budgeted Cost of Work Scheduled* (or BCWS).

$$Planned\ Value = Budgeted\ Cost\ of\ Work\ Scheduled$$

Using the initials we have the following.

$$PV = BCWS$$

The work BCWS represents is different from the work in ACWP or BCWP. BCWS represents the work that was *scheduled* (or planned) to be performed through the data date instead of the actual work performed. This scheduled work is expressed in budgeted dollars.

Equations 6-2a and 6-2b can now be rewritten in the Traditional Convention as Equations 6-5a and 6-5b.

$$\begin{array}{c}\text{Schedule}\\\text{Variance}\end{array} = \begin{array}{c}\text{Budgeted Cost}\\\text{of Work}\\\text{Performed}\end{array} - \begin{array}{c}\text{Budgeted Cost}\\\text{of Work}\\\text{Scheduled}\end{array} \qquad \text{(6-5a)}$$

$$SV = BCWP - BCWS \qquad \text{(6-5b)}$$

Like the other variances, the Traditional initials for Fiscal Variance are still FV. The Traditional initials for Planned Value (BCWS) and for Actual Cost (ACWP) have already been discussed.

Equations 6-3a and 6-3b can now be rewritten in the Traditional Convention as Equations 6-6a and 6-6b.

$$\begin{matrix} Fiscal \\ Variance \end{matrix} = \begin{matrix} Budgeted\ Cost \\ of\ Work \\ Scheduled \end{matrix} - \begin{matrix} Actual\ Cost \\ of\ Work \\ Performed \end{matrix} \quad (6\text{-}6a)$$

$$FV = BCWS - ACWP \quad (6\text{-}6b)$$

The Traditional Convention terms and their initials are summarized in Table 6-2, along with the equivalent term in the Modern Convention.

Initials	Term	Equivalent Term
BCWS	Budgeted Cost of Work Scheduled	Planned Value
ACWP	Actual Cost of Work Performed	Actual Cost
BCWP	Budgeted Cost of Work Performed	Earned Value
FV	Fiscal Variance	—
CV	Cost Variance	—
SV	Schedule Variance	—
BAC	Budget at Completion	—

Table 6-2: Traditional Convention Terms

Notice that in the Traditional Convention, the two-letter initials refer to the variances and the four-letter initials refer to the basic variables. So here, if we see the letter "V" it always refers to variance and never to value.

6-4 COST AND WORK COMPONENTS

Earlier we mentioned that the Traditional Convention is the more descriptive of the two. Now we'll explore more of the Traditional Convention and see how this is so.

Take a closer look at the three terms with four-letter initials BCWP, ACWP, and BCWS. Notice that they are each composed of two initial pairs. The first pair represents the cost component, and the last pair represents the work component.

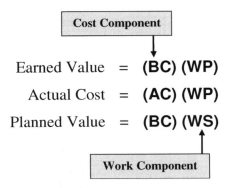

Earned Value = **(BC) (WP)**

Actual Cost = **(AC) (WP)**

Planned Value = **(BC) (WS)**

Be careful. We are not multiplying anything together here. We're just splitting up each four-initial name into two-initial pairs.

For Earned Value, the cost component (BC) indicates that it is expressed in terms of budgeted (or baseline) dollars. The work component (WP) indicates that we are looking at the work performed, or the work that was actually accomplished.

The Actual Cost term shows that the cost component (AC) is expressed in actual dollars, and the work component (WP) in terms of the work performed.

The cost component of the Planned Value term (BC) is expressed in terms of budgeted (or baseline) dollars, and the work component (WS) in terms of the work scheduled (or planned) to be performed. These are summarized in Table 6-3.

	Initials		Component	
Term	**Modern**	**Traditional**	**Cost**	**Work**
Planned Value	PV	BCWS	Planned	Planned
Earned Value	EV	BCWP	Planned	Actual
Actual Cost	AC	ACWP	Actual	Actual

Table 6-3: Cost and Work Components

6-5 COST VARIANCE

Let's take another look at the Cost Variance equation in light of the discussion on cost and work components. Notice that both terms reflect the same work, i.e. the work performed.

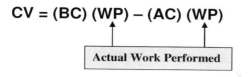

CV = (BC) (WP) – (AC) (WP)

Actual Work Performed

So, for the work that was actually done, we're taking the difference in cost. If the actual cost (AC) of that work is less than what was budgeted (BC) for that work, then the second term is smaller than the first term and the Cost Variance is a positive. That means that the project is under budget, for the work performed, by the magnitude of the Cost Variance.

If the Actual Cost (AC) is greater than the budgeted cost (BC), then the second term is greater than the first term and the Cost Variance is a negative. That means that the project is over budget by the magnitude of the Cost Variance.

6-6 SCHEDULE VARIANCE

In the Schedule Variance equation both terms are on the same cost basis i.e., the budgeted cost. In other words, they are both expressed in units of *value*.

SV = (BC) (WP) – (BC) (WS)

Value of Work Considered

Here we are comparing the value of the work actually performed with the value of the work that was scheduled to be performed as of a given date. If the work performed (WP) is greater than the work that was scheduled (WS), this is generally good. That means the first term is greater than the second term and the difference is positive. The magnitude of the Schedule Variance is then the value of the work by which the project is ahead of schedule.

If the work performed (WP) is less than the work scheduled (WS), that's bad. That means the first term is less than the second term, and the difference is a negative, i.e. the project is behind schedule. The magnitude of the Schedule Variance equals the value of the work that should have been done, but was not.

6-7 FISCAL VARIANCE

Now let us take a look at the Fiscal Variance. Notice that the terms have a different cost basis. One is expressed in budgeted dollars and the other in actual dollars. Also note that the terms are looking at different work. The only thing that both terms have in common (and of course this is true for the components of CV and SV as well) is the data date. The BCWS reflects the funding required as expressed in the baseline plan and ACWP reflects the actual funding required to perform the work actually accomplished.

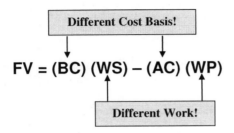

From this we can easily see that using the Fiscal Variance alone does not give an adequate picture of the status of the work in the project. There are too many things varying at once in order for us to get a clear comparison.

6-8 SUMMARY

PV, EV, and AC in the Modern Convention are known as BCWS, BCWP, and ACWP, respectively, in the Traditional Convention. The terms, FV, CV, SV, and BAC are the same in both conventions.

Both the Modern and Traditional Conventions are in widespread use and each EVM practitioner has his or her own preference on which to use. One convention is not inherently better than the other. To operate effectively in the real world, we should be familiar with both conventions since it is likely we could be exposed to either in certain situations.

For the purposes of expediency, we will be using the Modern Convention primarily while developing the concepts in the text. Formula summaries in the chapters and the Appendixes will reflect both conventions.

There are other items, yet to be developed, that are known by different terms in each convention. When these are presented, they will be described both ways. To give the reader practice with both conventions, the exercises at the end of each chapter will use a mix of the conventions.

Table 6-4 contains a summary of all the formulas introduced through this chapter using The Modern Convention, and Table 6-5 contains the same formulas, but using the Traditional Convention.

Modern
$FV = PV - AC$
$CV = EV - AC$
$SV = EV - PV$
$FV = CV - SV$
$CV = SV + FV$
$SV = CV - FV$
$PV = BAC \times (Planned\ \%\ Complete)$
$EV = BAC \times (Actual\ \%\ Complete)$

Table 6-4: Modern Convention Formulas

Traditional
$FV = BCWS - ACWP$
$CV = BCWP - ACWP$
$SV = BCWP - BCWS$
$FV = CV - SV$
$CV = SV + FV$
$SV = CV - FV$
$BCWS = BAC \times (Planned\ \%\ Complete)$
$BCWP = BAC \times (Actual\ \%\ Complete)$

Table 6-5: Traditional Convention Formulas

EXERCISES

6-1: Explain the difference between the two conventions. What are the advantages and disadvantages of each? Which do you prefer and why?

6-2: Perform some independent research on the origins of the Modern Convention. When was the first formal use? Who developed it? How has its acceptance grown over time?

6-3: What does it mean if
a) BCWP is greater than BCWS?
b) BCWP is less than ACWP?
c) ACWP is greater than BCWS?

6-4: Assume, for a project, BCWS = $2500, BCWP = $2250, and ACWP = $2400. Also the project BAC is $10,000.
a) What is the project status with respect to cost and schedule?
b) What per cent of the work (in terms of value) was planned to be complete?
c) What per cent of the work is actually complete?
d) What per cent of the project budget has been spent?

6-5: A task is budgeted to cost $80,000 and is currently 40% complete. The BCWS is $35,000 and the ACWP is $30,000.
a) What are the CV, SV, and FV?
b) Summarize the status of the work.

6-6: A $50,000 task was scheduled to be completed five days ago. It is currently 85% complete and $45,000 has been spent on this task so far.
a) What are BCWS, BCWP, and ACWP?
b) Determine FV, CV, and SV.
c) Characterize the status of the task.

Chapter 7

TASK-LEVEL ANALYSIS

So far we have been concentrating on the Earned Value indicators at the project level. While this is a good start, we may be highly misled if it is all we consider. The project-level figures may be flashing success, but it's still possible for the project to be in serious trouble.

In order to get a deeper understanding of the state of our project, we need to perform our analysis at a finer level of detail. In this chapter we're going to see how we can measure progress at the subproject, task summary, or even the individual task level.

7-1 WHY IS IT IMPORTANT TO LOOK AT MORE DETAIL?

Earlier, when we introduced the Schedule Variance, we learned that SV at the project level may not tell the whole story. Even though the project SV is positive, i.e. more work was performed than planned, it may not be the correct work. The project may be ahead of schedule for non-critical tasks, yet be behind schedule for tasks on the critical path.

A similar situation may also arise when dealing with cost. Consider a case where the project Cost Variance is zero. That means for all the work performed so far, the project is exactly on budget.

Now assume the project is composed of two equal (value-wise) subprojects: Subproject A and Subproject B. Let's also assume that Subproject A has a very high positive (out of tolerance) Cost Variance, and Subproject B has an equally high but negative (also out of tolerance) Cost Variance. See Figure 7-1.

Should we be worried? After all, they exactly offset each other. The answer is a very definitive YES! Let's see why.

Subproject B certainly has problems. The work is costing significantly more than we had planned. This subproject is either consuming more labor hours, units of material, etc. than planned, or the charge rate for these items is higher than planned, or both.

It's possible that this is a one-time occurrence never to be repeated. It's also possible that this is just the start of a trend and the situation could get considerably worse. Whatever the case, since it is out of tolerance on the bad side, it is necessary for us to intervene. Our approach to correct the problem will, of course, depend on what we discover following an investigation of the root cause.

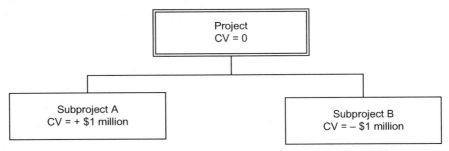

Figure 7-1: Acceptable tolerance for each subproject is CV = ± $100,000

Subproject A is out of tolerance on the "good" side, i.e. it is significantly under budget. What could possibly be the problem here? Maybe we should reward the manager of that subproject for a job well-done. Wouldn't we like to have all of our projects to be delivered under budget if possible? In fact, why should we even set tolerance limits on the good side to begin with?

We do for a very simple reason—*things are not going according to plan* and we need to find out why.

After our investigation, it's possible that we might be pleasantly surprised. In the real world, however, pleasant surprises don't seem to happen very often. It's also possible that something else could be terribly wrong.

There are many potential causes.

1) Maybe we didn't budget properly.

2) There may be a misunderstanding of the requirements, which may eventually result in a rejected deliverable.

3) The quality of the work products may be inferior. It is possible that someone is cutting corners or using substandard materials.

This is certainly not an exhaustive list. If variances are out of tolerance, even on the good side, it's too early to celebrate. We need to find out what's going on. Many projects have been able to identify quality problems in advance because it was noticed that the Cost Variance was positive, yet out of tolerance. The upshot is things are just looking too good to be true.

As we can see in this example, it's certainly possible to have two bad situations adding up to a seemingly good one. If we only look at the project-level indicators, the problems below the surface are masked.

Now that we appreciate the benefit of drilling down to lower levels of the

WBS, we need to determine the four basic indicators for each task, which are listed in Table 7-1.

Initials	Earned Value Element
BAC	Budget at Completion
PV or BCWS	Planned Value
EV or BCWP	Earned Value
AC or ACWP	Actual Cost

Table 7-1: Earned Value Management Elements

With these indicators, we can calculate the Cost Variance, Schedule Variance, Fiscal Variance and other items that we'll define later.

7-2 TASK STATUS EXAMPLE

Let's take a look at the sample project in Figure 7-2. This is a status report, incorporating a Gantt chart, which we might see for a project in progress. The tasks are identified by the letters A through G.

The *Budget* column represents the total amount of money that was budgeted to complete each task. As we now know, these are the values of each task. Each task was scheduled to take four weeks to complete, and we'll assume that the costs for each task were to be evenly distributed over that time.

The actual cost for the work performed so far (*Today* is the end of week 10) is given in the *Actual* column. The bars on the chart are positioned to indicate when each task is scheduled to be in progress according to the baseline plan.

Unlike the example used in Chapter 4, we will not move the task bars to show how the work is rescheduled. There, depicting the current plan, the bars were shifted to show when the work was actually accomplished. Here, depicting the baseline plan, the bars will remain on their originally scheduled dates. One method is not inherently better than the other; they just tell different stories. A comprehensive status report would show both sets of dates for each task, the planned and the actual.

The percentage to the right of each bar reflects the actual amount of work complete as of today in terms of the total value of the task. As a visual cue, the percentage of the bar that is shaded reflects this actual percentage complete.

It's easy to get a quick understanding of our schedule from this representation. Any *unshaded* area to the left of today (the end of week 10) is work that is behind schedule. Any *shaded* area to the right of today is work that is ahead of schedule. From this it is clear that tasks B and C are behind schedule, while tasks D, E, and F are ahead of schedule.

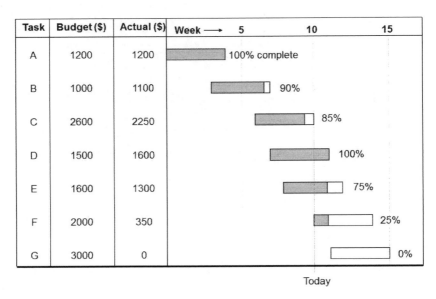

Figure 7-2: Project Status at the End of Week 10

7-3 BUDGET AT COMPLETION (BAC)

We will begin our analysis of project status by summarizing what we know. The BAC for each task is the easiest to determine. It is just the total budgeted cost for each task as expressed in the baseline plan. It is independent of actual cost, independent of when the work was scheduled to be performed, and independent of how much work was actually performed.

In Figure 7-2, the BAC for each task is simply the figure in the Budget column. In other words, the BAC represents the full value of each task. Table 7-2 below reflects this data.

Task	BAC [$]
A	1200
B	1000
C	2600
D	1500
E	1600
F	2000
G	3000
Project	**12,900**

Table 7-2: BAC by Task

We can see that the project BAC, or total budget, for this project is simply the sum of the task BACs, or $12,900.

7-4 ACTUAL COST (ACWP)

The Actual Cost is just the actual amount of money we spent in order to do the work that was performed. It is not something that can be obtained by examining a schedule. While it is conceptually easy to understand, it may be a challenge to obtain current data for this measure in a timely manner in our real-world projects.

As discussed in Chapter 3, the Actual Cost should include all of the costs associated with the work performed, whether or not we have actually yet paid for that work.

For those of us working in large organizations, the Actual Cost may be provided by the finance or accounting department. In this situation, it may be possible that the official figures we receive are delayed by a significant amount of time from when the work actually took place.

For most projects, we can't wait very long before we do our evaluations. Too much can happen to our project in the meantime, and we can't afford for circumstances to get too far away from us. So if there is a significant delay in us receiving official figures, we'll need to generate unofficial figures by estimating these actual costs. Later, we'll make any necessary adjustments when the official figures arrive. It's not that difficult to do, and we can't use delayed official data to be an excuse for not performing a timely analysis.

If we perform weekly evaluations, we may have our task managers send us a status report at the end of each week. This report should include an identification of the work accomplished, the actual labor hours charged, and any material used for that week's efforts. This, combined with the charge rates for each type of resource, will allow us to generate unofficial Actual Cost figures for the past week.

Later, when we receive the official figures, we can see if there are any differences, and make whatever adjustments that might be necessary. Once we understand the nature of those differences, we can then anticipate them as we generate our unofficial figures in the future.

If we are in a small organization, we or our team members are probably the ones generating the official figures directly anyway. In this case we won't have to wait. We just need to make sure we include all of the appropriate costs for the work actually accomplished.

In our sample project, Table 7-3 reflects the Actual Cost data provided to us, and here we'll just accept these figures as given.

With this information we can see that we have actually spent $7,800 of project funds to perform all of the work accomplished on the project so far. This is 7800/12,900 or approximately 60% of the project budget.

Task	BAC [$]	AC [$]
A	1200	1200
B	1000	1100
C	2600	2250
D	1500	1600
E	1600	1300
F	2000	350
G	3000	0
Project	**12,900**	**7,800**

Table 7-3: Adding Actual Costs

7-5 PLANNED VALUE (BCWS)

The Planned Value for a task is the value of the work that is *planned* to be complete as of today. This will be one of the easiest figures to obtain. This is because we know what we plan to achieve through any given date even before we start implementing the project.

Before the planned start date of any task, the Planned Value for that task is zero. During the period when the task is scheduled to be in progress, the Planned Value gradually increases from zero to the task BAC. From the task's scheduled completion date and beyond, the task Planned Value equals the task BAC.

In Figure 7-2, we can see that tasks A, B, and C were scheduled to be complete as of today. Therefore PV equals BAC for these tasks. Task D was scheduled to be in progress. Since task D should be three-fourths complete, PV is three-fourths of the BAC. Task E was also scheduled to be in progress. Since this task should be half complete, PV for Task E is half of the BAC. Tasks F and G were not yet scheduled to begin as of Today. For these, PV equals zero. These results are summarized in Table 7-4.

It is important to note that the *Planned % Complete* column identifies the percentage of *work* planned to be complete as of today, not the percentage of the duration that was planned to be concluded.

If the work distribution is not constant, we need to take that distribution into account. For example, if Task E were scheduled to perform 40% of the work in each of the first two weeks and 10% each of the last two weeks, then the Planned % Complete would be 80% and not 50%.

For simplicity in our example here, we are assuming that the work schedule is constant, i.e. the same amount of work is scheduled for each week for any given task. In this case the Planned % Complete and the planned percentage of the duration concluded are both the same.

Task	BAC [$]	AC [$]	Planned % Complete	PV [$]
A	1200	1200	100	1200
B	1000	1100	100	1000
C	2600	2250	100	2600
D	1500	1600	75	1125
E	1600	1300	50	800
F	2000	350	0	0
G	3000	0	0	0
Project	12,900	7,800		6,725

Table 7-4: Adding Planned Value

The Planned Value just expresses the Planned % Complete in dollar units. To calculate Planned Value we can use Equation 7-1, which we saw earlier as Equation 5-1.

$$Task\ PV = (Task\ BAC) \times (Planned\ \%\ Complete) \qquad (7\text{-}1)$$

After obtaining the Planned Value for each task, we can add up the PV column to determine the Planned Value for the project.

Notice that the value of the work we had planned to deliver as of today at the project level is $6,725. Since we always plan to perform work on budget, it also means that $6,725 of the budget was planned to have been spent. In percentage terms 6725/12,900 or approximately 52% of the work should have been performed and 52% of the budget should have been spent.

The fact that we spent more than we had planned as of today could be a real problem. We may be putting a strain on the funders of the project. We will put this into perspective later when we consider the Fiscal Variance.

7-6 EARNED VALUE (BCWP)

We need one more basic piece of data, the Earned Value, before we can determine all the variances.

For tasks that have not yet *actually* started, the Earned Value is zero. While a task is *actually* in progress, the Earned Value gradually increases from zero to the task's BAC. For tasks that are *actually* complete, the Earned Value is simply equal to the task's BAC.

Determining whether or not a task is actually complete should be simple and objective. Every task should have a well-defined and measurable work product associated with it. If a task is complete, the work product should be complete and meet all of the requirements of that product.

Likewise, it is easy to determine if a task has not yet begun, since there are no charges of any kind associated with the task.

Usually, the most inexact part of the process is determining the actual percent complete of a task in progress. The process we use will vary depending upon the nature of the task. Some tasks have well-defined intermediate milestones that we can use to objectively gauge progress. For example, if our task is to install 40 identically configured computer workstations, and 10 have already been installed, then we can confidently state that the task is actually 25% complete.

Other tasks may not be that straight forward. If the effort involves writing a computer program, it may not be very easy to determine how far along we are. It's possible that everything works correctly the first time we run it. On the other hand it may take a significant amount of time to troubleshoot problems and get all the bugs out.

For this type of task, we may need to confer with our task manager in order to generate an estimate of task progress. Keep in mind that sometimes this can be very subjective.

In this example, the Actual % Complete is given to us in Figure 7-2. We'll just accept these figures at face value and transcribe them into Table 7-5. The Earned Value expresses the Actual % Complete in dollar terms by taking that percentage of the task BAC. To calculate the Earned Value we can use Equation 7-2, which we saw earlier as Equation 5-2.

$$Task\ EV = (Task\ BAC) \times (Actual\ \%\ Complete) \qquad (7\text{-}2)$$

After obtaining the Earned Value for each task, we can add up the EV column to determine the Earned Value of the project.

The value of work that was actually delivered in the whole project is $7,510. This means that 7510/12,900 or approximately 58% of the project work has actually been performed.

Task	BAC [$]	AC [$]	PV [$]	Actual % Complete	EV [$]
A	1200	1200	1200	100	1200
B	1000	1100	1000	90	900
C	2600	2250	2600	85	2210
D	1500	1600	1125	100	1500
E	1600	1300	800	75	1200
F	2000	350	0	25	500
G	3000	0	0	0	0
Project	12,900	7,800	6,725		7,510

Table 7-5: Adding Earned Value

7-7 PROJECT-LEVEL ANALYSIS

Now that we have our basic variables, we can compute the variances, not only at the project level, but at the task level as well. The results are shown in Table 7-6.

Task	BAC [$]	AC [$]	PV [$]	EV [$]	CV [$]	SV [$]	FV [$]
A	1200	1200	1200	1200	0	0	0
B	1000	1100	1000	900	−200	−100	−100
C	2600	2250	2600	2210	−40	−390	350
D	1500	1600	1125	1500	−100	375	−475
E	1600	1300	800	1200	−100	400	−500
F	2000	350	0	500	150	500	−350
G	3000	0	0	0	0	0	0
Project	12,900	7,800	6,725	7,510	−290	785	−1,075

Table 7-6: Variance Calculations

Let's analyze the situation at the project level first.

If we recall, 52% of the project *should* have been complete with 52% of the budget spent. In fact, 58% of the work has actually been performed, but at a cost of over 60% of our budget. From this we can see that (at the project summary level) we are ahead of schedule, but over budget for the work performed so far.

These conclusions are confirmed by the project level CV and SV at the bottom of Table 7-6.

We had planned to perform work with a value of $6725 (Planned Value), and since we plan to deliver the work on budget, we planned to spend $6725 (Baseline Cost) to perform this work. The value of the work that was actually performed is $7510 (Earned Value), however, we actually spent $7800 (Actual Cost) to perform this work.

The variances add to our insight. For the work that was performed, it cost the project $290 more than planned (Cost Variance). The project is over budget by that amount, and if the rest of the work on this project is performed with the same level of cost efficiency, the project is on track to be delivered over budget.

On the other hand, $785 more value was delivered than planned (Schedule Variance) by the end of week 10. This means that, on average, the project is ahead of schedule. If this is representative of the critical path as well as the project overall, and the trend continues, the project will be on track to finish early.

Finally, we see that $1075 more was spent on the project than was planned (Fiscal Variance) through the end of Week 10. In Chapter 4 we saw the relationship between the variances. We can compute FV by this alternate method as follows.

$$FV = CV - SV$$

$$FV = -\$290 - \$785 = -\$1075$$

From this we can see what contributes to the excess spending. Of the additional $1075 required, $290 was due to being over budget for the work that was performed. This is not recoverable unless we can perform future work for a lower cost than planned in order to offset.

The remaining $785 was due to work being performed ahead of schedule. This is a temporary situation. Once the project reaches the planned completion date, the extra demand for funds due to schedule will disappear.

The impact of this negative Fiscal Variance will depend on the situation. Are we required to pay our costs immediately as they are incurred? Can we pass on cost increases to our customer? Can we get paid earlier if we deliver work earlier?

As we might imagine, there are many and varied considerations that will contribute to our interpretation of the severity of this situation. Every project is unique and must be assessed on a case-by-case basis.

7-8 TASK-LEVEL ANALYSIS

Let's now drill down and investigate what's happening at the task level. This will give us more insight than what we discover if we only look at project summary data.

Task A is complete, and its CV is equal to zero. What does this tell us? This means, of course, that the task was completed exactly on budget. We can clearly see this in Table 7-6 since the Actual Cost of the task equals its BAC.

Now let's look at Task A's schedule data. Note that the task's SV is equal to zero.

Question: With regard to schedule, when was Task A completed?

    a) Before the due date

    b) On the due date

    c) After the due date

    d) Not enough information to determine

Since SV is zero for Task A, the immediate response might be "b." From the information that we have available to us here, however, this is incorrect. The correct answer is in fact "d" (not enough information to determine).

What does it mean when SV equals zero for a task? Remember that all of these figures are associated with a data date. In this case the data date is the end of week 10. So, as of the end of week 10, Task A was planned to be complete (Planned Value equals BAC) and in fact it is complete (Earned Value equals BAC). Therefore, as of the end of week 10, there is no Schedule Variance.

SV loses memory over time. Once we get beyond both the planned completion date *and* the actual completion date, the Schedule Variance is always zero.

On the other hand, CV does not lose memory. Once a task is complete and over budget, it will always be on record as being over budget. Does this mean that the Schedule Variance is a useless indicator at the task level? Absolutely not! The purpose of the Schedule Variance here is to tell us which tasks are *currently* ahead or behind schedule. If we think about it, there's nothing we can do to correct tasks that are complete. We can still influence tasks that are in progress or have not yet begun. These are the ones that the task-level SV will point us toward.

This doesn't mean that there is no utility in looking at tasks that are already complete. If a current task is behind schedule, it may be because it started late due to a predecessor finishing late. We would then investigate that predecessor to obtain lessons-learned so that we can apply them to our project going forward.

Of course, we're not going to wait until we're 58% of the way through the project to take our first reading. Ideally, we should be assessing status every few percent or so.

Question: If a report similar to that in Table 7-6 is the only *type* of report available to us, how could we determine if Task A was completed behind schedule?

Obviously we cannot tell from this particular report. The key word in the question is "type." We need to obtain the report for the data date that matches the planned completion date for Task A. In this case we need to look at the report for the end of week 4. If SV equals zero for Task A in that report, then we would know that it was not completed late.

Let's now take a look at Tasks B and C. Both are in a similar situation having negative Schedule Variances. This means that each is currently behind schedule. The magnitudes of these Schedule Variances correspond to the values of the unfinished work. As we can see from Figure 7-2, both tasks should have been complete, but in fact they are still in progress. Any unshaded areas on the bars in the Gantt chart appearing earlier than today represent negative Schedule Variances.

Tasks B and C also have negative Cost Variances. This means that for the work performed so far, each cost more than planned. The Actual Cost for Task B is already more than its entire budget (BAC). While the Actual Cost for Task C is still below its BAC, it is on track to be delivered over budget if the trend continues. In this case, by intervening (and depending on what the problem is), we may be able to make enough modifications to alter the course of this task. It may be difficult, though, since this task is almost complete.

Notice that Task C has a favorable (positive) Fiscal Variance. It is putting a smaller demand on the organization for its funding than planned. We can see from the combination of CV and SV that the main reason for that is that much less work was performed than planned. For the work performed so far, the task is actually over budget.

Task D is complete even though the plan was for it to be only 75% complete. This is reflected in its positive Schedule Variance. In Figure 7-2, any shaded portion of the bar, later than the data date, is represented by a positive Schedule Variance. Tasks E and F are also in a similar situation in this respect.

Task D is over budget by $100. Since it is complete (Earned Value equals BAC) there is no opportunity to recover any of the overage from this task.

Task E is also over budget, but since there is 25% of that task left to be done, there may be a chance to make up at least some of the overage if the problem is addressed immediately.

Task F is early and on track to come in under budget. We certainly want to keep an eye on this one and be sure it does not begin to stray.

As we can see, there is a wealth of information that can be gleaned from looking at status reports at the task level. We will revisit this situation in later chapters as we introduce additional tools to help us analyze our status.

7-9 FIFTY-FIFTY RULE

Sometimes it can be difficult to get a good measure of the amount of value delivered for a task that is in progress. Some task managers will overestimate and others will underestimate, and it is easy for bias to sneak into the determination. When a task is complete, however, we have an objective measure. In that case, Earned Value equals the BAC.

This is a good argument for not making our tasks too large. For example, if our tasks are all about a week in duration and we do our formal evaluations on a weekly basis, then we will always within a week of knowing *objectively*, the status of our project.

If we must have long duration tasks, we should look for measurable milestones within the task that are spaced at regular intervals. This way we will have objective measures to give us the confidence in the progress taking place.

For tasks in progress without objective measures we can always make an educated guess or take the words of our task managers. Another popular approach, however, is to use the *50-50 Rule*.

The 50-50 Rule employs a simple mechanical scheme that will eliminate any bias. It works like this. Before a task starts, the Earned Value is zero just like before. As soon as a task actually begins, the Earned Value equals half of the BAC. In other words 50% of its value is considered to be earned. The other 50% is earned when the task is complete. Then the Earned Value equals the BAC, just like before.

The reasoning behind this is that at any time, some of the tasks in progress will be less than half done, and others will be more than half done. Hopefully, it will balance out statistically and we'll get a fairly realistic picture of the actual value delivered over the whole project. The attractiveness of this method is that it is simple, mechanical, and eliminates human bias.

This works well when our task durations are appropriately sized, i.e. they are relatively short in duration. The 50-50 rule breaks down if our task durations are too long. For instance, if all of our tasks are 8 week long, and we apply this rule the first week of the project, we can see that the result will be an unrealistically high estimate of the true Earned Value.

As an example of an application of the 50-50 Rule, we will use the sample project developed for this chapter. Table 7-7 shows the Earned Value and subsequent variances assuming that the 50-50 Rule was used. Notice from Figure 7-2 that Tasks B, C, E, and F are in progress. Therefore the Earned Values for these tasks are half of the task BAC.

Task	BAC [$]	AC [$]	PV [$]	EV [$]	CV [$]	SV [$]	FV [$]
A	1200	1200	1200	1200	0	0	0
B	1000	1100	1000	500	−600	−500	−100
C	2600	2250	2600	1300	−950	−1300	350
D	1500	1600	1125	1500	−100	375	−475
E	1600	1300	800	800	−500	0	−500
F	2000	350	0	1000	650	1000	−350
G	3000	0	0	0	0	0	0
Project	12,900	7,800	6,725	6,300	−1,500	−425	−1,075

Table 7-7: Earned Value Determined using 50-50 Rule

Compare Table 7-7 with Table 7-6. Notice that the Actual Costs and Planned Values are not affected. The Fiscal Variance is also unaffected because it is independent of the Earned Value. Cost Variance and Schedule Variance both depend on Earned Value, so obviously they are subject to modification. It is interesting to note that the differences between these two variances is not affected. That is "CV – SV" is the same whether the 50-50 rule is used or not. This difference, of course, is just the Fiscal Variance.

In this project there is a significant difference in Earned Values depending on the method used. Here the Earned Value is much less than before. So in this specific case, the 50-50 rule results in an underestimate of Earned Value. In other cases it could result in an overestimate.

Notice the Cost Variance. It went from slightly negative to significantly negative. The Schedule Variance is even more dramatic. It went from positive to negative.

This situation is obviously not representative of most projects. Here we have a majority of our tasks (4 of 7) in progress and subject to the 50-50 rule. The shorter the task durations, the smaller the average task BAC, and the smaller the number of tasks in progress, the less influence any difference in the methods will have in the project data.

If we choose to employ the 50-50 rule, we aren't obligated to use it for all of our tasks. We can have a mix. For example, we might use actual Earned Values where we have high confidence in the numbers, and use the 50-50 Rule in situations where we have low confidence or no information.

There are also variations on the 50-50 Rule. If the value to be delivered is not evenly distributed over the duration of the task, we may want to split up the value in unequal amounts. For instance, if the effort is front loaded, we may want to use a 60-40 Rule for that task. In this case, 60% of the task's value will be considered to be earned when the task begins. The remaining 40% will be earned when the task is complete.

On the other hand, the effort might be evenly distributed, but we want to be more conservative. In this case we might choose to use a 40-60 rule. We can use these or any other variant of the rule that may be appropriate for our situation.

Of course the ultimate conservative approach would be to use a 0-100 rule. Here no value is considered to be earned until the task is complete. Many practitioners like to use this approach in addition to their regular approach to give a "worst case" scenario.

7-10 SUMMARY

It is important to set tolerance limits on the "good" side as well as the "bad" side of a variance.

Looking at task-level EVM data will give us an insight into the internal workings of our projects. We now have tools to help us determine which tasks we should focus on if we realize we have a problem with cost or schedule.

This approach will also allow us to identify problems that are lurking under the surface, but might not reveal themselves if we're only looking at project-level data.

Schedule Variances indicate which tasks are currently ahead of or behind schedule. Since they lose memory over time, they will not indicate if a task finished on time.

The fifty-fifty rule is a tool that can be used to determine the Earned Value of tasks in progress. It can apply in situations where there is no information or there is low confidence in the actual percent complete figure provided for a task.

EXERCISES

7-1: Explain the importance of performing EVM analysis at the task level. What may we be missing if we only look at project-level data?

7-2: Why is it important to set tolerance limits on both the positive and negative sides of FV, CV, and SV?

7-3: Discuss the possible causes and impacts of each of the variances being out of tolerance on the positive side. Consider each one separately.

    a) SV

    b) CV

    c) FV

7-4: What data should be included and excluded when compiling the Actual Cost data for an EVM analysis?

7-5: A $2500 task is currently in progress. 40% of the work should have been completed and the actual cost so far is $1400. Using the 50-50 rule, analyze the status of this task.

7-6: Using the example project for this chapter, assume it is now the end of week 12. Tasks A through D are 100% complete. Task E is 95% complete, Task F is 45% complete, and Task G is 35% complete. The Actual Cost for Task B is $1200, for Task C is $2500, for Task E is $1500, for task F is $1200, and for Task G is $1100.

    a) Develop the equivalent of Table 7-6 for the end of Week 12.

    b) Determine the status of this project. What are the prospects of finishing within the original budget? Within the original schedule? Did the project gain or lose ground over the last two weeks?

7-7: Analyze the same situation in Exercise 7-6, but use the 50-50 rule instead of the actual percent complete. How does this affect the assessment of project status?

7-8: The plan for a project is given in the following table. Assume all tasks are scheduled to take place as soon as possible and that the budget for each task is evenly distributed over the life of the task.

Task ID	Duration [weeks]	Predecessor	Budget [$]
A	3		6,000
B	5		15,000
C	4	A, B	9,600
D	3	B	15,000
E	3	C	10,200
F	2	D	5,000

The next table displays the status of this project at the end of Week 7.

Task ID	Actual % Complete	Actual Cost [$]
A	100%	6,000
B	100%	15,500
C	30%	3,000
D	80%	11,600
E	0	0
F	0	0

Perform a comprehensive cost, schedule, and spending analysis of project status and the status of each task. Be sure to include the Schedule Variance of the critical path as well as the overall project Schedule Variance. Which tasks (if any) are causing problems? What are the prospects for finishing on budget and on schedule?

Chapter 8

VARIANCE PERCENTAGES

8-1 INTRODUCTION

The Cost Variance and Schedule Variance are very powerful indicators. They convey, in absolute terms, how much the project is under (or over) budget, or ahead of (or behind) schedule. What they don't do, however, is put into perspective how efficiently the work is progressing relative to the size of the project.

Let's say that as of today one of our projects should have spent $5 million for the work performed and we have a Cost Variance of –$5,000. This means that we spent $5,000 more than we planned for the work we did so far. Also assuming that this is a good representation of status at the task level, how worried should we be? Probably not very worried. This only represents 0.1% of the budget. Most of us would be very happy to be in this situation.

Now consider a different project where we should have spent $10,000 as of today. If we have that same –$5,000 Cost Variance, how worried would we be? Very worried! That is a 50% difference, which is significant in anyone's book.

Notice that in both cases we have the same variance but with two totally different interpretations. So, how do we put these variances into perspective for the size of project? One way is to look at the variances as a percentage of the values that we had planned to deliver. These *Variance Percentages* are normalized to the size of the project and provide a measure of performance independent of project size.

8-2 EXAMPLE # 1: WORKING WITH VARIANCE PERCENTAGES

In this example, we'll be using the sample project from the last chapter that is summarized in Figure 7-2 and Table 7-6. Table 7-6 is repeated here as Table 8-1. Recall that the data represented here is a snapshot in time at the end of Week 10.

Task	BAC [$]	AC [$]	PV [$]	EV [$]	CV [$]	SV [$]	FV [$]
A	1200	1200	1200	1200	0	0	0
B	1000	1100	1000	900	−200	−100	−100
C	2600	2250	2600	2210	−40	−390	350
D	1500	1600	1125	1500	−100	375	−475
E	1600	1300	800	1200	−100	400	−500
F	2000	350	0	500	150	500	−350
G	3000	0	0	0	0	0	0
Project	12,900	7,800	6,725	7,510	−290	785	−1,075

Table 8-1: Project Status at the End of Week 10

Let's assume that our acceptable tolerance limits are ±5% for cost, ±10% for schedule, and ±10% for spending. These will be measured by the Cost Variance Percentage, the Schedule Variance Percentage, and the Fiscal Variance Percentage respectively. How well are we doing? We'll see shortly, but first we need to define these variance percentages.

8-3 COST VARIANCE PERCENTAGE (CV%)

Just like any percentage difference, we take the difference from the original divided by the original. The Cost Variance is the difference between the amount of money that was budgeted for the work performed (Earned Value) and what it actually cost to perform that work (Actual Cost).

The Cost Variance Percentage (or CV%) then is simply the ratio of the Cost Variance to the Earned Value. This tells us how much we are over or under budget as a percentage of our original budget. In other words, it tells us if we're getting the proper value for the money we are spending.

Equation 8-1a gives us the CV% using the Modern Convention and Equation 8-1b using the Traditional Convention.

$$\textbf{Modern: } CV \% = \frac{CV}{EV} \tag{8-1a}$$

$$\textbf{Traditional: } CV \% = \frac{CV}{BCWP} \tag{8-1b}$$

The data in Table 8-1 gives us everything we need to easily calculate the Cost Variance Percentage. Notice that the project level CV = −$290 and EV = $7510. Since the CV is negative, the work performed cost $290 more than was budgeted for that work. We can now calculate the Cost Variance Percentage making sure to express the final result as a percentage.

$$CV\% = \frac{-\$290}{\$7510} = -0.039 = -3.9\%$$

CV% always has the same sign as CV since the Earned Value in the denominator can never be negative. The same convention applies here as with the cost variance: positive is good and negative is bad. If the cost is on target, then CV% is zero. If CV% is positive, the work is under budget, and if CV% is negative the work is over budget.

In this example, the work in question is over budget by 3.9%, or the work performed so far cost us 3.9% more than planned. If the rest of the project proceeds with the same average cost efficiency, we'll end up completing this project 3.9% over budget.

Since this project CV% is within our acceptable tolerance limits of ±5%, we can say that overall, our project is in control with respect to cost.

CV% can be expressed using a different formula, but of course yielding the same results. We can see that here in Equations 8-2a and 8-2b.

Modern: $CV\% = 1 - \dfrac{AC}{EV}$ (8-2a)

Traditional: $CV\% = 1 - \dfrac{ACWP}{BCWP}$ (8-2b)

The attractiveness of using this form is that the CV% is in terms of the basic data elements directly. The Cost Variance doesn't need to be calculated as an intermediate step. If we use the values in the example above we get the following.

$$CV\% = 1 - \frac{\$7800}{\$7510} = 1 - 1.039 = -.039 = -3.9\%$$

The maximum value for CV% on the positive side is 100%, since the project can't be more than 100% under budget. On the negative side, however, the value of CV% is unbounded, since there is no limit to how much the work can be over budget.

8-4 SCHEDULE VARIANCE PERCENTAGE (SV%)

Schedule Variance is the difference between the amount of work planned to be performed (Planned Value) and the amount of work actually performed (Earned Value). The Schedule Variance Percentage (or SV%) then is simply the ratio of the Schedule Variance to the Planned Value expressed as a percentage. This tells us how much we are ahead or behind schedule as a percentage of our original schedule.

The formulas for SV% are given in Equations 8-3a and 8-3b.

$$\textbf{Modern: } SV\% = \frac{SV}{PV} \tag{8-3a}$$

$$\textbf{Traditional: } SV\% = \frac{SV}{BCWS} \tag{8-3b}$$

Using the values given in Table 8-1 above, we have at the project level SV = $785 and PV = $6725. Since the SV is positive, we performed more work than planned and the project is ahead of schedule. The value of this extra work is $785. We can now calculate the Schedule Variance Percentage, making sure to express the final result as a percentage.

$$SV\% = \frac{\$785}{\$6725} = 0.117 = 11.7\%$$

SV% always has the same sign as SV since the Planned Value in the denominator can never be negative. The same convention applies here as with the schedule variance: positive is good and negative is bad. If the project is on schedule, then SV% is zero. If SV% is positive, we performed more work than planned, and if SV% is negative, we performed less work than planned.

In this example, the work in question is ahead of schedule by 11.7%. That is, we performed 11.7% more work (in terms of value) than we planned. If the rest of the project keeps to this trend, the project is on target to finish early. This assumes, of course, that the correct work is being performed along the way.

Since the SV% is outside of our acceptable tolerance limits of ±10% we would say that our project is out of control with respect to schedule.

Similar to CV%, SV% can be expressed using a different formula, but yielding the same results. This is given in Equations 8-4a and 8-4b.

$$\textbf{Modern: } SV\% = \frac{EV}{PV} - 1 \tag{8-4a}$$

$$\textbf{Traditional: } SV\% = \frac{BCWP}{BCWS} - 1 \tag{8-4b}$$

In this form SV% is in terms of the basic data elements directly, and the Schedule Variance does not need to be calculated as an intermediate step. If we use the values in the example above we get the following.

$$SV\% = \frac{\$7510}{\$6725} - 1 = 1.117 - 1 = 0.117 = 11.7\%$$

The maximum value for SV% on the positive side is unbounded, or we might say "at infinity." We would see this if no work was scheduled as of today, but some work was actually accomplished. The value of SV% cannot be less than −100%. This means that we can't be behind schedule by more than all of the planned work. SV% = −100% when we are beyond the planned start date of the work, but no work has *actually* been started.

8-5 FISCAL VARIANCE PERCENTAGE (FV%)

The Fiscal Variance tells us how much money we've actually spent (Actual Cost) vs. how much we had planned to spend (Planned Value) as of a given date. In other words, it indicates how much we're under-spending (or over-spending) our money with respect to the calendar, not the work performed. The Fiscal Variance Percentage then is simply the ratio of the Fiscal Variance to the Planned Value expressed as a percentage. This tells us how much more or less money we spent as a percentage of our original plan.

Equations 8-5a and 8-5b give us the FV% in each convention.

Modern: $FV\% = \dfrac{FV}{PV}$ $\hspace{4cm}$ (8-5a)

Traditional: $FV\% = \dfrac{FV}{BCWS}$ $\hspace{3cm}$ (8-5b)

From Table 8-1 we see that the Fiscal Variance is −$1075. Since the variance is negative, this means that we spent $1075 more than planned as of the end of Week 10.

Now computing the Fiscal Variance Percentage we have the following.

$$FV\% = \frac{-\$1075}{\$6725} = -0.160 = -16.0\%$$

FV% always has the same sign as FV since the Planned Value in the denominator can never be negative. If the spending rate is on target, then FV% is zero. If FV% is positive, we spent money less rapidly than we planned, and if FV% is negative, we spent money more rapidly than we planned.

In this example, we have spent 16.0% more money than we had planned to spend at the end of Week 10. We are clearly out of tolerance with respect to spending since our acceptable range is $\pm 10\%$.

We would need to look at the Cost Variance and Schedule Variance to see if this additional spending was due to us being over budget, by being ahead of schedule, or some combination. The FV% may give us an indication of the cash flow pressures we could experience.

From the calculations we performed earlier for CV% and SV%, we can see that the requirement for extra money came from a combination of the work performed being over budget and by being is ahead of schedule.

Like the other percentages, FV% can be expressed using a different formula, but yielding the same results. This can be seen in Equations 8-6a and 8-6b.

$$\textbf{Modern: } FV\% = 1 - \frac{AC}{PV} \tag{8-6a}$$

$$\textbf{Traditional: } FV\% = 1 - \frac{ACWP}{BCWS} \tag{8-6b}$$

Here FV% is in terms of the basic data elements directly. The Fiscal Variance does not need to be calculated as an intermediate step. If we use the values in the example above we get the following.

$$FV\% = 1 - \frac{\$7800}{\$6725} = 1 - 1.160 = -0.160 = -16.0\%$$

Table 8-2 provides a summary of the range of possible variance percentage values.

Variance %	Minimum Value	Maximum Value
CV%	$-$ infinity	$+ 100\%$
SV%	$- 100\%$	$+$ infinity
FV%	$-$ infinity	$+ 100\%$

Table 8-2: Variance % Range of Values

8-6 VARIANCE PERCENTAGES AT THE TASK LEVEL

We know that our sample project is over budget, but within tolerance with respect to cost. Also, more work was performed than planned, but the project is out of tolerance with respect to schedule. Finally, we're spending money faster than planned, again out of tolerance. We can see these project-level results summarized here in Table 8-3.

Task	BAC [$]	CV [$]	SV [$]	FV [$]	CV%	SV%	FV%
A	1200	0	0	0			
B	1000	−200	−100	−100			
C	2600	−40	−390	350			
D	1500	−100	375	−475			
E	1600	−100	400	−500			
F	2000	150	500	−350			
G	3000	0	0	0			
Project	12,900	−290	785	−1,075	−3.9%	11.7%	−16.0%

Table 8-3: Project Summary of Variance Percentages

We may now want to consider which tasks are the bad actors, i.e. contributing most to the problems. As we can see from Table 8-3, the cells for the variance percentages at the task level are vacant. The next obvious step is to calculate these variance percentages and see which of the tasks are out of tolerance.

Exercise: Do the calculations to complete Table 8-3; then compare the results with the answers in Table 8-4. What issue needs to be addressed when calculating the variance percentages for Tasks F and G?

Task	BAC [$]	CV [$]	SV [$]	FV [$]	CV%	SV%	FV%
A	1200	0	0	0	0.0%	0.0%	0.0%
B	1000	−200	−100	−100	−22.2%	−10.0%	−10.0%
C	2600	−40	−390	350	−1.8%	−15.0%	13.5%
D	1500	−100	375	−475	−6.7%	33.3%	−42.2%
E	1600	−100	400	−500	−8.3%	50.0%	−62.5%
F	2000	150	500	−350	30.0%	infinity	−infinity
G	3000	0	0	0	—	—	—
Project	12,900	−290	785	−1,075	−3.9%	11.7%	−16.0%

Table 8-4: Task-Level Variance Percentages

Notice that in Table 8-1, which is the source of the data for our calculations, there are several zeros. Zeros pose no problems when calculating variances, since zeros are well-behaved under subtraction. Zeros often do not play well with division, however. See Appendix D for guidance on how to handle division with zero.

Now we'll analyze what's happening at the task level using the data in Table 8-4. First of all, notice the dashes in the table for Task G. This means that we have no usable data; there is nothing to analyze.

Starting with the cost, we determined earlier that we were within our ±5% tolerance at the project level. Are all the tasks within tolerance? No. In fact we have four tasks that are out of tolerance with respect to cost: B, D, E, and F. As we can see, poor performance at the task level can be hidden at the project level. If we only look at project-level figures, we're not getting the whole story.

How about schedule? Notice that the project is out of the ±10% tolerance limits. So are four of the tasks: C, D, E, and F. We are giving the benefit of the doubt to task B which is on the border. Notice that Task E is out by 50%, and Task F is at infinity!

A variance percentage at infinity simply means that no matter how big the tolerance limits are, we are automatically out of tolerance on the good side. In this case Task F is out of tolerance ahead of schedule. This may or may not actually be a real problem. It's just an indicator that things are not going according to plan and we should investigate the cause. We can then determine how worried we should be, and whether corrective action is necessary.

The overall spending is out of tolerance at the project level as evidenced by the Project FV%. Four tasks are out: C, D, E, and F. Notice that E is out by a whopping 62.5% and F is at negative infinity!

A variance percentage at negative infinity simply means that no matter how big the tolerance limits are, we are automatically out of tolerance on the bad side. In this case Task F is over spending and out of tolerance. Again, this is an indication that things are not going according to plan and we should do our due diligence and investigate the situation.

The tasks that are out of tolerance are the ones to which we want to focus our attention. Our corrective action decisions will of course vary depending on our findings of the root causes. At least now, we'll know where we should be looking in order to find the problems.

Question: Is it possible for the project-level indicators to be within tolerance yet for every single task to be out of tolerance? By now we should quickly recognize that the answer is yes! Some tasks could be out of tolerance on the positive side and the others out of tolerance on the negative side. If they balance and nearly cancel each other out, the project will appear to be comfortably within tolerance. This is why it's important not to focus only on project-level indicators. They could be masking problems beneath the surface.

8-7 COMPARING THE VARIANCE PERCENTAGES

In Chapter 4 we saw that the CV, SV, and FV are related to each other. It is also the case that CV%, SV%, and FV% are related. If we know the values of any two of these, we can always find the third. The relationships are shown below. Note that Equations 8-7a and 8-7b are equivalent.

$$FV \% = 1 - (1 - CV \%)(1 + SV \%) \qquad (8\text{-}7a)$$

$$FV \% = CV \% - SV \% + (CV \%)(SV \%) \qquad (8\text{-}7b)$$

$$SV \% = \frac{1 - FV \%}{1 - CV \%} - 1 \qquad (8\text{-}8)$$

$$CV \% = 1 - \frac{1 - FV \%}{1 + SV \%} \qquad (8\text{-}9)$$

Recall that FV is simply the difference between CV and SV (see Equation 4-4). Notice that the relationship among the variance percentages is a little more complex. There is a correction term (CV%)(SV%) that must be included. Some practitioners use the difference between CV% and SV% to get a quick and dirty number for FV%. Omitting this correction term may give a result that's close enough if all we need a ballpark number, however we can see from Equation 8-7b that this is not exact.. Note that as the CV% and SV% decrease, the correction term becomes less important.

Let's investigate this for our Example # 1. To summarize what we already know, CV% = −3.9%, SV% = 11.7%, and FV% = −16.0%.

Without the correction term, the approximation for FV% is CV% − SV% = −3.9% − 11.7% = −15.6%. Notice that it is off by 0.4%. Once we include the correction term, we'll have the correct result of −16.0% for FV% (within rounding).

8-8 TOLERANCE LIMITS

The previous example illustrated how we can generate variance percentages at any point in time. These are just snapshots, however, valid for a specific date. The real power of these variance percentages comes by tracking them over time and generating trends.

It's good practice for our project plans to identify the acceptable tolerance limits for each of the indicators that we plan to employ in our tracking. For Earned Value Management, providing these acceptable ranges directly to the variances (CV and SV) is not the best approach. Acceptable ranges for CV and SV will vary depending on how much of the project has been completed.

It is far easier to work with the variance percentages. Acceptable ranges for CV% and SV% can be fixed for the life of the project. Also, we must remember to set acceptable tolerance limits on both the positive and negative sides.

For example, our acceptable tolerance may be ±10% for both cost and schedule variances. This means that if –10% ≤ CV% ≤ 10% and –10% ≤ SV% ≤ 10% then the project is within acceptable limits for cost and schedule. Figure 8-1 depicts a sample graph of cumulative CV% measurements for such a situation. This type of graph is known as a *Control Chart*. Notice that in this case CV% is never out of tolerance the entire time.

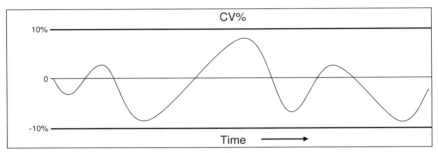

Figure 8-1: CV% is within Acceptable Tolerance Limits

If the CV% curve were to ever penetrate either 10% boundary we would have an intolerable situation. At this point we would say that the project is out of control with respect to cost and corrective action would need to be taken. Similar graphs could be constructed for SV% and FV%.

Intermediate levels can be used as warning indicators. For example, we might define ±5% as our warning level as shown in Figure 8-2. If CV% remains within ±5% the condition is satisfactory. Some like to use stop light colors to give a high-level indication. In this case we might say that the condition is "green."

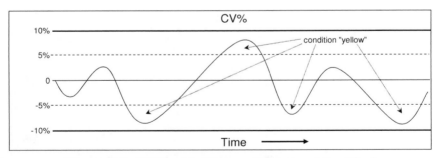

Figure 8-2: CV% with Times of Caution Identified

If CV% migrates outside of this band, but remains within ±10% then this would indicate condition "yellow." Technically we are still within tolerance so the situation is not dire, but the project has crossed over our self-imposed warning line. This indicates that we should take notice that our costs might be headed out of tolerance.

In Figure 8-2 there are four instances when CV% exceeded the 5% warning bands. We may be able to infer that proper action was taken to prevent the condition from turning to red. If that was the case, then those interventions were successful. By using an approach like this, we can be more proactive and not operate in a reactive crisis management mode.

If CV% penetrates the ±10% levels, then the condition is "red" or intolerable and we must take action immediately. If, in this case, we don't bring CV% within the acceptable tolerance limits before the project is over, we'll have a failed project with respect to cost.

8-9 WHAT ARE ACCEPTABLE RANGES FOR TOLERANCE LIMITS?

All the variances do not need to have the same tolerance limits. For example, if cost were more important than schedule, we might have tighter limits on CV% than we have on SV%. In this case the acceptable tolerance limits might be expressed as follows:

$$-7\% \leq CV\% \leq 7\%$$

$$-10\% \leq SV\% \leq 10\%$$

The bands do not even need to be symmetric about the centerline. We may feel that it is more acceptable to be under budget than over budget and more acceptable to be ahead of schedule than behind schedule. In this case the acceptable limits could be something like

$$-8\% \leq CV\% \leq 12\%$$

$$-5\% \leq SV\% \leq 10\%$$

The acceptable tolerance limits are negotiated items and should be agreed upon by the relevant stakeholders before project implementation begins. Every situation is unique, so limits that work in one project may not be applicable to another project. Most organizations have rules of thumb that they use for different types of projects.

These limits should also be included in the baseline plan, ensuring that all the participants know the ground rules going in. This will help to avoid confusion and prevent misunderstandings from developing later.

8-10 EXAMPLE # 2: WORKING WITH TOLERANCE LIMITS

Variance percentages can be charted on an incremental (e.g., weekly, biweekly, or monthly) basis as well as a cumulative basis. Although we judge the final project status by the cumulative variance percentages, the incremental figures can give us early warning, since trend changes will be noticed first in the incremental figures.

Here we'll look at an example of a project and chart the incremental CV% (inc CV%) and cumulative CV% (cum CV%). In this case, each incremental period will be one week. Table 8-5 gives us the Planned Value data for the project where "inc PV" designates the incremental Planned Value and "cum PV" is the cumulative Planned Value.

Week	inc PV [$K]	cum PV [$K]
1	90	90
2	115	205
3	165	370
4	175	545
5	190	735
6	225	960
7	240	1200
8	310	1510
9	250	1760
10	200	1960
11	160	2120
12	80	2200

Table 8-5: Baseline Project Plan

The incremental PV identifies the value of the work that is planned to be performed in any given week. The cumulative PV is the sum of the incremental Planned Values from the beginning of the project through the current week.

We can plot the cumulative Planned Value data and develop the graph that appears in Figure 8-3. As we can see, the Budget at Completion is $2.2 million and the Planned Duration of the project is 12 weeks.

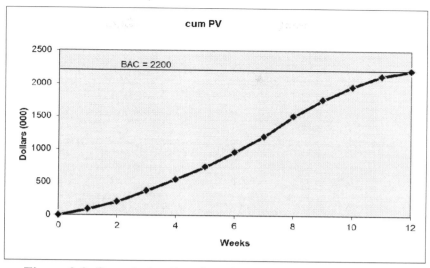

Figure 8-3: Cumulative Baseline Cost or Planned Value Curve

As part of our baseline plan, we should also include the acceptable tolerance limits for the indicators that we feel are important. In this case we'll assume that CV% and SV% must be within ±10%. If they go outside of these limits we'll consider the condition to be "red." We will also give ourselves a caution level at ±5%. If they exceed this range we'll say the condition is "yellow."

If we can maintain these tolerance limits all the way through the project, the final cost for the project will be within 10% of the BAC. The final Schedule Variance will always be zero of course.

8-11 COST EVALUATION OF EXAMPLE # 2

Let's assume we are six weeks into the project and have actual data to analyze. Table 8-6 gives us a summary of that data, which includes both incremental and cumulative figures for EV and AC.

Week	inc EV [$K]	cum EV [$K]	inc AC [$K]	cum AC [$K]
1	100	100	101	101
2	120	220	124	225
3	160	380	168	393
4	210	590	226	619
5	160	750	176	795
6	180	930	204	999

Table 8-6: EV and AC Data through Week 6

We can add the cumulative data for Earned Value and Actual Cost to Figure 8-3 to give us the three curves shown in Figure 8-4. As we can see, the bottom curve for the latest date is the Earned Value curve. This means that as of the end of Week 6, the project is both over budget and behind schedule. How significant are the variances in relation to our tolerance limits?

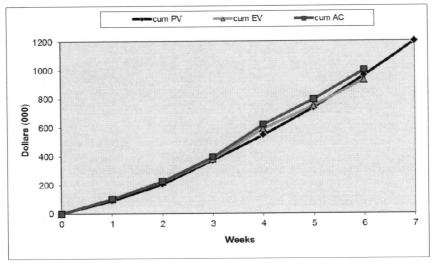

Figure 8-4: Cumulative Cost Curves through the End of Week 6

The best way to tell is to do the calculations. Let's first look at the project costs. We can generate a table with the Cost Variance data week by week as well as the figures for CV%. The results can be seen in Table 8-7.

Week	inc CV [$K]	cum CV [$K]	inc CV%	cum CV%
1	−1	−1	−1.0%	−1.0%
2	−4	−5	−3.3%	−2.3%
3	−8	−13	−5.0%	−3.4%
4	−16	−29	−7.6%	−4.9%
5	−16	−45	−10.0%	−6.0%
6	−24	−69	−13.3%	−7.4%

Table 8-7: CV and CV% Data through Week 6

As we can see, for the work performed so far, the project is $69,000 over budget. Also, while the cumulative CV% is within tolerance, the incremental (weekly) CV% for Week 6 is out of tolerance. If we plot the historical data on a control chart, we will be able to see the trends a lot easier. Figure 8-5 is a control chart through Week 6.

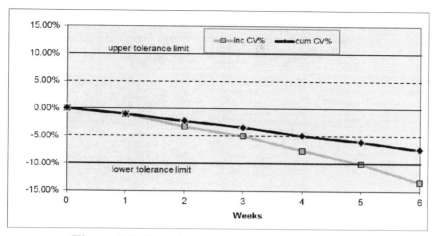

Figure 8-5: Cost Control Chart through Week 6

We can see that on a cumulative basis, our cost overage entered the "yellow" range at the end of Week 5 and remains there today. Our weekly, or incremental, data turned "yellow" on Week 4, giving us early warning. It went "red" this week (Week 6), giving us an indication that the project will be going "red" if we do not take immediate corrective action. Although the project is officially within tolerance, the trend doesn't look good. If the incremental percentage stays out of tolerance long enough, the cumulative is sure to follow.

Let's assume at this point that we have determined the root cause of the problem and we decide to take massive corrective action. Let's also assume that the result of this action generated the data for the rest of the project through Week 12, which is when the project was planned to be completed. The results are displayed in Table 8-8.

Notice that the project is not actually complete since the cumulative Earned Value is less than the project BAC of $2,200,000. Also notice that the cumulative Actual Cost to date is $2,220,000.

Table 8-9 allows us to evaluate the costs with the incremental and cumulative Cost Variances and their respective CV%. Notice that the latest cumulative CV% is −2.8%. This, of course indicates that the project is currently over budget by 2.8%. This was well within our acceptable tolerance levels of ±10%, so we can declare that our corrective action was successful in terms of cost control.

Week	inc EV [$K]	cum EV [$K]	inc AC [$K]	cum AC [$K]
1	100	100	101	101
2	120	220	124	225
3	160	380	168	393
4	210	590	226	619
5	160	750	176	795
6	180	930	204	999
7	240	1170	240	1239
8	300	1470	310	1549
9	260	1730	256	1805
10	180	1910	180	1985
11	150	2060	140	2125
12	100	2160	95	2220

Table 8-8: Project History through Week 12

Week	inc CV [$K]	cum CV [$K]	inc CV%	cum CV%
1	−1	−1	−1.0%	−1.0%
2	−4	−5	−3.3%	−2.3%
3	−8	−13	−5.0%	−3.4%
4	−16	−29	−7.6%	−4.9%
5	−16	−45	−10.0%	−6.0%
6	−24	−69	−13.3%	−7.4%
7	0	−69	0.0%	−5.9%
8	−10	−79	−3.3%	−5.4%
9	4	−75	1.5%	−4.3%
10	0	−75	0.0%	−3.9%
11	10	−65	6.7%	−3.2%
12	5	−60	5.0%	−2.8%

Table 8-9: CV and CV% Data through Week 12

We can also see that, while the incremental CV% was out of tolerance at one point, the cumulative CV% was never out of tolerance. Figure 8-6 depicts this data in the cost control chart through the end of Week 12.

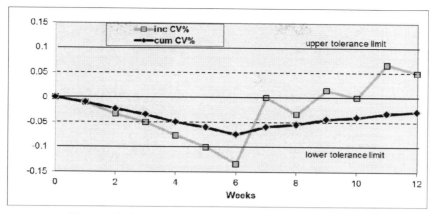

Figure 8-6: Cost Control Chart through Week 12

Here it is easy to see the trends. Notice that when the incremental CV% is above the cumulative CV%, then the cumulative will continue to rise. If the incremental CV% remains below the cumulative CV%, the cumulative will steadily drop. Also, note that the closer we get to the end of the project, the less influence each individual incremental value will have on the cumulative. This is because each incremental contribution is a smaller fraction of the cumulative as time goes by.

Remember the ultimate measure of success is where the cumulative winds up at the end of the project. Keeping track of these over time, though, will aid us in determining whether or not we're on a path to getting there successfully.

8-12 SCHEDULE EVALUATION OF EXAMPLE # 2

Let's analyze the same project during the same two sets of periods, but now from the scheduling perspective. This time we'll be interested in the Earned Value and Planned Value indicators which will combine to give us the SV and SV%.

First we'll look at the status at the end of Week 6. We can take the Planned Value data from Table 8-5 and the Earned Value data from Table 8-6 and repackage them as Table 8-10.

We can now calculate the Schedule Variances and Schedule Variance Percentages over time through this interval and arrive at the data in Table 8-11. Notice that the project is currently behind schedule as evidenced by the negative cumulative SV. The cumulative SV% is only –3.13% which indicates that we are currently within tolerance, however.

If we plot the SV% data on a control chart we can see graphically how these unfold over time. This is shown in Figure 8-7.

Week	inc EV [$K]	cum EV [$K]	inc PV [$K]	cum PV [$K]
1	100	100	90	90
2	120	220	115	205
3	160	380	165	370
4	210	590	175	545
5	160	750	190	735
6	180	930	225	960

Table 8-10: EV and PV Data through Week 6

Week	inc SV [$K]	cum SV [$K]	inc SV%	cum SV%
1	10	10	11.11%	11.11%
2	5	15	4.35%	7.32%
3	−5	10	−3.03%	2.70%
4	35	45	20.00%	8.26%
5	−30	15	−15.79%	2.04%
6	−45	−30	−20.00%	−3.13%

Table 8-11: SV and SV% Data through Week 6

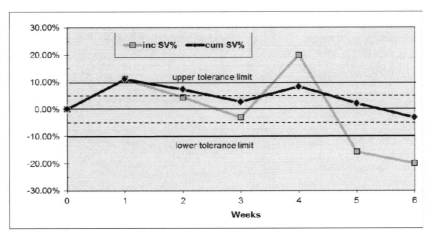

Figure 8-7: Schedule Control Chart through Week 6

Notice that the incremental SV% is very volatile. At the end of Week 1 and

Week 4, it was out of tolerance on the "good" side. The last two weeks it was out of tolerance on the "bad" side.

The cumulative SV% was slightly out of tolerance on the "good" side at the end of Week 1, giving us a reading of "red." Since then it has remained within tolerance, but has spent considerable time in the "yellow" region.

If we compute the incremental and cumulative SV% for weeks 7 through 12, we would get the figures given in Table 8-12.

Week	inc SV [$K]	cum SV [$K]	inc SV%	cum SV%
1	10	10	11.1%	11.1%
2	5	15	4.3%	7.3%
3	−5	10	−3.0%	2.7%
4	35	45	20.0%	8.3%
5	−30	15	−15.8%	2.0%
6	−45	−30	−20.0%	−3.1%
7	0	−30	0.0%	−2.5%
8	−10	−40	−3.2%	−2.6%
9	10	−30	4.0%	−1.7%
10	−20	−50	−10.0%	−2.6%
11	−10	−60	−6.3%	−2.8%
12	20	−40	25.0%	−1.8%

Table 8-12: SV and SV% Data through Week 12

The control chart in Figure 8-8 is a result of plotting the incremental and cumulative data in Table 8-12.

Question: Consider the data in Table 8-12 for the end of Week 12. Assuming a ±10% acceptable tolerance limit for cumulative SV%, is the schedule within tolerance?

a) Yes

b) No

c) Not enough information to determine

For the end of Week 12 the cum SV = −40, or there is $40,000 worth of value yet to be delivered. This tells us that the project is behind schedule. Cum SV% = −1.8%. This is well within the acceptable tolerance levels; therefore the answer is "a" or yes.

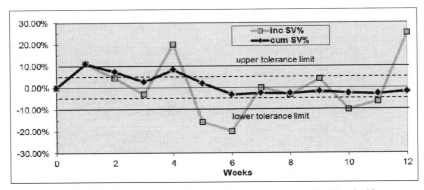

Figure 8-8: Schedule Control Chart through Week 12

Question: Assume that it is now the end of Week 20 and the final $40,000 of work was still not delivered. With the same ±10% acceptable tolerance level for cumulative SV%, is the schedule now within tolerance?

    a) Yes

    b) No

    c) Not enough information to determine

The project was originally planned to be complete in Week 12. It is now Week 20, and the project is 8 weeks behind schedule. If we calculate the cumulative Schedule Variance, we find cum SV = cum EV – cum PV = –40. This is the same result we found with the previous question at the end of Week 12. This of course indicates that there is $40,000 worth of work that should have been completed as of today that is not.

Cum SV% = cum SV/ cum PV = –40/2200 = –1.8%, so surprisingly, the answer is "a" or yes. Even though the project is 8 weeks behind schedule, SV% still shows the project SV% to be within tolerance! Obviously there is something lacking here. In fact, if no further work is done on this project, SV% will continue to be constant and indicate a result that is within tolerance.

Remember that the Schedule Variance is a measure of work accomplished and not of time. The SV% being within tolerance indicates that the project is within 10% of the *work* that should have been performed as of today. This is important to keep in mind as we apply SV and SV%.

This does not mean that the Schedule Variance is not a good indicator; we just have to be mindful of what it is telling us. In Chapter 11 we will be looking at time indicators. These time indicators will designate an out of tolerance condition if enough time goes by. They must be combined with SV and SV% to give a more complete picture of the schedule.

8-13 SUMMARY

Variance percentages normalize the variances to the size of the project giving us relative indications of performance.

Tolerance limits are negotiated items and should appear in the baseline plan.

Control charts give us a graphical depiction of project performance with respect to tolerance limits. Variance percentages are often used in control charts to indicate a project's performance over time.

While the cumulative variance percentages give us the ultimate measure of project success, the incremental variance percentages give us early warning. The incremental numbers will go out of tolerance before the cumulative and if they stay out of tolerance long enough the cumulative measures are sure to follow.

The questions that were addressed in this chapter are summarized in Table 8-13.

Question	Answer
What percentage under budget (or over budget) is the work that has been performed?	CV%
What percentage more work (or less work) was performed than planned?	SV%
What percentage less (or more) money was spent than planned for this date?	FV%

Table 8-13: Question Summary

Table 8-14 is a summary of the variance percentage formulas that were introduced in this chapter. Table 8-15 gives these formulas in the alternate form where they are expressed in terms of the basic data elements.

Modern	Traditional
$CV\% = \dfrac{CV}{EV}$	$CV\% = \dfrac{CV}{BCWP}$
$SV\% = \dfrac{SV}{PV}$	$SV\% = \dfrac{SV}{BCWS}$
$FV\% = \dfrac{FV}{PV}$	$FV\% = \dfrac{FV}{BCWS}$

Table 8-14: Variance % Formulas

Modern	Traditional
$CV\% = 1 - \dfrac{AC}{EV}$	$CV\% = 1 - \dfrac{ACWP}{BCWP}$
$SV\% = \dfrac{EV}{PV} - 1$	$SV\% = \dfrac{BCWP}{BCWS} - 1$
$FV\% = 1 - \dfrac{AC}{PV}$	$FV\% = 1 - \dfrac{ACWP}{BCWS}$

Table 8-15: Formulas Using Basic Data Variables

Table 8-16 shows how the various percentages relate to each other. If we know any two of these, we can always compute the third.

$FV\% = 1 - (1 - CV\%)(1 + SV\%)$
$FV\% = CV\% - SV\% + (CV\%)(SV\%)$
$SV\% = \dfrac{1 - FV\%}{1 - CV\%} - 1$
$CV\% = 1 - \dfrac{1 - FV\%}{1 + SV\%}$

Table 8-16: Variance Percentage Comparisons

EXERCISES

8-1: For a certain subproject BCWS = 500, BCWP = 560, and ACWP = 580. Determine the following indicators and interpret the status of the subproject.

– CV	– CV%
– SV	– SV%
– FV	– FV%

8-2: Show that

a) Equation 8-1a is equivalent to 8-2a

b) Equation 8-3a is equivalent to 8-4a

c) Equation 8-5a is equivalent to 8-6a

8-3: What is the CV% for a task that has not actually started?

8-4: What is the SV% when no work was scheduled to be performed and no work was actually performed? What would it be if the task actually started?

8-5: Prove that Equations 8-7a, 8-7b, 8-8, and 8-9 are true.

8-6: Look at Figure 8-8 in the text. Notice that the wild swings of the incremental SV% in the last few weeks have relatively little effect on the cumulative SV% compared to those near the beginning. Why is that?

8-7: Using the data in Table 8-5 and Table 8-6 in the text, calculate the FV and FV% data on a weekly and cumulative basis for each week through the end of Week 6. Draw the Fiscal Control Chart through Week 6 and assess the status of the project spending history through that time. Assuming an acceptable tolerance limit of ±10%, is the project spending in or out of control as of the end of Week 6?

8-8: A project has a BAC of $5,000K and a project Planned Duration of 15 weeks. Using the project data in the table below, draw control charts for CV%, SV%, and FV% (incremental and cumulative) through the end of week 7. Describe the status of the project throughout its history. Assume that the tolerance limits for all indicators is ±10%.

Week	cum PV [$K]	cum EV [$K]	cum AC [$K]
1	100	95	105
2	250	220	270
3	625	575	625
4	1,040	960	1,010
5	1,425	1,285	1,510
6	1,750	1,490	1,830
7	1,970	1,830	2,140

Chapter 9

INDEXES

9-1 INTRODUCTION

As we saw in the last chapter, the variances that we have been using (CV, SV, and FV) do not put the work status into perspective relative to the size of the project. To address this issue, we introduced the variance percentages (CV%, SV%, and FV%). These additional indicators expand the set of tools from which we can draw in order to more fully assess the status of our projects.

There is another set of indicators that give us yet one more view into project performance. These are known as the indexes. The indexes offer us a unique perspective on our projects by providing us with a measure of efficiency.

Indexes are very popular with EVM practitioners. Their formulas are closely related to the variances and are easy to remember. The indexes are also widely used in forecasting, which we'll discuss in later chapters.

First we will define the indexes and show how they can be used to indicate project status and efficiency with a sample project. Later in this chapter we'll discuss the relationship between the indexes and the variance percentages.

9-2 COST PERFORMANCE INDEX (CPI)

Remember the formula for Cost Variance.

$$\textbf{Modern: } CV = EV - AC \qquad\qquad (9\text{-}1a)$$

$$\textbf{Traditional: } CV = BCWP - ACWP \qquad\qquad (9\text{-}1b)$$

We can change the Cost Variance to the Cost Performance Index (or CPI) simply by changing the subtraction operation to division. The elements are the same, so it's easy to remember.

Modern: $CPI = EV \div AC = \dfrac{EV}{AC}$ (9-2a)

Traditional: $CPI = BCWP \div ACWP = \dfrac{BCWP}{ACWP}$ (9-2b)

Notice that the CPI has no units—it's a pure number. Since we are dividing dollars by dollars the units cancel. If the work we are evaluating is on budget, then the CPI equals 1.

If the CPI is less than 1, then the denominator will be greater than the numerator, indicating that the cost was higher than planned. This is equivalent to a negative CV. In this case, the project is over budget for the work performed.

A CPI greater than 1 means that the cost is lower than was planned for a given amount of work, or the work is under budget.

Basically, we are shifting the neutral point from zero (for the variances or variance percentages) up to 1 for the indexes. In all cases, a result greater than the neutral point is on the good side (i.e., the work is being delivered under budget). A result lower than the neutral point is on the bad side, and indicates that the work is being delivered over budget.

By the way, the CPI can never be negative; the lowest value it can have is zero. It is unbounded on the high side. The CPI is undefined when both the Earned Value and Actual Cost are zero.

What is the meaning of the CPI number? For instance, how would we interpret a situation where CPI equals 0.85? It is obvious that the work is over budget since the CPI is less than 1.

The proper interpretation is that of a measure of cost efficiency. In other words, how efficient are we in producing work for the money we are actually spending? A CPI of 0.85 would mean that *for every dollar actually spent, the project only delivered 85 cents of value.* Since this is an average over each individual dollar that was expended, it doesn't matter what the size of the project is. Equivalently, we could say that our project is operating with an 85% cost efficiency.

If the CPI equals 1.07, this would mean that we are delivering $1.07 in value for every dollar we are actually spending on average. In this case we could say that our project is operating with a 107% cost efficiency. Obviously, we would normally prefer to have a CPI greater than 1 than less than 1.

9-3 SCHEDULE PERFORMANCE INDEX (SPI)

Like the CPI, the Schedule Performance Index (or SPI) is also a number that has no units, and in some ways it relates to the SV like the CPI relates to the CV. As we'll see later, however, the relationship between the schedule variables is not exactly the same as between the cost variables in every way.

Let's begin by defining the SPI. Remember the formula for Schedule Variance.

Modern: $SV = EV - PV$ (9-3a)

Traditional: $SV = BCWP - BCWS$ (9-3b)

Like with cost, we can change the Schedule Variance to the Schedule Performance Index simply by changing the subtraction operation to division. Again the elements are the same.

Modern: $SPI = EV \div PV = \dfrac{EV}{PV}$ (9-4a)

Traditional: $SPI = BCWP \div BCWS = \dfrac{BCWP}{BCWS}$ (9-4b)

Notice that, similar to CPI, if SPI equals 1, then the project is on target with respect to schedule. If SPI is less than 1, our project is performing less work than planned. If SPI is greater than 1, our project is performing more work than planned.

Again, just like with the cost, we moved the neutral point from zero (for SV and SV%) up to 1 for the SPI. In all cases, a number greater than the neutral point is good (ahead of schedule) and less than the neutral point is bad (behind schedule).

SPI can never be negative. The minimum value for SPI is zero, and the maximum value for SPI is unbounded. SPI is undefined when both the Planned Value and Earned Value are zero.

The proper interpretation of the SPI is that of a measure of schedule efficiency. In other words, how efficient are we in using our time to deliver the work that we had planned to deliver. An SPI of 0.90 would obviously mean that we were behind schedule since the SPI is less than 1. A more precise interpretation would be that we only delivered 90% of the work that we had planned to deliver (in terms of value) as of today. In this case we would be 10% behind schedule.

If the SPI were 1.04, we could say that we've performed 104% of the work that we had planned to perform, or we are 4% ahead of schedule.

9-4 FISCAL PERFORMANCE INDEX (FPI)

The Fiscal Performance Index (or FPI) is a measure of our spending rate relative to the plan (with respect to the calendar and not the work). Like the

CPI and SPI, FPI is also a unit-less number, and it is analogous to the FV like the CPI is to the CV and SPI is to SV.

Remember the formula for Fiscal Variance.

Modern: $FV = PV - AC$ (9-5a)

Traditional: $FV = BCWS - ACWP$ (9-5b)

We can change the Fiscal Variance to the Fiscal Performance Index simply by changing the subtraction operation to division. Again the factors are the same.

Modern: $FPI = PV \div AC = \dfrac{PV}{AC}$ (9-6a)

Traditional: $FPI = BCWS \div ACWP = \dfrac{BCWS}{ACWP}$ (9-6b)

Like the other indexes, we've moved the neutral point up from zero (for FV and FV%) to 1 for the FPI. The Fiscal Performance Index can never be negative. If FPI is less than 1, we are spending money faster than planned according to the calendar. If FPI equals 1, we are spending at a rate exactly as planned. Finally, if FPI is greater than 1, we are spending our money less rapidly than planned.

Let's say the FPI were equal to 0.80. How would we interpret that? Since FPI is less than 1, it is obvious that the project is spending money faster than planned. The correct interpretation is that of a measure of relative spending rates, comparing the actual with the plan. For every dollar we actually spent, we had only planned to spend $0.80. In other words, our performance at controlling our spending is only 80%.

On the other hand, if we had an FPI of 1.15, then for every dollar we actually spent, we had planned to spend $1.15. Our performance at controlling our spending is 115%.

Remember, just like the Fiscal Variance, the FPI could be explained by differences in schedule as well as with differences in cost. The FPI alone allows us to reference our spending only with respect to the calendar.

9-5 EXAMPLE PROJECT: WORKING WITH INDEXES

Now we'll apply these indexes to a sample project. It's the same project we worked with in Chapters 7 and 8. It was introduced in Figure 7-2 and Table 7-6. Table 7-6 is repeated here as Table 9-1. Remember that this data represents a snapshot in time, in this case the end of Week 10 of the project.

Task	BAC [$]	AC [$]	PV [$]	EV [$]	CV [$]	SV [$]	FV [$]
A	1200	1200	1200	1200	0	0	0
B	1000	1100	1000	900	−200	−100	−100
C	2600	2250	2600	2210	−40	−390	350
D	1500	1600	1125	1500	−100	375	−475
E	1600	1300	800	1200	−100	400	−500
F	2000	350	0	500	150	500	−350
G	3000	0	0	0	0	0	0
Project	**12,900**	**7,800**	**6,725**	**7,510**	**−290**	**785**	**−1,075**

Table 9-1: Project Status at the end of Week 10

The data in Table 9-1 gives us everything we need to easily calculate the Cost Performance Index. Notice that at the project level, EV equals $7510 and AC equals $7800. Also CV equals –$290 showing that the project is over budget by $290. Now let's calculate the Cost Performance Index.

$$CPI = \frac{\$7510}{\$7800} = 0.96$$

Here we are rounding to two decimal places. How far we carry it out in real-world applications will depend on the need, but two decimal places is sufficient to give a good indication of status in most cases.

Let's interpret what this means. Since the index is less than 1, the project is over budget. This agrees with what we found with the Cost Variance. In fact the two will always confirm each other. It is impossible to have a situation where the CV and CPI disagree on the status of the cost.

The magnitude of the CPI gives us an indication of how efficiently we are performing the work for the money we are actually spending. In this case, we are operating with a 96% cost efficiency. Another way to express this is that for every dollar we are actually spending, on average we are only delivering 96 cents of value.

As we can see we are not receiving the full value we had planned for each dollar we are spending. If this trend were to continue, we are on target to deliver this project over budget.

Now let's look at the project schedule. We can see from Table 9-1 that SV equals $785. Since this is positive, the project is ahead of schedule. More precisely, $785 more in value was delivered than was planned. This indicates that we should expect an SPI greater than 1.

When we do the calculation we get the following.

$$SPI = \frac{\$7510}{\$6725} = 1.12$$

This confirms the SV assessment that we delivered more work than planned. We can say that we performed 112% of the work that was planned to be performed as of the end of Week 10. Since we performed 12% more work than planned, this indicates that we are 12% ahead of schedule.

Before we celebrate our good performance and forecast that we are going to finish this project early, we would want to verify that the correct work was performed. Remember, this is just an aggregate figure for the project as a whole. It is possible to be behind schedule for tasks on the critical path, but be ahead of schedule enough on non-critical tasks to give us an SPI greater than 100%. If this were the case, it might still be a challenge to bring the project in on schedule, never mind ahead of schedule.

Now, let's see how well we are pacing ourselves with respect to our project's spending rate relative to the calendar. From Table 9-1 we can see that FV equals –$1075. This means that we are spending money more rapidly than planned, so we expect our FPI to be less than 1.

Let's do the calculation.

$$FPI = \frac{\$6725}{\$7800} = 0.86$$

The FPI being less than 1 confirms that we are spending money more rapidly than we had planned. For every dollar we spent so far we had only planned to spend 86 cents, or our performance at controlling our spending is only 86%. As we can see from what we discovered earlier, this is due to a combination of being over budget for the work we did as well as by being ahead of schedule. Both of these lead to an increased rate of spending over what we had planned.

9-6 INDEXES AT THE TASK LEVEL

Just like we did earlier with variances and variance percentages, we can calculate the indexes for each individual task. This will allow us to evaluate our performance at the task level and help us to better understand the true status of our project internally. We are now aware that looking only at project-level figures may be misleading.

Table 9-2 summarizes our findings thus far. Notice that the variances and the indexes confirm each other. We can see that the project is over budget, ahead of schedule, and is spending money at a rate faster than planned.

Task	BAC [$]	CV [$]	SV [$]	FV [$]	CPI	SPI	FPI
A	1200	0	0	0			
B	1000	−200	−100	−100			
C	2600	−40	−390	350			
D	1500	−100	375	−475			
E	1600	−100	400	−500			
F	2000	150	500	−350			
G	3000	0	0	0			
Project	**12,900**	**−290**	**785**	**−1,075**	**0.96**	**1.12**	**0.86**

Table 9-2: Project Summary of Indexes

The index results are more like the variance percentages than like the variances themselves. This is because the indexes give us results that are normalized to the size of the effort (like the variance percentages) and not in absolute terms (like the variances). Since the indexes are normalized, they can be used to set tolerance limits just like the variance percentages.

For example, we could have specified that the acceptable tolerance limits for this project's indexes are ±0.05 for cost, ±0.10 for schedule, and ±0.10 for spending. This is equivalent to stating that the following ranges are within tolerance.

$$0.95 \le CPI \le 1.05$$

$$0.90 \le SPI \le 1.10$$

$$0.90 \le FPI \le 1.10$$

If the results are within these ranges, the work in question is within tolerance. Notice that in this case, the cost is within tolerance, but both the schedule and spending are out of tolerance.

We don't need to set tolerance limits using both the indexes and variance percentages. Either will do. Some EVM practitioners prefer to work with indexes and others prefer to work with the variance percentages. As we will see later in this chapter, the indexes and variance percentages are related and one can easily be converted into the other.

We can now calculate the indexes for each individual task. This will allow us to assess which tasks are the bad actors.

Exercise: Perform the calculations to complete Table 9-2; then compare your results with the answers in Table 9-3. The source data can be found in Table 9-1. See Appendix D for guidance on how to handle division with zero.

Task	BAC [$]	CV [$]	SV [$]	FV [$]	CPI	SPI	FPI
A	1200	0	0	0	1.00	1.00	1.00
B	1000	−200	−100	−100	0.82	0.90	0.91
C	2600	−40	−390	350	0.98	0.85	1.16
D	1500	−100	375	−475	0.94	1.33	0.70
E	1600	−100	400	−500	0.92	1.50	0.62
F	2000	150	500	−350	1.43	infinity	0.00
G	3000	0	0	0	−	−	−
Project	**12,900**	**−290**	**785**	**−1,075**	**0.96**	**1.12**	**0.86**

Table 9-3: Task-Level Indexes

Now that we have this data, we can evaluate the status of each task to see if it is in or out of tolerance. Using the index tolerances specified above, we can see that Tasks B, D, E, and F are out of tolerance with respect to cost. Also, Tasks C, D, E, and F are out of tolerance with respect to schedule. Tasks C, D, E, and F are out with respect to their spending rate. There is no information that can be obtained from Task G for any index.

A result of zero or infinity for an index automatically means that the task is out of tolerance. Infinity means that the task is automatically out of tolerance on the "good" side, while zero means that the task is automatically out of tolerance on the "bad" side. Remember, the indexes can never be negative.

The project-level variances can be generated by adding the task-level variances together. The project-level indexes **cannot** be obtained by adding or even averaging the task-level indexes together. The only proper way to do it is the way we did it earlier, i.e. by taking the ratios of the project-level basic elements.

9-7 COMPARING THE INDEXES

In Chapter 4 we saw that the variances are related to each other and in Chapter 8 that the variance percentages are related to each other. It's probably no surprise, then, to find that the indexes are also related to each other. If we know the value of any two of them, we can always find the third. The relationships among the indexes are given in Equations 9-7, 9-8, and 9-9.

$$CPI = SPI \times FPI \tag{9-7}$$

$$SPI = \frac{CPI}{FPI} \qquad\qquad (9\text{-}8)$$

$$FPI = \frac{CPI}{SPI} \qquad\qquad (9\text{-}9)$$

Notice that these relationships are much simpler than those between the variance percentages and no correction terms are necessary.

We can use the example project to show that this works. Recall that CPI equals 0.96 and SPI equals 1.12. Now we can calculate FPI using Equation 9-9.

$$FPI = \frac{0.96}{1.12} = 0.86$$

This is exactly the result we obtained earlier when we calculated FPI directly. Keep in mind that in some cases the comparison of the results from the two methods might differ slightly due to rounding.

In addition to the indexes being related to each other, the indexes are also related to the variance percentages. The next several sections explore how each index can be converted to its counterpart variance percentage and vice versa.

9-8 CPI VS. CV%

As mentioned earlier, the indexes can serve a similar purpose as the variance percentages. This implies that they should be closely related. In fact the relationship between CPI and CV% is simple to express. Recall the formula for CV% from the last chapter.

$$\textbf{Modern: } CV\% = 1 - \frac{AC}{EV} \qquad\qquad (9\text{-}10a)$$

$$\textbf{Traditional: } CV\% = 1 - \frac{ACWP}{BCWP} \qquad\qquad (9\text{-}10b)$$

By substituting for CPI we find the relationship between CV% and CPI.

$$CV\% = 1 - \frac{1}{CPI} \qquad\qquad (9\text{-}11)$$

This can also be rewritten as follows in order to express CPI in terms of

CV%.

$$CPI = \frac{1}{1 - CV\%} \qquad (9\text{-}12)$$

The relationship between CPI and CV% is graphically represented in Figure 9-1. As we can see, the relationship is not linear, i.e. a graph that depicts the relationship between the two variables does not form a straight line.

If we know the value of one variable, it is easy to determine the value of the other through one of these three methods—table, formula, or graph. Table 9-4 displays some common values of CV% in terms of CPI.

CPI vs. CV%

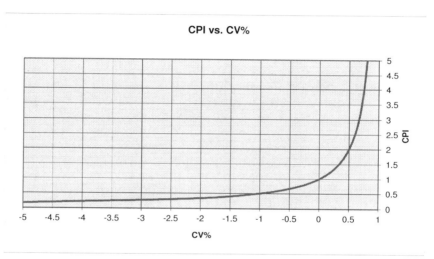

Figure 9-1: Relationship between CPI and CV%

Let's explore the relationship between CPI and CV% a little bit. If we calculated a CPI to be 0.80, we might be tempted to conclude that the work is over budget by 20%, since the difference between the CPI and 1 is 20%. This is not correct, however. Notice that from Table 9-4 that a CPI of 0.80 is equivalent to a CV% of –25%! In other words, the work is actually 25% over budget.

So for cost evaluations, it is *not* true that the difference between the CPI and 1 equals the percentage that the work is over or under budget. We must convert to CV% for this purpose.

However, as we can see from Table 9-4, if the variance is relatively small (within 10% or so) this might be a very acceptable approximation. For example, if the CPI were computed to be 0.95, we can say that the work is *approximately* 5% over budget. While in actuality, it is 5.26% over budget (using Equation 9-11 to get this figure), this might be close enough for our immediate needs. This approximation, or rule of thumb, breaks down once the cost gets beyond about 10% either way.

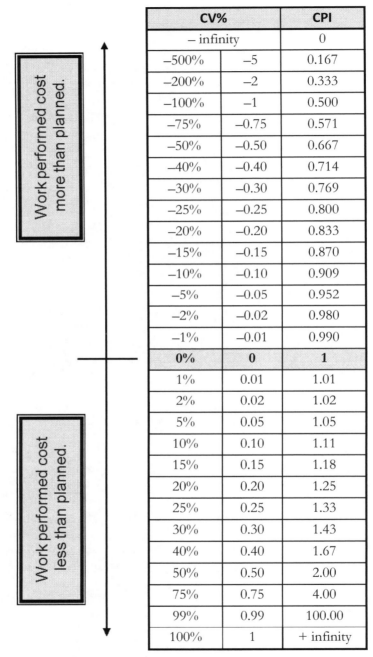

CV%		CPI
– infinity		0
–500%	–5	0.167
–200%	–2	0.333
–100%	–1	0.500
–75%	–0.75	0.571
–50%	–0.50	0.667
–40%	–0.40	0.714
–30%	–0.30	0.769
–25%	–0.25	0.800
–20%	–0.20	0.833
–15%	–0.15	0.870
–10%	–0.10	0.909
–5%	–0.05	0.952
–2%	–0.02	0.980
–1%	–0.01	0.990
0%	**0**	**1**
1%	0.01	1.01
2%	0.02	1.02
5%	0.05	1.05
10%	0.10	1.11
15%	0.15	1.18
20%	0.20	1.25
25%	0.25	1.33
30%	0.30	1.43
40%	0.40	1.67
50%	0.50	2.00
75%	0.75	4.00
99%	0.99	100.00
100%	1	+ infinity

Table 9-4: Comparison of CV% and CPI values

Work performed cost more than planned.

Work performed cost less than planned.

While it was mentioned earlier that we can use CPI to set and track tolerance limits, we need to be careful that we understand the relationship with CV% so that we are confident that we are specifying the correct figures.

In summary, we have three different ways to convert between CPI and CV%. The graph allows us to see how the relationship varies over a wide range of values, the table lets us quickly convert one to the other for common values, and the formula allows us to calculate an exact answer for any value we desire.

9-9 SPI VS. SV%

Just as CPI is related to CV%, SPI is also related to SV%. As we'll see, these two sets of relationships are not exactly parallel, however.

Like with cost, we can express SPI in terms of SV% with an equation. Remember Equations 9-13a and 9-13b that were developed in the last chapter.

$$\textbf{Modern: } SV\% = \frac{EV}{PV} - 1 \tag{9-13a}$$

$$\textbf{Traditional: } SV\% = \frac{BCWP}{BCWS} - 1 \tag{9-13b}$$

By substituting for SPI we get Equation 9-14.

$$SV\% = SPI - 1 \tag{9-14}$$

This can be rewritten to express SPI in terms of SV%.

$$SPI = SV\% + 1 \tag{9-15}$$

Notice that these are different in form than Equations 9-11 and 9-12. The range of values of SPI can be seen in Table 9-5 along with the corresponding values of SV%.

How do we interpret the value of SPI? Let's first look at an SPI that equals 0.85. Obviously, less work has been performed than was planned. Unlike with CPI, however, here it *is* correct to interpret this project as being 15% behind schedule. We can see this by looking at Equation 9-14.

$$SV\% = 0.85 - 1 = -0.15 = -15\%$$

Notice that the difference between SPI and 1 is just SV%. If the SPI were 1.1, this would mean that we performed 10% more work than planned, or we could say we were 10% ahead of schedule. Some common values are displayed in Table 9-5.

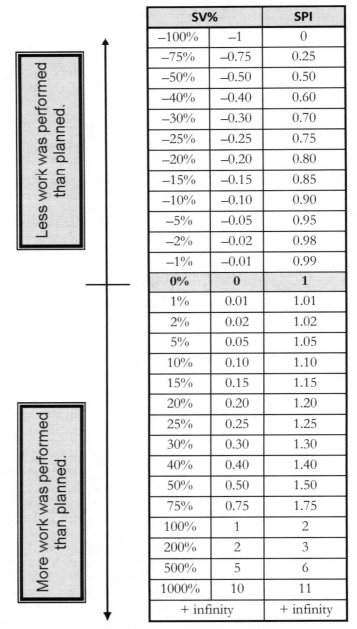

SV%		SPI
−100%	−1	0
−75%	−0.75	0.25
−50%	−0.50	0.50
−40%	−0.40	0.60
−30%	−0.30	0.70
−25%	−0.25	0.75
−20%	−0.20	0.80
−15%	−0.15	0.85
−10%	−0.10	0.90
−5%	−0.05	0.95
−2%	−0.02	0.98
−1%	−0.01	0.99
0%	0	1
1%	0.01	1.01
2%	0.02	1.02
5%	0.05	1.05
10%	0.10	1.10
15%	0.15	1.15
20%	0.20	1.20
25%	0.25	1.25
30%	0.30	1.30
40%	0.40	1.40
50%	0.50	1.50
75%	0.75	1.75
100%	1	2
200%	2	3
500%	5	6
1000%	10	11
+ infinity		+ infinity

Less work was performed than planned.

More work was performed than planned.

Table 9-5: Comparison of SV% and SPI values

We can see from Equations 9-14 and 9-15 that the relationship between SPI and SV% **is** linear (i.e., the graph forms a straight line). This is shown in Figure 9-2.

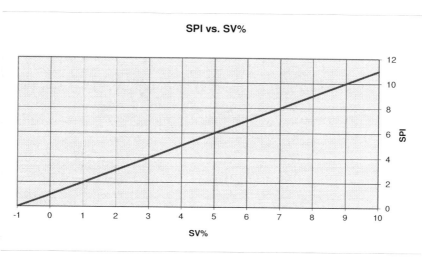

SPI vs. SV%

Figure 9-2: Relationship between SPI and SV%

9-10 FPI VS. FV%

To conclude the comparisons between indexes and variance percentages, let's now look at FPI and FV%. From the last chapter we get Equations 9-16a and 9-16b.

Modern: $FV\% = 1 - \dfrac{AC}{PV}$ (9-16a)

Traditional: $FV\% = 1 - \dfrac{ACWP}{BCWS}$ (9-16b)

By substituting for FPI we get Equation 9-17.

$$FV\% = 1 - \dfrac{1}{FPI}$$ (9-17)

This can be rewritten to express FPI in terms of FV%.

$$FPI = \frac{1}{1 - FV\%} \qquad (9\text{-}18)$$

The relationship between these two indicators can be seen graphically in Figure 9-3. As we can see, the relationship between FPI and FV% is not linear, but is similar to that between CPI and CV%. Common values of FPI and FV% can be found in Table 9-6.

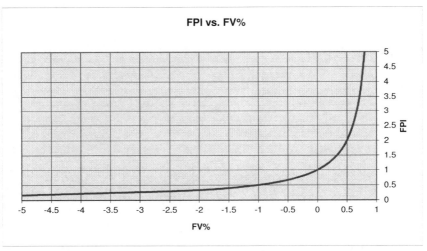

Figure 9-3: Relationship between FPI and FV%

Here we must be careful with analyzing spending like we were with the cost. If our FPI equals 0.80, this is an indication that we are spending our money 25% faster than planned, **not** 20% faster! Again, just like with cost, if we are looking at values within about 10% of plan, then the error is not great and may be an acceptable approximation for our needs.

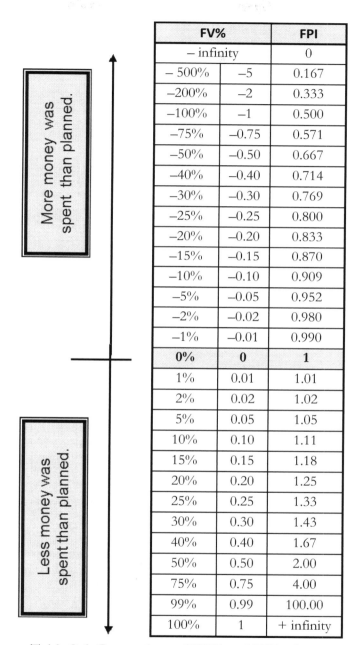

FV%		FPI
– infinity		0
– 500%	–5	0.167
–200%	–2	0.333
–100%	–1	0.500
–75%	–0.75	0.571
–50%	–0.50	0.667
–40%	–0.40	0.714
–30%	–0.30	0.769
–25%	–0.25	0.800
–20%	–0.20	0.833
–15%	–0.15	0.870
–10%	–0.10	0.909
–5%	–0.05	0.952
–2%	–0.02	0.980
–1%	–0.01	0.990
0%	**0**	**1**
1%	0.01	1.01
2%	0.02	1.02
5%	0.05	1.05
10%	0.10	1.11
15%	0.15	1.18
20%	0.20	1.25
25%	0.25	1.33
30%	0.30	1.43
40%	0.40	1.67
50%	0.50	2.00
75%	0.75	4.00
99%	0.99	100.00
100%	1	+ infinity

More money was spent than planned.

Less money was spent than planned.

Table 9-6: Comparison of FV% and FPI values

9-11 EXAMPLE PROJECT: COMPARING INDEXES WITH VARIANCE PERCENTAGES

Now we are briefly going to look at our sample project again (Table 9-1). Remember that we computed the indexes and summarized them in Table 9-3. We also computed the variance percentages for the same project in the last chapter and summarized them in Table 8-4.

Let's use Equations 9-11, 9-14, and 9-17 to generate the variance percentages from the indexes and see how well they compare to the percentages we computed in the last chapter.

$$CV\% = 1 - \frac{1}{0.963} = 1 - 1.038 = -0.038 = -3.8\%$$

$$SV\% = 1.117 - 1 = 0.117 = 11.7\%$$

$$FV\% = 1 - \frac{1}{0.862} = 1 - 1.160 = -0.160 = -16.0\%$$

Notice that these results match what we produced in the last chapter when we calculated the variance percentages directly. Any differences that we get between the methods will just be due to rounding.

9-12 SUMMARY

Indexes offer another perspective on the status of our projects. They give us a measure of efficiency.

The neutral point for the indexes is 1 instead of zero, like it is for the variances and variance percentages. The indexes can never be negative.

Indexes can be expressed in terms of one another. If we know the value of two indexes, we can always compute the third.

Like the variance percentages, the indexes normalize the data to the size of the project. Many EVM practitioners favor the indexes over the variance percentages for use in control charts to track progress over time. Either will do—it's just a matter of personal preference.

Indexes and variance percentages are related to one another. If we know one index, we can always find its corresponding variance percentage. If we know the variance percentage, we can always determine its index partner.

There are three different ways to convert between the Indexes and Variance Percentages. The graph allows us to see how the relationship between the two varies over a wide range of values, the table lets us quickly convert one to the other for common values, and the formula allows us to calculate an exact answer for any value we desire that may not be in the table.

The questions that were addressed in this chapter are summarized in Table 9-7. Table 9-8 summarizes the index formulas for each of the conventions. The indexes and variance percentages are related to each other. The relationships between them are summarized in Table 9-9.

Question	Answer
How much value was received for each dollar actually spent?	CPI
What percentage of the scheduled work has been actually performed?	SPI
How much money was planned to have been spent for each dollar actually spent through today?	FPI

Table 9-7: Question Summary

Modern	Traditional
$CPI = \dfrac{EV}{AC}$	$CPI = \dfrac{BCWP}{ACWP}$
$SPI = \dfrac{EV}{PV}$	$SPI = \dfrac{BCWP}{BCWS}$
$FPI = \dfrac{PV}{AC}$	$FPI = \dfrac{BCWS}{ACWP}$

Table 9-8: Index Formulas

Variance %	Index
$CV\% = 1 - \dfrac{1}{CPI}$	$CPI = \dfrac{1}{1 - CV\%}$
$SV\% = SPI - 1$	$SPI = SV\% + 1$
$FV\% = 1 - \dfrac{1}{FPI}$	$FPI = \dfrac{1}{1 - FV\%}$

Table 9-9: Relationships between Indexes and Variance %

EXERCISES

9-1: Determine the cost, schedule, and spending status of the work in the following cases. Assume that the tolerance limits are ±5% for cost, schedule, and spending variance percentages.

    a) CPI = 0.93 and SPI = 1.02

    b) CPI = 1.05 and FPI = 1.08

    c) SPI = 0.96 and CV% = 4%

    d) FV% = –11%and SPI = 1.03

    e) FV% = 3% and SPI = 0.92

9-2: Compute the indexes and determine the status for each of the following cases.

    a) EV = $8000, PV = $9900, AC = $8500

    b) BCWS = $7500, ACWP = $7500, BCWP = $7600

    c) AC = $2600, EV = $2650, PV = $2700

9-3: Show that

    a) Equation 9-11 is correct using Equation 9-10a (or 9-10b) and the definition of CPI.

    b) Equation 9-14 is correct using Equation 9-13a (or 9-13b) and the definition of SPI.

    c) Equation 9-17 is correct using Equation 9-16a (or 9-16b) and the definition of FPI.

9-4: What is the CPI and status for a task that has not actually started? What is the SPI and status for a task that has started, but nothing was scheduled to be performed?

9-5: Explain the relationship between the indexes and the variance percentages. How are they similar and how do they differ? What can they be used to indicate?

9-6: Explain how the relationship between SPI and SV% is different from that between CPI and CV%.

9-7: A project has a CV% of –11% and a SV% of 5%. Compute FV%, CPI, SPI, and FPI. Characterize the project status with respect to cost, schedule, and spending. Assume that all tolerance limits are ±10%. Would the results differ if the acceptable range were defined to be ±0.10 in terms of the indexes?

9-8: Using the data in the table below, generate control charts for cost, schedule, and spending, using cumulative and incremental indexes. Assume that the acceptable tolerance limits for all indexes are ±0.10 (i.e. the acceptable range is between 0.90 and 1.10).

Week	cum PV [$K]	cum EV [$K]	cum AC [$K]
1	90	100	101
2	205	220	225
3	370	380	393
4	545	590	619
5	735	750	795
6	960	930	999

Characterize the status of the project over time. Are there any dates where the status would be different if variance percentages were used with an acceptable range of ±10%? If so, when?

As a practical matter, how significant of a difference would our conclusions be if the tolerance limits were chosen to be ±10% with respect to the variance percentages vs. ±0.10 with respect to the indexes?

Chapter 10

PERCENTS COMPLETE AND SPENT

In this chapter we introduce some very simple measures commonly used to indicate the overall status of a piece of work on a proportionate basis. They can be applied at any level, whether we are dealing with the whole project, a subproject, or an individual task.

10-1 PERCENTAGE INDICATORS

There are four percentage indicators that we will discuss in this chapter. They are:

Planned Percent Complete (Planned % Complete): The percentage of the total work scheduled to be performed (in terms of value) as of any given date. We may also see this referred to as *Percent Scheduled* or *Percent Planned*.

Since we always plan to perform our work on-budget, the Planned Percent Complete is always numerically equal to the percentage of the total budget planned to be spent through the same date, or **Planned Percent Spent (Planned % Spent)**.

We usually refer to Planned Percent Complete when dealing with work and Planned Percent Spent when dealing with funding.

Actual Percent Complete (Actual % Complete): The percentage of work actually performed as of a particular date (in terms of value). This is often, but ambiguously, referred to as simply *Percent Complete*.

Actual Percent Spent (Actual % Spent): The percentage of the budget actually spent. This is also commonly, but ambiguously, known as *Percent Spent*.

10-2 PLANNED PERCENT COMPLETE (OR SPENT)

Sometimes we are interested in the percentage of work that *should* have been performed (or the percentage of the budget that should have been spent) as of today. Since PV represents the portion of the BAC that was planned to be delivered through a given date, a simple ratio gives us this indicator. This is expressed in Equations 10-1a and 10-1b.

$$\textbf{Modern: } Planned~\%~Complete = \frac{PV}{BAC} \qquad (10\text{-}1a)$$

$$\textbf{Traditional: } Planned~\%~Complete = \frac{BCWS}{BAC} \qquad (10\text{-}1b)$$

After performing the calculations, we simply express the results in percentage terms. For instance, if the Planned Value is two-thirds of the BAC, then two-thirds of the work was planned to be complete, two-thirds of the budget was planned to have been spent, and Planned Percent Complete is approximately 67%.

If the Planned Value is one quarter of the BAC, then a quarter of the work was planned to have been complete, a quarter of the budget was planned to have been spent, and Planned Percent Complete (or Planned Percent Spent) is 25%.

Also, since the Planned Value cannot exceed the BAC, Planned Percent Complete cannot exceed 100%. Therefore, our plan is to never spend more than 100% of our budget, and never to perform more than 100% of the total work in the project. This 100% mark will be achieved on the planned completion date.

In the example shown in Figure 10-1, the BAC is $1,000,000 and the Planned Value is $500,000. Substituting these values into equation 10-1a or 10-1b we get the following.

$$Planned~\%~Complete = \frac{\$500,000}{\$1,000,000} = 0.50 = 50\%$$

This tells us that, in this case, we had planned to deliver 50% of the value of the project as of today. Also, since Planned % Spent is always numerically equal to Planned % Complete, we had planned to spend 50% of the budget.

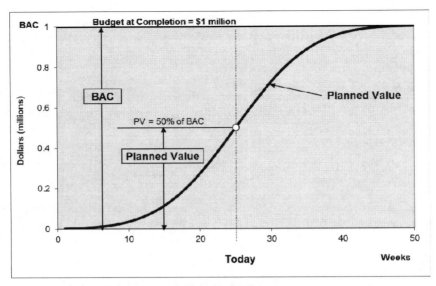

Figure 10-1: Planned Percent Complete = 50%

10-3 ACTUAL PERCENT COMPLETE

Very often we want to be able to determine the percentage of total work that was *actually* completed as of a given date. We can calculate this through a very simple ratio involving the Earned Value, and displaying the result as a percentage. This is expressed in Equations 10-2a and 10-2b.

$$\textbf{Modern: } Actual \ \% \ Complete \ = \frac{EV}{BAC} \qquad (10\text{-}2a)$$

$$\textbf{Traditional: } Actual \ \% \ Complete \ = \frac{BCWP}{BAC} \qquad (10\text{-}2b)$$

We can see this graphically in Figure 10-2. Here the BAC represents the value of all the work. The Earned Value represents the value of work actually performed. The ratio of the two just represents the fraction of total work complete. If the Earned Value is half of the BAC, the work is 50% complete. If the Earned Value is two thirds of the BAC, the work is approximately 67% complete.

Remember that the range of values for the Earned Value is from zero through BAC. When the Earned Value is equal to the BAC, EV/BAC equals 100%, and the work is actually 100% complete. Of course the Actual Percent Complete will reach 100% on the actual completion date as opposed to the planned completion date. Also, since the Earned Value cannot exceed the

BAC, it's impossible to be more than 100% complete.

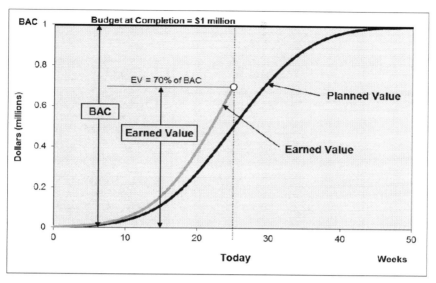

Figure 10-2: Actual Percent Complete = 70%

From Figure 10-2, the BAC equals $1,000,000 and the Earned Value equals $700,000. Substituting these values into equation 10-2a or 10-2b we get the following.

$$Actual\ \%\ Complete\ = \frac{\$700,000}{\$1,000,000} = 0.70 = 70\%$$

This tells us that the project is actually 70% done, or we actually completed 70% of the work of this project through today.

10-4 ACTUAL PERCENT SPENT

In addition to measuring the fraction of work performed, we are often interested in the fraction of the budget that we've spent so far. This is also available through a very simple ratio using the Actual Cost. The formula in Equation 10-3a or 10-3b tells us the percentage of our budget that we have actually spent so far.

$$\textbf{Modern:}\ Actual\ \%\ Spent = \frac{AC}{BAC} \qquad (10\text{-}3a)$$

Traditional: $Actual \ \% \ Spent = \dfrac{ACWP}{BAC}$ (10-3b)

This is very easy to see graphically in Figure 10-3.

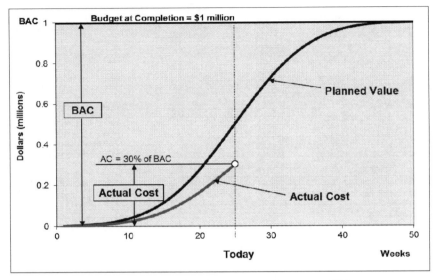

Figure 10-3: Actual Percent Spent = 30%

If the Actual Cost equals the BAC, this means that we have spent all of our budget and the Actual Percent Spent equals 100%. If the Actual Cost is half of the BAC, we have spent 50% of the budget. If the Actual Cost is one third of the BAC, we have spent approximately 33% of the budget.

The Actual Percent Spent has one significant difference from the other percentages we introduced in this chapter. It is the only one that can be greater than 100%.

Since the Actual Cost *can* exceed the BAC, the maximum value of Actual Percent Spent is unbounded. In other words, it is possible for us to spend more than the total original budget. For instance, if the Actual Cost is 10% greater than the BAC, that means that we have spent 110% of our budget, or Actual Percent Spent equals 110%. Theoretically, there is no upper limit to the percentage of our original budget that we can spend.

From Figure 10-3, the BAC equals $1,000,000 and the Actual Cost equals $300,000. Substituting these values into equation 10-3a or 10-3b we get the following.

$$Actual \ \% \ Spent = \dfrac{\$300,000}{\$1,000,000} = 0.30 = 30\%$$

This tells us that we spent 30% of the project's budget as of today.

10-5 EXAMPLE PROJECT

As an example, we will use a sample project that we considered earlier. Refer back to the project introduced in Figure 7-2 in Chapter 7. The data in Tables 7-2 through 7-5 are consolidated here in Table 10-1. All of the information in this table is valid for the end of Week 10.

Let's review what we have here.

Task	BAC [$]	Planned % Comp.	PV [$]	Actual % Comp.	EV [$]	Actual % Spent	AC [$]
A	1200	100%	1200	100%	1200		1200
B	1000	100%	1000	90%	900		1100
C	2600	100%	2600	85%	2210		2250
D	1500	75%	1125	100%	1500		1600
E	1600	50%	800	75%	1200		1300
F	2000	0%	0	25%	500		350
G	3000	0%	0	0%	0		0
Proj.	**12,900**		**6,725**		**7,510**		**7,800**

Table 10-1: Project Status for Week 10

The first two columns are not functions of time. That is, if we change the date, the data in these two columns will be unaffected. The rest of the columns will change as the date changes.

The next two columns (Planned % Complete and PV) can be completed while we are still in the planning phase of the project. Remember that we first determined the Planned % Complete of each task from the schedule, then we computed the Planned Value using Equation 10-4, below, which we saw earlier as Equation 7-1.

$$PV = BAC \times (Planned \% \ Complete) \qquad (10\text{-}4)$$

Notice that this is the same relationship as Equation 10-1a. When we introduced Equations 10-1a and 10-1b earlier in this chapter, we knew the Planned Value but wanted to compute the Planned % Complete. In our current example project, we already have the Planned % Complete for each task and need to compute the Planned Value.

As we can see, this relationship can be used either way depending on the information we have available to us. If we know two of the items, we can always determine the third.

The columns to the right of PV in Table 10-1 contain no data until work actually begins. At that point we are able to determine the Actual % Complete of each task based on the amount of work performed. After populating that column, we are able to shade in the bars on the Gantt Chart in order to record progress. Then we are able to compute the Earned Value based on Equation 10-5, which is the same as Equation 7-2.

$$EV = BAC \times (Actual\ \%\ Complete) \tag{10-5}$$

Notice that Equation 10-5 relates the same factors as Equation 10-2a. It's just that here the unknown item is the Earned Value, while in Equation 10-2 the unknown item was the Actual % Complete.

When assembling Table 10-1, we had to handle the Actual Cost a different way. Since we can't determine the Actual % Spent from the schedule, we have no way to populate that column directly. We needed to generate a figure for the Actual Cost of each task individually from some external source. These could be employee time cards, invoices, or reports from the accounting department. Once we obtain that data we can then fill in the AC column.

In summary, PV and EV were derived from the Planned % Complete and Actual % Complete, respectively, of each task. The AC, however, was not; it was measured directly. The final result is Table 10-1.

Notice the glaring omission of the blank Actual % Spent column. While AC is not normally determined from the Actual % Spent of the BAC, the reverse calculation can always be performed. We can use Equation 10-3a or 10-3b to fill in that column. The result is given as Table 10-2.

Task	BAC [$]	Planned % Comp.	PV [$]	Actual % Comp.	EV [$]	Actual % Spent	AC [$]
A	1200	100%	1200	100%	1200	100%	1200
B	1000	100%	1000	90%	900	110%	1100
C	2600	100%	2600	85%	2210	87%	2250
D	1500	75%	1125	100%	1500	107%	1600
E	1600	50%	800	75%	1200	81%	1300
F	2000	0%	0	25%	500	18%	350
G	3000	0%	0	0%	0	0%	0
Proj.	12,900		6,725		7,510		7,800

Table 10-2: Actual % Spent Calculated for each Task

Now that we have all this data, there is just one more step to complete the table. This is to generate the project-level figures for Planned % Complete, Actual % Complete, and Actual % Spent. To do this we use the formulas in Equation 10-1a or 10-1b, Equation 10-2a or 10-2b, and Equation 10-3a or 10-3b.

$$Planned\ \%\ Complete = \frac{6725}{12,900} = 52\%$$

$$Actual\ \%\ Complete = \frac{7510}{12,900} = 58\%$$

$$Actual\ \%\ Spent = \frac{7800}{12,900} = 60\%$$

These results are posted in Table 10-3.

Task	BAC [$]	Planned % Comp.	PV [$]	Actual % Comp.	EV [$]	Actual % Spent	AC [$]
A	1200	100%	1200	100%	1200	100%	1200
B	1000	100%	1000	90%	900	110%	1100
C	2600	100%	2600	85%	2210	87%	2250
D	1500	75%	1125	100%	1500	107%	1600
E	1600	50%	800	75%	1200	81%	1300
F	2000	0%	0	25%	500	18%	350
G	3000	0%	0	0%	0	0%	0
Proj.	12,900	52%	6,725	58%	7,510	60%	7,800

Table 10-3: Complete Project Status Table

If we recall from our discussion of this project in Chapter 7, we concluded that the project was over budget due to a negative Cost Variance, ahead of schedule due to a positive Schedule Variance, and spending at a rate more rapidly than planned due to a negative Fiscal Variance. Let's see how we can use our new data to draw the same conclusions.

From Table 10-3 we can see that 52% of the total project work should have been completed as of week 10. Since 58% of the work was actually performed, this means that our project is ahead of schedule. This checks out.

Since we spent 60% of the budget to produce 58% of the work, we are over budget for what we performed so far. This checks out too.

Finally, we had planned to spend 52% of the budget as of week 10, but we actually spent 60% of the budget. This indicates that we are spending money faster than planned, which could indicate a potential cash flow problem. Part of the reason for the additional spending is that our work is costing more than planned. In addition, we are ahead of schedule and have to account for that spending earlier than planned. Both cost and schedule are pulling in the same direction of increased spending.

Notice that all of these indicators (variances, variance percentages, indexes, and percents complete/spent) confirm each other, as they should, but they each give us a little different perspective into the state of our project.

10-6 RELATION TO INDEXES

There are several ways that we can combine these percentages to give us an indication of how well the project is progressing. As we did above, we can take any two and compare them directly. For example, given that the Actual Percent Complete is 58% and Actual Percent Spent is 60%, we inferred that we are over budget and have an unfavorable cost efficiency.

Remember that cost efficiency was measured earlier by the Cost Performance Index or CPI. In fact the ratio of the Actual Percent Complete to the Actual Percent Spent is the Cost Performance Index.

$$\frac{Actual\ \%\ Complete}{Actual\ \%\ Spent} = CPI \qquad (10\text{-}6)$$

This is an alternate and perfectly acceptable definition of CPI. Using the values above we get the following.

$$CPI = \frac{58\%}{60\%} = \frac{0.58}{0.60} = 0.97$$

This is the same result we obtained for CPI in the last chapter, within rounding of course.

The schedule efficiency was identified earlier as the Schedule Performance Index or SPI. If we look at the ratio of the Actual Percent Complete to the Planned Percent Complete, we will also see the schedule efficiency.

$$\frac{Actual\ \%\ Complete}{Planned\ \%\ Complete} = SPI \qquad (10\text{-}7)$$

This, too, is an acceptable definition of SPI. Using the values from Table 10-4 above we get the following, which matches the results found in Chapter 7.

$$SPI = \frac{58\%}{52\%} = \frac{0.58}{0.52} = 1.12$$

The third possible combination is the relationship between the Planned Percent Spent (which is numerically equal to the Planned Percent Complete) and the Actual Percent Spent. The ratio of the two indicators yields, and is an alternate definition of the Fiscal Performance Index.

$$\frac{Planned\ \%\ Spent}{Actual\ \%\ Spent} = FPI \tag{10-8}$$

Using the values from Table 10-4 above we again obtain a result consistent with that found in Chapter 7.

$$FPI = \frac{52\%}{60\%} = \frac{0.52}{0.60} = 0.87$$

10-7 SUMMARY

We can use our basic indicators to express the progress made or the money spent in percentage terms. These percentages can be combined to give us alternate definitions of the indexes.

The questions that were addressed in this chapter are summarized in Table 10-4. The formulas introduced in this chapter can be found in Table 10-5.

Question	Answer
What portion of the work was planned to be complete through today?	Planned % Complete
What portion of the budget was planned to be spent through today?	Planned % Spent
What portion of the work was actually completed through today?	Actual % Complete
What portion of the budget was actually spent through today?	Actual % Spent

Table 10-4: Question Summary

Modern	Traditional
$Planned\ \%\ Complete = \dfrac{PV}{BAC}$	$Planned\ \%\ Complete = \dfrac{BCWS}{BAC}$
$Planned\ \%\ Spent = \dfrac{PV}{BAC}$	$Planned\ \%\ Spent = \dfrac{BCWS}{BAC}$
$Actual\ \%\ Complete = \dfrac{EV}{BAC}$	$Actual\ \%\ Complete = \dfrac{BCWP}{BAC}$
$Actual\ \%\ Spent = \dfrac{AC}{BAC}$	$Actual\ \%\ Spent = \dfrac{ACWP}{BAC}$
$CPI = \dfrac{Actual\ \%\ Complete}{Actual\ \%\ Spent}$	
$SPI = \dfrac{Actual\ \%\ Complete}{Planned\ \%\ Complete}$	
$FPI = \dfrac{Planned\ \%\ Spent}{Actual\ \%\ Spent}$	

Table 10-5: Formula Summary

EXERCISES

10-1: Explain why the Actual Cost for tasks is usually gathered directly and not as a result of the Actual % Spent.

10-2: A $50,000 task has a Planned Value of $28,000, an Earned Value of $30,000, and an Actual Cost of $29,000. Compute the following and determine the status of the task.

a) Planned % Complete

b) Planned % Spent

c) Actual % Complete

d) Actual % Spent

10-3: A project has a Planned Percent Spent of 75%, an Actual Percent Complete of 70%, and an Actual Percent Spent of 72%. Compute CPI, SPI, and FPI. What can be said of the project status?

10-4: We have been given a status report with the following data. Calculate the variances and indexes. What would be our concerns in this project?

BAC = $100,000

Planned % Complete = 52%

Actual % Complete = 55%

Planned % Spent = 54%.

10-5: Use the data in the following table for this exercise. The project BAC is $2200.

Week	cum PV [$]	cum EV [$]	cum AC [$]
1	90	100	101
2	205	220	225
3	370	380	393
4	545	590	619
5	735	750	795
6	960	930	999

a) Determine Planned % Complete, Actual % Complete, and Actual % Spent of the project at the end of Week 3.

b) What percentage of the project work was completed in Week 3 alone? What percentage of the budget was spent in Week 3? What percentage of the project work should have been completed in Week 3?

c) Characterize the status of the project using the percentages alone.

d) Compute the indexes using Equations 10-6, 10,7, and 10-8. What is the project status based on the indexes?

e) Repeat all of the above for Week 6.

Chapter 11

TIME INDICATORS

So far, when we've been looking at schedule performance, we focused on the value of the work performed with respect to the work scheduled. Any variances were associated with the difference in the work accomplished rather than with respect to time. In this chapter we're going to introduce some time-based indicators that will give us a different perspective on our schedule performance.

11-1 VALUE-BASED INDICATORS

First, let us review a term we defined in Chapter 4 called the Value-Based Schedule Variance, or SV($). SV($) is identical to the Schedule Variance we've been working with all along up to this point, as can be seen in the following expression.

$$SV(\$) = SV = EV - PV$$

SV is often referred to as the implicit form of the Value-Based Schedule Variance, while SV($) is referred to as the explicit form. In this chapter we will be introducing the Time-Based Schedule Variance, so we want to be clear to which we are referencing. From now on we will be using SV($) for emphasis any time we are referring to the Value-Based Schedule Variance to differentiate it from the Time-Based Schedule Variance.

The same goes for the Value-Based Schedule Variance Percentage. Up to this point we've been using the implicit form, or SV%, but from now on we'll be using the explicit form, or SV($)%. Likewise, the implicit form of the Value-Based Schedule Performance Index, or SPI, will be referred to in its explicit form of SPI($).

11-2 LIMITATIONS OF VALUE-BASED INDICATORS

In Example #2 of Chapter 8 we observed a major drawback in using value-based indicators. As a reminder, let's review that situation.

Table 11-1 shows the cumulative schedule status of the project at the end of Week 12, which is the planned completion date. The total project BAC is $2.2 million.

PV	$2,200K
EV	$2,160K
SV($)	−$40K
SPI($)	0.982
SV($)%	−1.8%

Table 11-1: Project Status at Week 12

Notice that the Planned Value equals the BAC, which indicates that the project is planned to be complete. The PV will remain constant at this level from now on.

We can see that the project is not *actually* complete yet, since the EV is less than the BAC. The Value-Based Schedule Variance tells us that $40,000 worth of work is still yet to be done.

The SPI($) indicates that only 98.2% of the work that should have been done so far is actually done. Since the entire project was planned to be complete, this also means that 98.2% of the whole project is actually done.

The SV($)% indicates that we performed 1.8% less work than what was scheduled. If our tolerance limits are ±5%, this indicates that we are well within tolerance. So in summary it appears that the project is in pretty good shape with respect to schedule.

Now, let's go into the future. Assume that it is now the end of Week 20 and no additional work was performed on the project. The project schedule status is given in Table 11-2.

PV	$2,200K
EV	$2,160K
SV($)	−$40K
SPI($)	0.982
SV($)%	−1.8%

Table 11-2: Project Status at Week 20

Notice that none of the numbers have changed! This is because these indicators give us status in terms of the *work* that was accomplished and not in terms of time. In fact, we can allow as much time as we would like to pass and the project will continue to remain only 1.8% behind schedule, using this measure, and still well within tolerance. Obviously there is something lacking with this approach.

In this chapter we are going to investigate schedule performance in terms of time units. With these new tools we *will* get an indication that we are out of tolerance if enough time elapses. After we develop the terms and relationships, we'll return to this example and see how it works.

11-3 PLANNED DURATION (PD)

As we discussed in an earlier chapter, we refer to the scheduled duration of the project as expressed in the baseline plan as the Planned Duration or PD. This represents the interval in time between the planned start date of the project and the planned finish date of the project. It is analogous to BAC, but in terms of time instead of value.

As an aid in developing some new concepts, we'll use the example project whose plan is given in Table 11-3. Here we can see a baseline project plan with a Planned Duration of 50 weeks and a total budget (BAC) of $1,000,000. The cumulative Planned Value is given on a week-by-week basis. This is the money we're planning to spend or equivalently, the value of the work we are planning to deliver through a given week. This data is exhibited graphically in Figure 11-1.

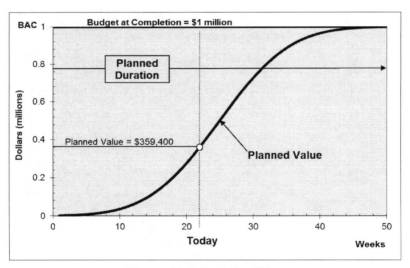

Figure 11-1: Baseline Plan

If we assume that today is the end of Week 22, we can see that the project should be 44% of the way through its planned duration (22 weeks/50 weeks). Also, Table 11-3 indicates that the plan is to have spent $359,400, which is the project Planned Value.

Week	cum PV [$K]	Week	cum PV [$K]
1	2.0	26	547.8
2	2.9	27	594.8
3	4.1	28	640.6
4	5.9	29	684.4
5	8.2	30	725.7
6	11.3	31	764.2
7	15.4	32	799.5
8	20.7	33	831.5
9	27.4	34	859.9
10	35.9	35	884.9
11	46.5	36	906.6
12	59.4	37	925.1
13	74.9	38	940.6
14	93.4	39	953.5
15	115.1	40	964.1
16	140.1	41	972.6
17	168.5	42	979.3
18	200.5	43	984.6
19	235.8	44	988.7
20	274.3	45	991.8
21	315.6	46	994.1
22	359.4	47	995.9
23	405.2	48	997.1
24	452.2	49	998.0
25	500.0	50	1000.0

Table 11-3: Cumulative Planned Value by week

11-4 ACTUAL TIME (AT) AND EARNED SCHEDULE (ES)

Let's now consider the actual progress. Figure 11-2 shows a situation where the project is behind schedule. We can see in this case that the Earned Value is equal to $215,000. The Schedule Variance, or SV($), is –$144,400. The negative sign indicates that we performed $144,400 less work than planned. This was obtained, of course, by taking the difference between the two indicators on the vertical (dollar) axis.

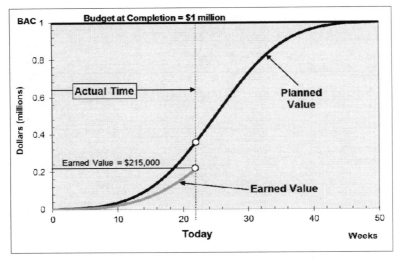

Figure 11-2: Project is behind schedule

Now, instead of concentrating on the vertical axis, let's look at the horizontal (time) axis.

We refer to the interval of time from the project start through today as the *Actual Time* (or AT) using the Modern Convention. It is also known as the *Actual Time for Work Performed* (ATWP) in the Traditional Convention. That is, this is the actual time it took deliver the work we performed. It represents the data date.

$$\text{Actual Time} \quad = \quad AT \quad = \quad ATWP$$

So in our example here we can say that today's Actual Time is 22 weeks.

Next, we will define the time it *should* have taken to perform that amount of work as the *Earned Schedule* (or ES) using the Modern Convention. It is also known as the *Planned Time for Work Performed* (PTWP) in the Traditional Convention.

$$\text{Earned Schedule} \quad = \quad ES \quad = \quad PTWP$$

We can find the Earned Schedule by drawing a horizontal line from the end of the Earned Value curve. The date at which this horizontal line intersects the Planned Value curve gives us the Earned Schedule.

Since the Earned Value is $215,000 we want to find the date at which the Planned Value also equals $215,000. From Figure 11-3 we can see that the Actual Time is 22 weeks, and Earned Schedule is a little more than 18 weeks.

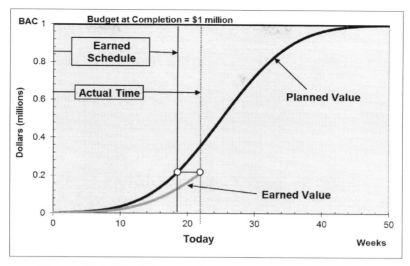

Figure 11-3: Work is over three weeks behind schedule

To get a more precise answer, we will use the cumulative Planned Value data in Table 11-3. From the table, we can see that the cumulative Planned Value of $215,000 occurs somewhere between the end of Week 18 and the end of Week 19. We can interpolate to find a more precise time. Equation 11-1a gives us the interpolation formula using the Modern Convention.

$$ES = Date_1 + (Date_2 - Date_1) \times \frac{(EV - PV_1)}{(PV_2 - PV_1)} \qquad (11\text{-}1a)$$

Date$_1$ refers to the planned date at the beginning of the range of interest and Date$_2$ to the planned date at the end of the range of interest. PV$_1$ is the Planned Value at Date$_1$ and PV$_2$ is the Planned Value at Date$_2$. We can now substitute the values from Table 11-3.

$$ES = 18 \ weeks + (19 \ weeks - 18 \ weeks) \times \frac{(215.0 - 200.5)}{(235.8 - 200.5)}$$

$$ES = 18 \ weeks + (1 \ week) \times \frac{14.5}{35.3}$$

$$ES = 18 \ weeks + (1 \ week) \times 0.4$$

$$ES = 18 \ weeks + 0.4 \ week$$

$$ES = 18.4 \ weeks$$

This means that the amount of work that was actually performed through Week 22 should have taken 18.4 weeks.

For the record, Equation 11-1b gives the interpolation formula in the Traditional Convention.

$$PTWP = Date_1 + (Date_2 - Date_1) \times \frac{(BCWP - BCWS_1)}{(BCWS_2 - BCWS_1)} \quad \text{(11-1b)}$$

11-5 TIME-BASED SCHEDULE VARIANCE [SV(t)]

Here we'll define another new term called the *Time-Based Schedule Variance* or SV(t). This is the difference between the time it took to perform the work actually accomplished and the time in which the same amount of work was planned to have been performed in the baseline plan.

A note of caution is needed here. It is very possible that the work actually accomplished was not the correct work. In some cases it may be possible that more work was performed than planned, but if the critical path is behind schedule the project still has a good likelihood of coming in late. So SV(t) applied to the entire project is not a fool-proof indicator.

One way to protect against this possible shortcoming is to use the tools in this chapter two different ways. First, apply it to the entire project like we are doing here, and secondly apply it using only the tasks on the critical path. Since the critical path defines the project duration, any delay along the critical path will indicate that the project is in danger of being completed behind schedule.

The Time-Based Schedule Variance is calculated using Equation 11-2a or 11-2b. SV(t) has time units instead of monetary units as is the case with SV($). We can think of SV(t) as the amount of time the project is ahead or behind schedule.

Modern: $SV(t) = ES - AT$ (11-2a)

Traditional: $SV(t) = PTWP - ATWP$ (11-2b)

The convention is the same as the other variances that we've been working with. A negative result is generally considered to be bad and a positive is good. In this case a negative result means that it took longer to perform the work than planned, or we are behind schedule.

If we substitute the values generated in our example project we find the following.

$$SV(t) = 18.4 \; weeks - 22.0 \; weeks = -3.6 \; weeks$$

Since SV(t) is negative, this means that it took 3.6 weeks longer than planned to perform the amount of work actually accomplished, or the project is 3.6 weeks behind schedule. Assuming a 5 day standard work week, this is equivalent to being behind schedule by 3 weeks and 3 days or 18 work days.

If the SV(t) is negative, it is often said that the schedule has slipped by the magnitude of SV(t). So, in this case, we might say that the schedule has slipped by 3.6 weeks, or that the schedule slippage equals 3.6 weeks.

Notice that in the Traditional terms, the four letter initials (ATWP and PTWP) can be divided into two initial pairs. The first pair represents the time and the last pair represents the work. In both cases, the work is the same (i.e. the work that was actually performed) the difference is just in the time it took to perform that amount of work.

SV(t) = (PT) (WP) − (AT) (WP)

Actual Work Performed

11-6 TIME-BASED SCHEDULE VARIANCE PERCENTAGE [SV(t)%]

SV(t) gives us the time, in absolute terms, that the project is ahead or behind schedule. Just as in the earlier variances, this falls short in giving us a complete picture. For example, let's assume that our project is 2 days behind schedule. If it is a year since the project began, this is a small fraction of the total and may not be significant. However, if our project is only one week old, this is a very significant portion of the total.

To remedy this, we use the same approach as with the other variances, i.e. by taking the Time-Based Schedule Variance as a percentage of the planned time. To get this Time-Base Schedule Variance Percentage, or SV(t)%, we simply divide the SV(t) by the Earned Schedule and express the result as a percentage. Equations 11-3a and 11-3b give us the formulas for SV(t)%.

Modern: $SV(t)\% = \dfrac{SV(t)}{ES}$ $\hspace{2cm}$ (11-3a)

Traditional: $SV(t)\% = \dfrac{SV(t)}{PTWP}$ $\hspace{2cm}$ (11-3b)

Using the example given above, we find that SV(t)% = −3.6/18.4 = −19.6%. In other words, it took 19.6% longer than planned to perform the work accomplished. Another way of expressing this is that the schedule has slipped by 19.6%.

If we want to set tolerance limits on our schedule, we should use SV(t)% rather than SV(t). SV(t)% always has the same sign as SV(t) since the Earned Schedule can never be negative.

SV(t)% can be expressed in a different form, but of course yielding the same result. See Equations 11-4 a and 11-4b.

$$\textbf{Modern: } SV(t)\% = 1 - \frac{AT}{ES} \tag{11-4a}$$

$$\textbf{Traditional: } SV(t)\% = 1 - \frac{ATWP}{PTWP} \tag{11-4b}$$

The attractiveness of using this form of the equation is that the SV(t)% is in terms of the basic elements directly. The Time-Based Schedule Variance does not need to be calculated as an intermediate step. If we use the values in the example above we get the following.

$$SV(t)\% = 1 - \frac{22}{18.4} = 1 - 1.196 = -0.196 = -19.6\%$$

As we can see, the result is the same.

11-7 TIME-BASED SCHEDULE PERFORMANCE INDEX [SPI(t)]

Analogous to the other variances, there is also an index that can be used for tracking tolerance limits. Here we use the same factors as in the Time-Based Schedule Variance, but take the ratio instead of the difference. It indicates how efficient we are with our time. The formulas for SPI(t) are given in Equations 11-5a and 11-5b.

$$\textbf{Modern: } SPI(t) = \frac{ES}{AT} \tag{11-5a}$$

$$\textbf{Traditional: } SPI(t) = \frac{PTWP}{ATWP} \tag{11-5b}$$

SPI(t) is a pure number (i.e. it has no units). If SPI(t) equals 1, then the project is on schedule. If SPI(t) is greater than 1 the project is ahead of schedule, and if SPI(t) is less than 1 the project is behind schedule. SPI(t) can never be negative.

Let's compute the value of SPI(t) in our sample project. Since SPI(t) =

18.4/22 = 0.84, this means that for each day actually spent working on the project, only 0.84 days worth of progress was being made on average. In other words, we are progressing through our project with only an 84% time efficiency.

11-8 RELATIONSHIP BETWEEN SV(t)% AND SPI(t)

Just as we can relate the indexes to the variance percentages in the dollar-denominated indicators, we can also relate SV(t)% to SPI(t). By substituting equation 11-5a into 11-4a we can see that we get the relationship in Equation 11-6.

$$SV(t)\% = 1 - \frac{1}{SPI(t)} \tag{11-6}$$

Equivalently, we can represent SPI(t) in terms of SV(t)% as shown in Equation 11-7.

$$SPI(t) = \frac{1}{1 - SV(t)\%} \tag{11-7}$$

In addition to expressing this relationship as an equation, we can also put it in the form of a table or depict it in a graph.

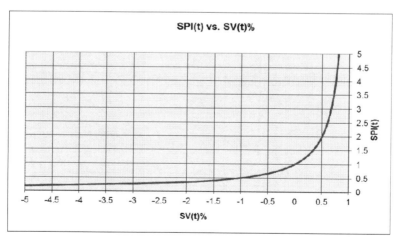

Figure 11-4: Relationship between SPI(t) and SV(t)%

As we can see the relationship between SV(t)% and SPI(t) is *not* analogous to the relationship between SV($) and SPI($) which is linear. It is, however, analogous to the relationship between CV% and CPI as well as the one between FV% and FPI. This is easy to see graphically in Figure 11-4.

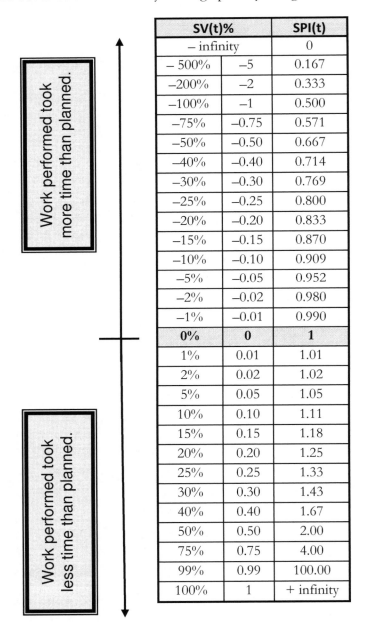

SV(t)%		SPI(t)
− infinity		0
− 500%	−5	0.167
−200%	−2	0.333
−100%	−1	0.500
−75%	−0.75	0.571
−50%	−0.50	0.667
−40%	−0.40	0.714
−30%	−0.30	0.769
−25%	−0.25	0.800
−20%	−0.20	0.833
−15%	−0.15	0.870
−10%	−0.10	0.909
−5%	−0.05	0.952
−2%	−0.02	0.980
−1%	−0.01	0.990
0%	**0**	**1**
1%	0.01	1.01
2%	0.02	1.02
5%	0.05	1.05
10%	0.10	1.11
15%	0.15	1.18
20%	0.20	1.25
25%	0.25	1.33
30%	0.30	1.43
40%	0.40	1.67
50%	0.50	2.00
75%	0.75	4.00
99%	0.99	100.00
100%	1	+ infinity

Work performed took more time than planned.

Work performed took less time than planned.

Table 11-4: Comparison of SV(t)% and SPI(t) values

Table 11-4 displays some common values of SV(t)% in terms of SPI(t). For example, if the work actually performed to-date took 10% more time than planned, SPI(t) would have a value of 0.909.

11-9 PERCENT ELAPSED AND PERCENT CONCLUDED

In an earlier chapter we saw how we could measure our progress through the project by tracking the Actual % Complete. This is a measure of how much of the total work in the project we delivered so far. When compared to the Planned % Complete, we were given a sense of how much we were ahead or behind schedule. These were generated by looking at project work and not the time.

We have an analogous way of expressing our progress through the project using time factors with Percent Elapsed (or % Elapsed) and Percent Concluded (% Concluded). Percent Elapsed is a measure of how far along we are through the project Planned Duration, while Percent Concluded indicates how far we should have been through the project duration based on the work accomplished.

Equations 11-8a and 11-8b define Percent Elapsed while Equations 11-9a and 11-9b define Percent Concluded.

$$\textbf{Modern: } \%\ Elapsed = \frac{AT}{PD} \tag{11-8a}$$

$$\textbf{Traditional: } \%\ Elapsed = \frac{ATWP}{PD} \tag{11-8b}$$

$$\textbf{Modern: } \%\ Concluded = \frac{ES}{PD} \tag{11-9a}$$

$$\textbf{Traditional: } \%\ Concluded = \frac{PTWP}{PD} \tag{11-9b}$$

Using our sample project we can compute values for each of these indicators.

$$\%\ Elapsed = \frac{AT}{PD} = \frac{ATWP}{PD} = \frac{22}{50} = 44\%$$

This means that as of today (the end of Week 22) 44.0% of the time through the project's planned duration of 50 weeks has elapsed, or we are 44.0% of the way through the project's planned duration. The % Elapsed figure progresses at a constant rate along with the clock, regardless of how much work is actually being accomplished.

$$\% \ Concluded \ = \frac{ES}{PD} = \frac{PTWP}{PD} = \frac{18.4}{50} = 36.8\%$$

This means that we have actually concluded an equivalent of only 36.8% of the planned project duration. That is, the actual amount of work performed though today was planned to have been delivered when the project was 36.8% of the way through its planned duration. The % Concluded figure progresses at a variable rate. This rate is dependent upon how much work is actually being accomplished per unit time with respect to what was planned to be accomplished within that same time.

Since we have concluded less of the project than was planned, we are behind schedule.

We can combine Percent Elapsed and Percent Concluded to give us another, and equally valid, definition of the Time-Based Schedule Performance Index, or SPI(t). This is shown here in Equation 11-10.

$$SPI \ (t) = \frac{\% \ Concluded}{\% \ Elapsed} \tag{11-10}$$

We can see that if we perform this calculation, we'll arrive at the same value we determined for SPI(t) earlier.

$$SPI \ (t) = \frac{0.368}{0.440} = 0.84$$

11-10 EXAMPLE PROJECT REVISITED

Now that we have laid the groundwork, let's go back to the situation we introduced at the beginning of the chapter. We found that by looking at measures of work alone, we would not get any warning if too much time had passed. Even when the 12 week project was 8 weeks late, everything was still within tolerance.

When we employ our new time indicators, we will now see that we are alerted when too much time passes by.

First, we need to obtain the Planned Value data over time for the project. In Chapter 8 it was given in Table 8-5. That data is reproduced here in Table 11-5.

Week	inc PV [$K]	cum PV [$K]
1	90	90
2	115	205
3	165	370
4	175	545
5	190	735
6	225	960
7	240	1200
8	310	1510
9	250	1760
10	200	1960
11	160	2120
12	80	2200

Table 11-5: Planned Value data

From Table 11-1 earlier in this chapter, we saw that the cumulative Earned Value at the end of Week 12 (the Actual Time) was $2160K. Using our interpolation method, we can compute the Earned Schedule which indicates when the Planned Value should have equaled $2160K.

$$ES = 11\ weeks + 1\ week \times \frac{(2160 - 2120)}{(2200 - 2120)}$$

$$ES = 11\ weeks + \frac{40}{80}\ weeks = 11.5\ weeks$$

This tells us that the total amount of work that was actually performed through the end of Week 12 should have been completed in 11.5 weeks.

We can compute the Time-Based Schedule Variance for Week 12. SV(t) = 11.5 − 12.0 = −0.5 weeks. This indicates that the project is half of a week behind schedule.

The Time-Based Schedule Variance Percentage will allow us to see this delay in relative terms. SV(t)% = −0.5/11.5 = −4.3%, which means that the project is 4.3% behind schedule. In Chapter 8 we determined that at Week 12, SV($)% = −1.8%. Even though the Time-Based Schedule Variance Percentage is greater, we are still within our ±5% tolerance limits.

Next we'll compute the Time-Based Schedule Performance Index. SPI(t) = 11.5/12.0 = 0.958. We can interpret this as meaning for every day we've actually worked the project, on average only 0.958 days of planned work were accomplished. In other words, we are 95.8% efficient with our time.

Now let's look at Week 20, remembering our assumption from the beginning of the chapter that no more work was accomplished over the intervening 8 weeks. Also recall that SV($), SV($)%, and SPI($) all gave the same results that were calculated for Week 12, thereby masking any slippage.

Let's look at our new indicators to see if they alert us to the problem. Our Actual Time is now 20 weeks. Since no additional work was performed, the Earned Value is the same as that for Week 12. Since we use the Earned Value to compute the Earned Schedule, the Earned Schedule is the same as for Week 12, i.e. 11.5 weeks.

Now, however, when we compute the Time-Based Schedule Variance, we get a different result because the Actual Time has changed. SV(t) = 11.5 weeks − 20.0 weeks = −8.5 weeks. So now we know that the project is 8.5 weeks behind schedule, a significant amount. If no further work is accomplished, the magnitude of this indicator will continue to grow, because the Actual Time will continue to grow.

Putting this in perspective relative to the size of the project, we can compute the Time-Based Schedule Variance Percentage. SV(t)% = −8.5/11.5 = −73.9%. We are now well beyond our tolerance limits of ±5%, so this project is significantly out of tolerance with respect to time. The magnitude of this too will continue to grow if no more work is accomplished.

Finally, let's compute the Time-Based Schedule Performance Index. SPI(t) = 11.5/20.0 = 0.575, which means that we are operating at only a 57.5% time efficiency. This is significantly worse than what we had at Week 12. This will also continue to degrade with time if no more work is performed.

So, as we can see, these time indicators give us an additional set of tools that more accurately reflect project schedule status with respect to the calendar.

11-11 SUMMARY

Time indicators, while sometimes more challenging to compute, add another important dimension to analyzing project progress.

As we saw, if the work in a project is 98% complete, but progress has stopped, the work-related indicators will continue to designate a 98% completion level. In this case the SV($), SV($)%, and SPI($) will be frozen at their current values forever. On the other hand, if the project is 98% concluded and the work has stopped, the SV(t), SV(t)%, and SPI(t) will not be frozen. Time marches on.

The % Elapsed will continue to grow, causing the SPI(t) to continually diminish. This shrinking SPI(t) will eventually get someone's attention. As such, these time indicators are an important component in every EVM toolbox.

The questions that were addressed in this chapter are summarized in Table

11-6. Tables 11-7 and 11-8 contain summaries of the formulas introduced in this chapter.

Question	Answer
How much time has passed since the beginning of the project?	AT
How much time should it have taken to perform the work that was actually accomplished?	ES
How much time is the project ahead of (or behind) schedule?	SV(t)
By what percentage of time is the project ahead of (or behind) schedule?	SV(t)%
How efficiently is the project making use of its time?	SPI(t)
What portion of the project's duration has gone by so far?	% Elapsed
At what point along the project's duration was the work performed scheduled to be done?	% Concluded

Table 11-6: Question Summary

Modern Convention
$$ES = Date_1 + (Date_2 - Date_1) \times \frac{(EV - PV_1)}{(PV_2 - PV_1)}$$
Traditional Convention
$$PTWP = Date_1 + (Date_2 - Date_1) \times \frac{(BCWP - BCWS_1)}{(BCWS_2 - BCWS_1)}$$

Table 11-7: Interpolation Formula Summary

Modern	Traditional
$SV(t) = ES - AT$	$SV(t) = PTWP - ATWP$
$SV(t)\% = \dfrac{SV(t)}{ES}$	$SV(t)\% = \dfrac{SV(t)}{PTWP}$
$SV(t)\% = 1 - \dfrac{AT}{ES}$	$SV(t)\% = 1 - \dfrac{ATWP}{PTWP}$
$SPI(t) = \dfrac{ES}{AT}$	$SPI(t) = \dfrac{PTWP}{ATWP}$
$\%\ Elapsed = \dfrac{AT}{PD}$	$\%\ Elapsed = \dfrac{ATWP}{PD}$
$\%\ Concluded = \dfrac{ES}{PD}$	$\%\ Concluded = \dfrac{PTWP}{PD}$
$SV(t)\% = 1 - \dfrac{1}{SPI(t)}$	
$SPI(t) = \dfrac{1}{1 - SV(t)\%}$	
$SPI(t) = \dfrac{\%\ Concluded}{\%\ Elapsed}$	

Table 11-8: Formula Summary

EXERCISES

11-1: Explain the difference between the value-based schedule indicators and the time-based schedule indicators. What are the strengths and short-comings of each?

11-2: Why should our schedule analysis be performed using all of the tasks in the project and be repeated for the critical tasks? What would it mean if the critical path has a positive SV(t), but the entire project has a negative

SV(t)? What would it mean if the signs were reversed?

11-3: Use the data in the table below to calculate ES, SV($), SV(t), SV($)%, and SV(t)% for each point in time given. Interpret the status of the project. How do the time-based indicators compare to the value-based indicators?

Week	cum PV [$]	cum EV [$]
1	600	550
3	2200	2100
5	3400	3200
8	5500	5400

11-4: It is currently the end of Week 7 of a 20-week project. Using the data in the table below, compute the following cumulative indicators for the end of Week 3 and interpret the results. Repeat for Week 7. How did the schedule status of this project change over the intervening weeks?

Week	cum PV [$K]	cum EV [$K]
1	100	105
2	220	228
3	350	370
4	500	498
5	650	635
6	820	792
7	1100	990

a) AT

b) ES

c) % Elapsed

d) % Concluded

e) SV($)

f) SV(t)

g) SPI($)

h) SPI(t)

i) SV($)%

j) SV(t)%

11-5: Using the data in Exercise 11-4, draw a control chart for SV(t)%. Include data points for each week for both incremental and cumulative curves. Assuming ±5% tolerance limits, characterize the evolution of the project's schedule status over time. Repeat using SV($)%. How do the time-based indicators compare with the value-based indicators?

11-6: Using the data in the following table, generate a report for the end of Week 12 and interpret the results. Perform your analysis using the data for all the tasks, then repeat for only the critical tasks. Include the project-level indicators below in your assessment. [Assume that the tasks are scheduled as soon as possible and that the budget for each task is evenly distributed over the life of the task.]

Task ID	Duration [weeks]	Budget [$]	Predecessor(s)	Actual % Complete (Week 12)
A	3	6,000	–	100%
B	4	10,000	–	100%
C	5	12,000	A, B	100%
D	2	3,000	B	100%
E	4	6,000	C	80%
F	6	9,000	C, D	10%
G	3	5,400	D	90%
H	5	8,500	E, F	0%
I	6	10,500	F, G	0%

a) PV

b) EV

c) AT

d) ES

e) Planned % Complete

f) Actual % Complete

g) % Elapsed

h) % Concluded

i) SV($)

j) SV(t)

k) SPI($)

l) SPI(t)

m) SV($)%

n) SV(t)%

Chapter12

FORECASTING COST: DEFINITIONS

12-1 INTRODUCTION TO FORECASTING

Up until now, we have been working within the Earned Value system to help us analyze and communicate project status. As we have discovered, it is very valuable to know how our project is progressing with respect to cost, schedule, and spending.

The ultimate measure of our project's success will be determined by how the variances compare to their acceptable tolerance limits when the project is complete. For example, if our project budget is $10 million and the acceptable limits for cost are ±5%, then our project will be deemed a success with respect to cost if the final cumulative actual cost is between $9.5 million and $10.5 million, i.e. within 5% either side of the budget.

Of course, we don't want to wait until we're near the end of the project in order to determine whether or not we're going to be successful. If we wait until we see the light at the end of the tunnel before we take our first reading, it will be too late to do anything about it if we find that the project is in trouble.

The process of making predictions about how our project will behave in the future is called forecasting. It is similar to the estimating process that we employed during planning. The principal difference is that we can now take advantage of lessons-learned and data generated in the current project. By coupling trends with some reasonable assumptions about the future, we will be equipped to make forecasts of how our project will unfold.

This is not much different than forecasting the weather. Meteorologists collect data about current atmospheric conditions and trends. Then by utilizing models that simulate atmospheric behavior, they can make predictions about future weather conditions.

We can do same thing with our projects. Near-term forecasts can be pretty good. Longer term forecasts will by nature be less accurate. Since we cannot know for sure how the future will unfold, the accuracy of our forecasts will depend on the quality of our data and the assumptions that we make.

As an example, by using the forecasting tools presented here, we'll be able to tell in the first reporting period where the project will end up if things keep going the way they have been going. Then if we don't like what we see, we have plenty of time remaining in order to make the adjustments necessary in order to get back on track.

If we act early, our adjustments won't need to be as great as they would be if we waited. The closer we get to the end of the project, the less work we have left to influence and the more difficult it will to be to recover if we have a problem. Therefore, to be useful as a project management tool we need to make our forecasts early and frequently.

In this chapter we'll begin our discussion of forecasting cost by defining some terms and formulas. In the next chapter, we'll look at examples where we can apply what we learn here to make some specific forecasts. In later chapters we'll discuss how to forecast our schedule.

12-2 BUDGET REMAINING (BR)

After working on a portion of the project, we may be interested in knowing how much of our baseline budget is as yet unspent. This amount is known as the Budget Remaining, or BR. It is clear that our total project budget (Budget at Completion) is simply the sum of the money we've spent so far (Actual Cost) plus the unspent portion of the budget (Budget Remaining) as shown in the following expression.

$$\begin{matrix} Budget \\ at \\ Completion \end{matrix} = \begin{matrix} Actual \\ Cost \end{matrix} + \begin{matrix} Budget \\ Remaining \end{matrix}$$

We can see this relationship displayed graphically in the project depicted in Figure 12-1. Here we have a project where the Budget at Completion equals $1 million and the Planned Duration is 50 weeks. As of today, the end of Week 25, the cumulative Actual Cost equals $300,000.

Stating the relationship above using the initials, we get Equation 12-1a in the Modern Convention.

$$BAC = AC + BR \qquad (12\text{-}1a)$$

Budget Remaining to-Complete, or BRTC, is the equivalent term to Budget Remaining in the Traditional Convention, as can be seen in the following expression.

$$BRTC = BR$$

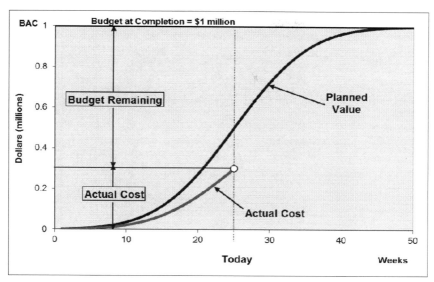

Figure 12-1: BAC = AC + BR

The relationship in Equation 12-1a expressed in the Traditional Convention is shown in Equation 12-1b.

$$BAC = ACWP + BRTC \qquad (12\text{-}1b)$$

At this point BAC and AC are known quantities. We can then use this relationship to compute the Budget Remaining from the other terms. To do this it is more convenient to rewrite the relationship as shown in Equations 12-2a and 12-2b.

Modern: $BR = BAC - AC$ $\qquad (12\text{-}2a)$

Traditional: $BRTC = BAC - ACWP$ $\qquad (12\text{-}2b)$

The Budget Remaining indicates how much of our original budget is left to be spent. If the BR is zero, then we have spent our entire budget. If BR is negative, we have overspent our budget, and the magnitude of BR equals the amount of the overage so far.

Using the data from our example in Figure 12-1 we can now calculate the Budget Remaining using Equation 12-2a.

$$BR = \$1,000,000 - \$300,000$$

$$BR = \$700,000$$

Since the result is positive, we have $700,000 of our budget left unspent. We'll need to do all the remaining work for this amount of money if we want to finish our project on budget.

12-3 ESTIMATE AT COMPLETION (EAC)

We saw in Chapter 5 that the cumulative Planned Value curve terminates on the dollar axis at BAC when the project is *planned* to be completed. We also saw that the cumulative Earned Value curve also terminates at BAC, but when the project is *actually* completed. They both top out at BAC because they are expressed in baseline or budgeted dollars.

We also previously noted that the cumulative Actual Cost curve can terminate anywhere on the dollar axis. This is obviously true because the project can finish below budget, on budget, or over budget.

We are going to define the cost at which we are forecasting the Actual Cost to terminate as the Estimate at Completion, or EAC. Because this forecast is based upon assumptions that we make about the future, there will be some uncertainty involved. This uncertainty will decrease as we get closer to the end of the project, because the cost of the unfinished work will be a smaller and smaller fraction of the entire cost of the project.

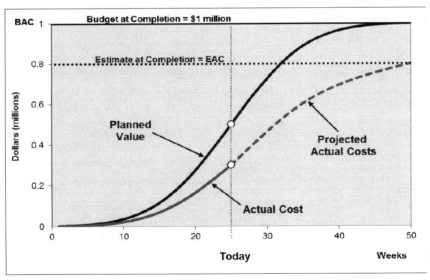

Figure 12-2: EAC is the projected total Actual Cost of the project

Figure 12-2 shows our project with our cost forecast. Here we are assuming that the project finishes on schedule at the original 50 week mark, and that the Actual Cost is forecasted to equal $800,000 at that time. In other words, we are predicting that the project EAC will equal $800,000.

170

Here we've just been given the number. The trick will be to figure out how we can actually generate that number. That we will discuss in the next chapter. For now we are just defining terms.

12-4 ESTIMATE TO COMPLETE (ETC)

At this time we'll define a related term called Estimate to Complete or ETC. While EAC is our forecast for the *total* Actual Cost of the project when it is finished, the ETC is our forecast for how much money we will need from today to complete the remaining project work.

The difference is that EAC includes the amount of money that we already spent through today, i.e. the Actual Cost, while the ETC does not. See Figure 12-3 to see a depiction of this with the cumulative cost curves.

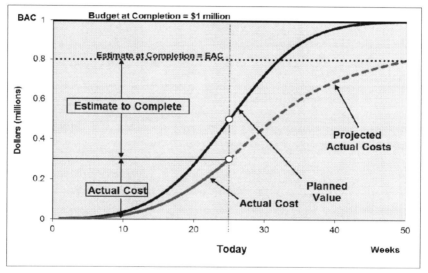

Figure 12-3: EAC = AC + ETC

From this graph we can see an obvious relationship among the terms.

$$\begin{array}{ccc} Estimate \\ at \\ Completion \end{array} = \begin{array}{c} Actual \\ Cost \end{array} + \begin{array}{c} Estimate \\ to \\ Complete \end{array}$$

This expression is restated using our initials in Equations 12-3a and 12-3b.

Modern: $EAC = AC + ETC$ (12-3a)

Traditional: $EAC = ACWP + ETC$ (12-3b)

These formulas are true all the time. They are independent of any assumption we make about the future. All it says is the total projected cost (EAC) is equal to the actual cost of the work already performed (AC) plus the projected cost of the work yet to be done (ETC). In other words the past plus the future equals the total.

The problem here is that we have two unknowns. While we can measure the Actual Cost, EAC and ETC both have yet to be determined. It's clear that we can't use these formulas unless we find a number for either ETC or EAC first by using some other means. Once we do, we can use these formulas to find the other term.

If we generate a value for ETC, we can then use Equation 12-3a or 12-3b to find EAC. Sometimes, however, it's easier to find EAC first. In this case, we can use a related form of the equations above where we have solved for ETC. See Equations 12-4a and 12-4b.

Modern: $ETC = EAC - AC$ (12-4a)

Traditional: $ETC = EAC - ACWP$ (12-4b)

Again, these formulas are true all the time and are independent of any assumptions we make about the future.

Using the sample project depicted in Figure 12-3, we can see that an assumption has already been made about how the Actual Cost will progress. We can then use these formulas to make a calculation. We can gather the following data from Figure 12-3.

$EAC = \$800,000$

$AC = \$300,000$

From this we can calculate ETC using Equation 12-4a or 12-4b.

$ETC = \$800,000 - \$300,000$

$ETC = \$500,000$

This matches with what we can see graphically. The implication is that, assuming the future will unfold as depicted, we will need $500,000 more in actual funds in order to finish the project.

12-5 VARIANCE AT COMPLETION (VAC)

The difference between our baseline budget (BAC) and what we are currently forecasting to spend (EAC) we will define as the Variance at Completion, or VAC. Figure 12-4 depicts the VAC relative to BAC and EAC. We can express this relationship using the formula in Equation 12-5.

$$VAC = BAC - EAC \qquad (12\text{-}5)$$

The VAC has the same convention as CV, i.e. positive is good and negative is bad. A positive VAC means that we are expecting to deliver the project under budget by the amount of the VAC. Conversely, a negative VAC indicates that we are expecting to deliver the project over budget by that amount. If the VAC is zero, we're forecasting to bring the project in on budget.

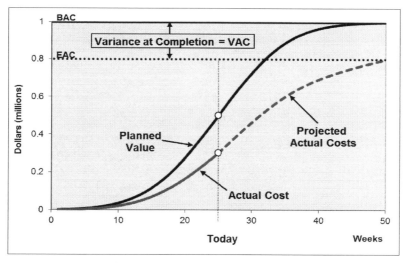

Figure 12-4: VAC = BAC − EAC

Taking the data from Figure 12-4, we can see that we are expecting to complete the project under budget since EAC is less than BAC. We can use the formula above to calculate the magnitude of the difference.

$$BAC = \$1,000,000$$

$$EAC = \$800,000$$

$$VAC = \$1,000,000 - \$800,000$$

$$VAC = \$200,000$$

Since the result is positive, we are expecting to deliver the project under budget by $200,000. Technically, the Variance at Completion is just our forecast of what the Cost Variance will be at the end of the project.

This is easy to see. Recall that the Cost Variance is the amount of money we are currently over or under budget for the work performed so far. This is expressed in the following formula.

$$CV = EV - AC$$

At the end of the project EV equals BAC and AC equals EAC. Therefore, at the end of the project, CV = BAC − EAC, which is just our definition of VAC.

Notice that the VAC will also be the Fiscal Variance after both the planned and actual completion dates have been passed. The Value-Based Schedule Variance at that time will of course always be zero.

Another way to calculate the Variance at Completion is to work with the Budget Remaining. We can see this relationship in Equations 12-6a and 12-6b.

Modern: $VAC = BR - ETC$ (12-6a)

Traditional: $VAC = BRTC - ETC$ (12-6b)

We can see that this makes sense. BR represents the amount of funding remaining in our budget and ETC is the amount of funding we need to finish the project. If we need more money to finish the project than we have available, we will end up over budget by the difference, which is just the VAC. If we have more funds available than we need, the project will be under budget by the difference.

Using the data in our sample project we can now calculate the VAC for our sample project.

$$BR = \$700,000$$

$$ETC = \$500,000$$

$$VAC = \$700,000 - \$500,000 = \$200,000$$

This is just what we discovered earlier using the first method.

12-6 VARIANCE AT COMPLETION PERCENTAGE (VAC%)

The Variance at Completion is a very useful indicator. It tells us exactly how many dollars over budget or under budget we are expecting our project to finish. If our original project budget is $50 million and the VAC is –$5000 we may not be worried. However, if our original budget is $10,000 and we are projecting that same –$5000 VAC we would be very worried.

While VAC gives us the amount our project is projected to come in over or under budget in absolute terms, it does not put it into perspective relative to the size of our project. The VAC% will do this for us.

To get the Variance at Completion Percentage, simply divide the Variance at Completion by the Budget at Completion and express the result as a percentage. The formula is seen here as Equation 12-7.

$$VAC\% = \frac{VAC}{BAC} \qquad (12\text{-}7)$$

Similar to the CV%, a VAC% equal to zero indicates a forecast to finish on budget. A positive VAC% predicts the project will finish under budget, while a negative VAC% predicts a finish over budget.

Let's look at a numerical example. From Figure 12-4 we found the following.

$$BAC = \$1,000,000$$

$$EAC = \$800,000$$

$$VAC = \$200,000$$

From these we can calculate a value for VAC%.

$$VAC\% = \frac{\$200,000}{\$1,000,000} = 0.2 = 20\%$$

Since the result is positive, this indicates that we are forecasting to bring the project in 20% under budget.

The same equation for VAC% can be expressed in a different form, but of course yielding the same results as shown in Equation 12-8.

$$VAC\% = 1 - \frac{EAC}{BAC} \qquad (12\text{-}8)$$

The attractiveness of this equation is that VAC% is expressed in directly in terms of the basic elements. The VAC does not need to be calculated as an intermediate step.

Using the same example above, we can now compute VAC% using the alternate method.

$$VAC\% = 1 - \frac{\$800{,}000}{\$1{,}000{,}000} = 1 - 0.8 = 0.2 = 20\%$$

We can set acceptable tolerance levels for cost using VAC%. By calculating VAC% on a regular basis, we can get early warning when our projected cost is expected to be out of tolerance.

One final note, using an argument similar to the one between VAC and CV discussed earlier, VAC% is simply our forecast of what the CV% will be at the end of the project.

VAC% also represents what the FV% will be after both the planned and actual completion dates have been reached. At that time the SV($)% will always be zero.

12-7 SUMMARY

Forecasting is an estimating process that utilizes data and lessons-learned generated in the current project. It is important to perform our forecasts early and often in order to minimize the magnitude of the corrections we may need to make to keep our project on track.

In this chapter, we introduced a number of terms that will allow us to interpret our forecasting results. In the next chapter we will apply these using some example scenarios.

The questions that were addressed in this chapter are summarized in Table 12-1.

Question	Answer
How much money in the budget has not yet been spent?	BR
What is the total project expected to cost when it is complete?	EAC
What is the remaining work expected to cost?	ETC
How much is the project expected to be under (or over) budget when it is complete?	VAC
By what percentage is the project expected to be under (or over) budget when it is complete?	VAC%

Table 12-1: Question Summary

Table 12-2 summarizes the equations that we introduced in this chapter. All of these formulas are true all of the time, i.e. they are independent of any assumptions we make about the future. The scenarios in the next chapter will be based on certain assumptions about how the future will unfold. Certain formulas presented there will not be true all the time, but only true if those assumptions are true.

Modern	Traditional
$BAC = AC + BR$	$BAC = ACWP + BRTC$
$BR = BAC - AC$	$BRTC = BAC - ACWP$
$EAC = AC + ETC$	$EAC = ACWP + ETC$
$ETC = EAC - AC$	$ETC = EAC - ACWP$
$VAC = BAC - EAC$	
$VAC\% = \dfrac{VAC}{BAC}$	
$VAC\% = 1 - \dfrac{EAC}{BAC}$	

Table 12-2: Forecasting Equations by Convention (Always True)

EXERCISES

12-1: What is forecasting? Why is it performed? When should it be performed?

12-2: Explain the difference between EAC and ETC.

12-3: What is VAC? How does it relate to CV?

12-4: What are the impacts of schedule variances on forecasting project costs?

12-5: $6,000 has been spent so far in a $20,000 project. The project is expected to be completed $1,000 over budget. Determine the following indicators and interpret the meaning of each.

a) BAC   d) ETC

b) AC   e) EAC

c) BR   f) VAC

                      g) VAC%

12-6: A $100,000 project is two-thirds complete and has $30,000 of its budget remaining to be spent. The current forecast is predicting that the project will finish $10,000 over budget. Determine the following indicators and interpret the meaning of each.

a) BAC   e) CV   h) ETC

b) AC   f) CV%   i) EAC

c) EV   g) CPI   j) VAC

d) BR   k) VAC%

12-7: A status report on a $50,000 project indicates that it is 30% complete with a Cost Variance Percentage of +6%. The manager of this effort is forecasting that $33,900 will be required to perform the remaining work. Determine the following indicators and interpret the meaning of each.

a) BAC   e) CV   h) ETC

b) AC   f) CV%   i) EAC

c) EV   g) CPI   j) VAC

d) BR   k) VAC%

Is this project forecasted to perform better or worse in the future than it has performed in the past? By how much?

Chapter 13

FORECASTING COST: SCENARIOS

13-1 INTRODUCTION

In the last chapter we defined some terms used in forecasting cost. Estimate at Completion (EAC) is our estimate for the Actual Cost at project completion. Estimate to Complete (ETC) is the amount of money we believe the project needs after today in order to complete all remaining work. Variance at Completion (VAC) indicates how much under (or over) budget the project will be when it is completed.

In the examples that we used in the last chapter, the forecast was already provided to us. Our job there was to interpret the results of that forecast. In this chapter we'll explore how to arrive at values for ETC or EAC based upon assumptions we'll make about how the future of the project unfolds. Once we generate a figure for one of these, the other is easy to calculate using either Equation 13-1 or 13-2, whichever is appropriate. These are the relationships, using the Modern Convention, that were introduced in the last chapter.

$$EAC = ETC + AC \tag{13-1}$$

$$ETC = EAC - AC \tag{13-2}$$

13-2 ESTIMATING FROM SCRATCH

One way to determine the Estimate to Complete is to re-estimate the cost of all remaining work from scratch, taking into account any lessons-learned from the previously performed work. This may well be the most accurate way of determining ETC (and then EAC), but generating detailed estimates can take a significant amount of time and effort.

In this chapter we'll investigate some simpler ways of utilizing our baseline budgets in order to generate forecasts. We'll look at some of the different assumptions we could make and how those translate into formulas and finally specific numbers.

179

First, however, we need to define a new term we will be using to represent the value of all the work remaining.

13-3 REMAINING VALUE (RV)

We know that the project Budget at Completion, or BAC, represents the value (or budgeted cost) of all of the work in the project. The Earned Value, or EV, represents the value of the work already performed. The Remaining Value, or RV, represents the value of the work yet to be done, i.e. the amount of work whose cost we are interested in estimating. Just from the definition of the terms we can see that the following relationship is an obvious result.

$$
\begin{array}{ccccc}
\textit{Value of} & & \textit{Value of} & & \textit{Value of} \\
\textit{Total} & = & \textit{Work} & + & \textit{Work} \\
\textit{Work} & & \textit{Performed} & & \textit{Remaining}
\end{array}
$$

This is restated, using the Modern Convention initials, in Equation 13-3a.

Modern: $BAC = EV + RV$ (13-3a)

We can see this relationship depicted graphically in Figure 13-1.

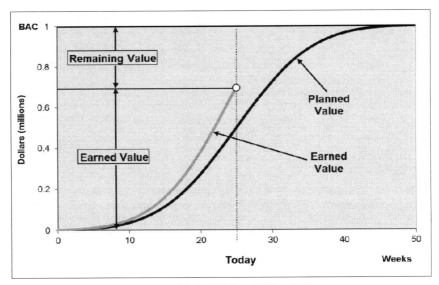

Figure 13-1: BAC = EV + RV

In the Traditional Convention we use the term *Budgeted Cost of Work Remaining*, or BCWR, to designate Remaining Value.

$$BCWR = RV$$

Expressing Equation 13-3a in Traditional Convention terms gives us Equation 13-3b.

Traditional: $BAC = BCWP + BCWR$ (13-3b)

Since the Budget at Completion and the Earned Value are both known, we can use this relationship to find the Remaining Value. To facilitate this, it is convenient to reconfigure Equations 13-3a and 13-3b as Equations 13-4a and 13-4b respectively.

Modern: $RV = BAC - EV$ (13-4a)

Traditional: $BCWR = BAC - BCWP$ (13-4b)

Let's now determine the Remaining Value using the example depicted in Figure 13-1. From the graph we can extract the following figures.

$$BAC = \$1,000,000$$

$$EV = \$700,000$$

We now have what we need to calculate the Remaining Value using Equation 13-4a or 13-4b.

$$RV = \$1,000,000 - \$700,000 = \$300,000$$

This means that we had originally budgeted $300,000 for all the work remaining in the project. This Remaining Value can never be negative. When it drops to zero, it means that there is no work remaining in the project and the project is actually complete.

If all the remaining work is performed on its original budget, the amount of money that will be spent in the future will also be equal to the Remaining Value. In this case, if we believe we can perform all the remaining work on budget, we will need $300,000 in funding in order to finish the project. This will be one of the scenarios we will investigate later in this chapter.

If we can't make the assumption that all future work will be performed on budget, we can use RV as a starting point and adjust it for differences in cost efficiency in order to make a forecast of ETC. Specifically, we will use the formula given in Equation 13-5.

$$ETC = \frac{Remaining\ Value}{Future\ Cost\ Efficiency} \qquad (13\text{-}5)$$

If we can perform all the remaining work on its original budget, or with a Future Cost Efficiency of 100%, the denominator will just be 1 and the ETC is just the Value of the Work Remaining. This is just the case we discussed above.

If on the other hand, the future work cannot be performed on its original budget, then we must adjust the Future Cost Efficiency to reflect this. To take a simple, but extreme example, let's assume that the Future Cost Efficiency will only be 50%. This means that all future work will cost double of what was in the plan.

If we put 50% in the denominator of Equation 13-5, the ETC will be twice the Value of the Work Remaining. We can see that conceptually this makes sense.

13-4 TO-COMPLETE COST PERFORMANCE INDEX (TCPI)

There is another name we give to the Future Cost Efficiency seen in the denominator of Equation 13-5. We call it the To-Complete Cost Performance Index, or TCPI. The TCPI is the cost efficiency that we are assuming for work yet to be performed. Think of it as the equivalent of the CPI but for future work.

As we'll see later, there is a schedule analog to this known as the To-Complete Schedule Performance Index, or TSPI.

While the formal name for TCPI is the To-Complete Cost Performance Index, it is sometimes called simply the To-Complete Performance Index. While this is admittedly ambiguous, chances are the reference will be to the TCPI as opposed to the TSPI. Of course, best usage indicates not using ambiguous terms if at all possible.

TCPI is also sometimes called the Target CPI. If we believe we can meet this target cost efficiency for future work, then we can confidently use it to forecast our future costs.

If we assume that the future work will be performed on its original budget, then the TCPI will equal 1. If we assume that the future work will cost more money than planned, the TCPI will be less than 1. If we assume that the future work will cost less money than planned, the TCPI will be greater than 1. As we can see, the interpretation of the TCPI tracks that of the CPI.

Once we have a target value for the cost efficiency (it's an assumed number), we can calculate the ETC using Equation 13-6a, or 13-6b, which is the same relationship as Equation 13-5. A little later we will discuss how we can go about determining a value of TCPI for our forecast.

Modern: $ETC = \dfrac{RV}{TCPI}$ (13-6a)

Traditional: $ETC = \dfrac{BCWR}{TCPI}$ (13-6b)

If we substitute Equations 13-4a and 13-4b into Equations 13-6a and 13-6b respectively, we get Equations 13-7a and 13-7b.

Modern: $ETC = \dfrac{BAC - EV}{TCPI}$ (13-7a)

Traditional: $ETC = \dfrac{BAC - BCWP}{TCPI}$ (13-7b)

Equation 13-7a (or 13-7b) is the most common general formula used to calculate ETC because the numerator is expressed in known quantities. Notice that there are still two unknowns in the equation. While BAC and EV are both known, ETC and TCPI are unknown. If we can find the value for one of these, we can use this relationship to find the other.

In this chapter we'll look at several scenarios that will allow us to assume a number for TCPI. Then we can calculate a result for ETC. In the next chapter, we'll do the reverse. There we will generate a number for ETC and see what TCPI will be necessary in order to achieve that result.

Once we have a figure for ETC we can then substitute it into Equation 13-1 to generate a number for EAC. We can also express the formula for generating EAC directly by substituting the formula for ETC in Equation 13-7a or 13-7b into Equation 13-1. The result gives us Equations 13-8a and 13-8b.

Modern: $EAC = \dfrac{BAC - EV}{TCPI} + AC$ (13-8a)

Traditional: $EAC = \dfrac{BAC - BCWP}{TCPI} + ACWP$ (13-8b)

These formulas are true all the time and can be considered a generalized set of formulas for determining ETC or EAC, and can be used once we obtain a value for TCPI.

The value of TCPI, and thus ETC and EAC, depends upon the assumptions we make about the future. Let's take a look at some simple scenarios.

13-5 SCENARIOS

To investigate the upcoming scenarios, we'll use the sample project shown in Table 13-1 below. The data represents the project status at the end of the second week of a forty week project. The figures for PV, EV, and AC are cumulative through the end of Week 2.

BAC	$120,000
PV	$5,500
EV	$5,450
AC	$6,000

Table 13-1: Sample Project Status
for Week 2 (of 40 weeks)

Using Equation 13-4a or 13-4b we can calculate the Remaining Value or BCWR as follows.

$$RV = \$120,000 - \$5,450 = \$114,550$$

This indicates that the work yet to be performed was budgeted to cost $114,550 in our baseline plan. We can also determine our Budget Remaining or BRTC from Equation 12-2a or 12-2b as follows.

$$BR = \$120,000 - \$6,000 = \$114,000$$

This means that we have $114,000 of our project funding remaining to finish the project.

We can add these indicators as well as CV, CV%, and CPI to Table 13-1 and get Table 13-2 as a result. Notice that we dropped PV since it is not relevant to a cost analysis. These represent cumulative figures through the end of week 2.

The data in Table 13-2 will now provide the basis for the assumptions that we will make in the upcoming scenarios that can be used to illustrate the forecasting process. As we can see, the project is over budget by $550 (or 10.1%) for the work performed so far and operating at a 90.8% cost efficiency.

BAC	$120,000
EV	$5,450
AC	$6,000
RV	$114,550
BR	$114,000
CV	−$550
CV%	−10.1%
CPI	0.9083

**Table 13-2: Expanded Sample Project
Cost Data for Week 2**

13-6 SCENARIO #1: PAST PERFORMANCE CONTINUES (TCPI = CPI)

The notion that past performance will continue may well be the most common assumption that many of us make. If this turns out to be true in this case, then all future work will be performed at a cost efficiency of 90.8%. We can then make a prediction for ETC.

This scenario is valid if we determine that the project has a systemic issue that cannot be corrected. For example, we may have made incorrect assumptions when estimating the costs for our tasks. If these are embedded throughout the entire plan, and we don't have an expectation of making a recovery, the plan will need to be adjusted in order to reflect reality.

By substituting CPI for TCPI in Equation 13-6 (a or b) or Equation 13-7 (a or b), we get the following.

$$ETC = \frac{\$114,550}{0.9083} = \$126,115$$

This indicates that if past performance were to continue, we are going to need $126,115 in funding to complete the remaining work of the project. Now that we have a number for ETC, we can use Equation 13-1 in order to compute EAC.

$$EAC = \$6,000 + \$126,115 = \$132,115$$

If our assumption (that past performance will continue) is correct, the project will end up costing a total of $132,115 when it is complete.

We are now in a position to compute VAC.

$$VAC = \$120,000 - \$132,115 = -\$12,115$$

The negative sign indicates that the project is forecasted to be \$12,115 over budget when it is complete. To complete the process, let's now calculate a value for VAC%.

$$VAC\% = \frac{-\$12,115}{\$120,000} = -0.101 = -10.1\%$$

As we can see, the project will end up being 10.1% over budget if the forecast is correct. Notice that this is the same as CV% in Table 13-2, as it should be. If we are currently 10.1% over budget, and past performance continues, it makes sense that we'll end up being the same 10.1% over budget when the project is complete.

This leads us to another way to calculate VAC% that is only valid for the assumption that TCPI equals CPI.

$$VAC\% = CV\%$$

With the assumption that past performance will continue, there is a much simpler formula that we can use to calculate the EAC directly. This is given as Equation 13-9 below.

$$EAC = \frac{BAC}{CPI} \tag{13-9}$$

In some texts, when EAC is discussed, this is the only formula that is given. While this is understandably a very popular one, we must remember that **this formula is not true all the time!** It is only true when the assumption that this scenario is based upon is true, i.e. future performance equal past performance. This may be true many times, but certainly not true all the time.

In other words, this formula is only true when we use the actual CPI based upon the values of Earned Value and Actual Cost to date. If the cost efficiency for future work (TCPI) is assumed to be different from the CPI for past work, we must use a different formula.

Calculating EAC assuming that past performance will continue can be very useful. It's certainly valuable to know where the project is going to end up if things keep going the way they have been going, If we do not like the forecast that we see, we are going to do the best we can to find out why there is a problem, and to take actions to prevent this prediction from becoming reality.

Let's use the numbers in Table 13-2 to calculate EAC using Equation 13-9.

$$EAC = \frac{\$120,000}{0.9083} = \$132,115$$

As we can see, both methods yield the same result. Sometimes we may find that each method yields a slightly different result due to rounding errors. We can get the two to match more closely if we carry out the CPI to more significant figures.

Now that we have generated a number for EAC first, we can use Equation 13-2 in order to compute ETC.

$$ETC = \$132,115 - \$6,000 = \$126,115$$

VAC and VAC% will, of course, also be the same as we computed earlier.

13-7 SCENARIO #2: FUTURE WORK ON BUDGET (TCPI = 1)

Here we're going to use the same sample project summarized in Table 13-2, but make a different assumption. In this case we will assume that we are able do discover the cause of the cost overrun and get it fixed so that all future tasks will be able to be performed on their original budgets. We will not be able to recover any losses we have already incurred, but at least we will not get any further in the hole. In this case our future cost efficiency will be 100% or TCPI equals 1.

This scenario will apply if we have a situation where certain events may have occurred that generated an over-budget condition. In this case, we are confident that the past will not be repeated, and that all future work will be performed on budget.

By substituting 1 for TCPI in Equation 13-7a we get Equation 13-10.

$$ETC = BAC - EV \qquad\qquad (13\text{-}10)$$

This formula is not true all the time, only when our assumption that TCPI equals 1 is true. We can now calculate ETC.

$$ETC = \$120,000 - \$5,450 = \$114,550$$

So the amount of money we need to finish the remaining work of the project is simply the Remaining Value which is the amount of money we budgeted for the remaining work. This makes sense.

If we add to the ETC the amount of money we've already spent (AC) we can calculate the EAC.

$$EAC = AC + ETC = \$6,000 + \$114,550 = \$120,550$$

If this assumption is correct, the project will cost a total of $120,550 when it is complete. Notice that this is significantly less than the forecast in the previous scenario because here we are assuming we fixed the problem. In Scenario #1 the problem persisted.

Now let's calculate VAC and VAC%.

$$VAC = BAC - EAC = \$120,000 - \$120,550 = -\$550$$

$$VAC\% = \frac{VAC}{BAC} = \frac{-\$550}{\$120,000} = -0.46\%$$

This indicates that the project will end up being $550 or 0.46% over budget if this assumption is correct. This makes sense as well. If we are currently over budget by $550 (CV) and all future work will be performed on its original budget, we will end up being the same $550 over budget.

So, for this scenario only we have another formula for VAC.

$$VAC = CV$$

Again this is not true all the time, only when this assumption (TCPI = 1) is true.

13-8 SCENARIO #3: ARBITRARY VALUE FOR TCPI.

Our sample project, depicted in Table 13-2, is currently 10.1% over budget at the end of Week 2. In this case we will naturally want to determine the cause so that we can take corrective action and get the project back on track. If this is possible, we should be able to improve upon the forecast made in Scenario #1. If we're able to fix all of the problems, then we'll go the way of Scenario #2.

In many projects, reality is likely to be somewhere in between. We may be able to fix some of the problems, but maybe not all. In this case, our TCPI will not be CPI or 100%, but something in between.

Even if this is the case, analyzing Scenarios #1 and #2 are still worthwhile performing. First, the calculations are relatively simple. Secondly, in many cases, they will bracket where we are likely to end up, and give us an indication of best and worst cases.

The current CPI is 0.9083. Let's assume that, based on our findings, we believe we can perform all future work at a cost efficiency of 95%. In other words, our TCPI is 0.95. We can now make a forecast.

$$ETC = \frac{RV}{TCPI} = \frac{\$114,550}{0.95} = \$120,579$$

$$EAC = AC + ETC = \$6,000 + \$120,579 = \$126,579$$

$$VAC = BAC - EAC = \$120,000 - \$126,579 = -\$6,579$$

$$VAC\% = \frac{VAC}{BAC} = \frac{-\$6,579}{\$120,000} = -5.48\%$$

Notice that this scenario forecasts that the project will finish over budget by $6,579, which is in between Scenarios #1 and #2. This is as we expected.

13-9 SCENARIO #4: MOST RECENT PERFORMANCE CONTINUES

We are going to use the same sample project here as described in Table 13-2. Remember it had a duration of 40 weeks and a BAC of $120,000. In the three preceding scenarios we were very early in the project, the end of the second week to be specific, and didn't have enough time to see any appreciable trends develop. This time we'll look at the project at the end of Week 8.

Table 13-3 shows the incremental (weekly) data for project performance and Table 13-4 gives a summary for the cumulative values at the end of Week 8.

Week	inc EV [$]	inc AC [$]	inc CPI
1	2,200	2,450	0.898
2	3,250	3,550	0.915
3	3,300	3,600	0.917
4	3,500	3,800	0.921
5	3,550	3,900	0.910
6	4,000	4,200	0.952
7	4,500	4,700	0.957
8	4,440	4,650	0.955
Weeks 1 - 8	28,740	30,850	0.932
Weeks 6 - 8	12,940	13,550	0.955

Table 13-3: Weekly Sample Project Cost Data

Notice that for the first five weeks the incremental CPI was hovering in a range between 0.898 and 0.921. Since we were tracking progress early, we discovered soon on that there was a problem with cost performance. By intervening, we can see that we had a noticeable improvement beginning on Week 6.

BAC	$120,000
EV	$28,740
AC	$30,850
RV	$91,260
BR	$89,150
CV	–$2,110
CV%	–7.34%
CPI	0.932

Table 13-4: Sample Project Status for Week 8

How should we proceed from here to make our forecast? If we believe that the performance in Weeks 6-8 is a good representation of how the project will unfold going forward, then that's the data we should use when formulating our TCPI. In this case, our best assessment is to use a TCPI of 0.955 when making our forecast. This value for TCPI was obtained by dividing the Earned Value for Weeks 6-8 ($12,940) by the Actual Cost for Weeks 6-8 ($13,550).

This is preferable to taking the average of the three incremental CPI values because our result will be weighted by the amount of work performed each period.

Note: Even though we're using an existing CPI as the basis for TCPI, we **cannot** use Equation 13-9. That only works if the CPI we are using is for the *entire* project and not for a portion as we have here. We must use the general formula. Here are the results of our calculations.

$$ETC = \frac{RV}{TCPI} = \frac{\$91,260}{0.955} = \$95,560$$

$$EAC = AC + ETC = \$30,850 + \$95,560 = \$126,410$$

$$VAC = BAC - EAC = \$120,000 - \$126,410 = -\$6,410$$

$$VAC\% = \frac{VAC}{BAC} = \frac{-\$6,410}{\$120,000} = -5.3\%$$

So in this case, the project is expected to be completed $6,410 (or 5.3%) over budget.

13-10 SUMMARY

These are only examples of the types of scenarios we may encounter as we generate our forecasts. They certainly don't represent an exhaustive set. The key is for us to be as realistic as possible when generating our forecasts

We don't have to wait to see the light at the end of the tunnel in order to predict how much the project will cost. We can make a forecast at the end of the very first reporting period. It is important to forecast early and often. The earlier we are in the project, the more likely we are able to alter the outcome if we don't like what we see. As we get closer to the end of the project, there is less and less work remaining to influence. As time goes by, we will see the forecasts from all of our scenarios converging.

The questions that were addressed in this chapter are summarized in Table 13-5. Table 13-6 summarizes the formulas introduced in this chapter that are true all the time. Tables 13-7 and 13-8 give formulas that are applicable only in very specific situations. If we are not sure whether a situational formula applies, it is best to use the general formulas.

Question	Answer
How much money was budgeted to perform the remaining work?	RV
What is the projected average cost efficiency of all future work?	TCPI

Table 13-5: Question Summary

Modern Convention	Traditional Convention
$BAC = EV + RV$	$BAC = BCWP + BCWR$
$RV = BAC - EV$	$BCWR = BAC - BCWP$
$ETC = \dfrac{RV}{TCPI}$	$ETC = \dfrac{BCWR}{TCPI}$
$ETC = \dfrac{BAC - EV}{TCPI}$	$ETC = \dfrac{BAC - BCWP}{TCPI}$

Table 13-6: General Forecasting Equations (Always True)

Modern	Traditional
$EAC = \dfrac{AC}{Actual\% \, Complete}$	$EAC = \dfrac{ACWP}{Actual\% \, Complete}$
$EAC = \dfrac{BAC}{CPI}$	
$VAC\% = CV\%$	

**Table 13-7: Specific Forecasting Equations
(Only True when TCPI = CPI)**

Modern	Traditional
$ETC = RV$	$ETC = BCWR$
$ETC = BAC - EV$	$ETC = BAC - BCWP$
$EAC = BAC - CV$	
$VAC = CV$	

**Table 13-8: Specific Forecasting Equations
(Only True when TCPI = 1)**

EXERCISES

13-1: When would it be appropriate to do a forecast by re-estimating the cost of the remaining work from scratch?

13-2: Beginning with Equation 13-8a or 13-8b, show that if past performance is assumed to continue (i.e., TCPI = CPI), then $EAC = \dfrac{BAC}{CPI}$.

13-3: Show that if TCPI = 1, then $VAC = CV$

13-4: Show that the following are true if TCPI = CPI.

a) $VAC = BAC \times CV\%$

b) $EAC = \dfrac{AC}{Actual\% \, Complete}$

13-5: A $100,000 project has an Earned Value of $60,000 and an Actual Cost of $63,000. Determine the ETC, EAC, VAC, and VAC% in the following cases.

a) Past Performance will continue

b) All future work will be performed on budget

c) The future work will be performed at a 90% cost efficiency

13-6: A $200,000 project was planned to be 60% complete as of today, but is actually only 55% complete. $104,000 has been spent so far.

a) What is the cost and schedule status of this project?

b) If the cost and (value-based) schedule tolerance limits are ±5%, is this project out of tolerance with either cost or schedule?

c) Assuming that past performance will continue, develop a forecast for project cost and interpret the results. Be sure to include ETC, EAC, VAC, and VAC% in the assessment.

d) Repeat the forecast in c), but this time assume that all future work will be performed on its original budget.

13-7: The table below contains the cumulative Earned Value and Actual cost figures for the end of each two-week reporting period through today, the end of week 14. The project BAC is $500,000.

Develop a forecast including ETC, EAC, VAC, and VAC% for each of the three following approaches. Comment on the differences among them.

a) All future work will be performed on budget.

b) The future cost efficiency will equal the average cost efficiency of the past.

c) The future cost efficiency will likely track recent performance.

Week	cum EV [$]	cum AC [$]
2	8,000	8,900
4	16,500	18,200
6	25,500	28,100
8	35,000	38,300
10	45,000	48,900
12	55,500	60,000
14	66,500	71,700

Chapter 14

EASE OF MEETING COST TARGETS

In the last chapter, we assumed a cost efficiency for future work. This allowed us to determine how much funding would be necessary to finish the project. Here, we are going to do the reverse. Given an amount of funding available, we will determine the cost efficiency that will be needed for all future work in order to meet that target. We can then assess if this efficiency is something that can realistically be achieved.

14-1 TO-COMPLETE COST PERFORMANCE INDEX (TCPI)

If we recall, the TCPI is an index or cost efficiency factor like the CPI. The difference is that the CPI represents the actual cost efficiency for the work already performed, while the TCPI represents a target cost efficiency for work yet to be performed.

In the last chapter we were given Equation 13-6a relating ETC with TCPI. It is repeated here as Equation 14-1. Remember that RV is the value of the work remaining.

$$ETC = \frac{RV}{TCPI} \qquad (14\text{-}1)$$

Notice that in this equation there are two unknowns, ETC and TCPI. In the last chapter we generated a figure for TCPI first and then used this equation to calculate ETC. This was our forecast for the actual cost of the work to be performed to complete the project.

Now we will do the reverse. We'll first generate a figure for ETC, which now represents how much funding we can obtain to perform the remaining work of the project. Then we will back-calculate the TCPI, which represents the cost efficiency that must be achieved in order to reach that target.

If the TCPI is reasonable, then we have a realistic chance of achieving our goal. If not, then we must either acquire more funding or generate an alternate approach.

First, let's rewrite Equation 14-1 by solving for TCPI. This gives us Equation 14-2.

$$TCPI = \frac{RV}{ETC} \qquad (14\text{-}2)$$

Stating this in words, we get the following relationship.

$$TCPI = \frac{Work\ Remaining}{Funding\ Available}$$

TCPI here represents the ratio of the value of work remaining to the funding available to perform that work. Another way to think of it is the amount of value that must be delivered, on average, for each dollar of funding expended.

Let's recall the equation for CPI which is simply the ratio of the value of the work performed to the funding expended to perform that work.

$$CPI = \frac{EV}{AC} = \frac{Work\ Performed}{Funding\ Expended}$$

As we can see, the TCPI given above is simply the complement of CPI.

Recall the following relationships that were presented in earlier chapters.

$$RV = BAC - EV$$

$$ETC = EAC - AC$$

By substituting these into Equation 14-2 we get the expression shown in Equation 14-3.

$$TCPI = \frac{BAC - EV}{EAC - AC} \qquad (14\text{-}3)$$

This is a general formula for TCPI that is true all the time. While it will always yield the same results as Equation 14-2, this is the most common form that is cited, and will be the form we'll be using as we investigate several scenarios.

BAC is known from our plan. EV and AC can be measured. Once we determine how much money we can gather together to do the whole project (EAC), we are in a position to compute TCPI.

14-2 TCPI(BAC)

A common special case for this calculation is to determine the cost efficiency that we need going forward in order to deliver our project on budget, i.e. where EAC equals BAC. In this case we can rewrite Equation 14-3 as Equation 14-4.

$$TCPI\,(BAC) = \frac{BAC - EV}{BAC - AC} \qquad (14\text{-}4)$$

We are using the designation TCPI(BAC) to indicate that the target cost we are aiming for is BAC. Note that this equation is not true all the time, but only for this specific case where EAC equals BAC.

If the project is exactly on budget, CPI equals 1 and TCPI(BAC) also equals 1.

If the Project is over budget, CPI is less than 1 and TCPI(BAC) is greater than 1. This is obvious since there has to be a higher efficiency for future work to make up for a lower efficiency in past work.

If the project is currently under budget, CPI is greater than 1 and TCPI(BAC) is less than 1. This too makes sense. If we've been overly efficient in the past, we can afford to be somewhat less efficient in our future work and still come in on budget.

14-3 COST EFFICIENCY IMPROVEMENT FACTOR (CIF)

Once we obtain a figure for TCPI, we can then gauge how difficult it may be to achieve that target. One simple way to quantify the extent of the challenge is by a measure that we call the Cost Efficiency Improvement Factor or CIF. It is calculated using Equation 14-5.

$$CIF = \frac{TCPI - CPI}{CPI} \qquad (14\text{-}5)$$

The result is usually expressed as a percentage. The higher the factor, the greater the challenge we face.

Of course, we don't want to oversimplify and imply that all of our challenges can be reduced to a single number. Many qualitative factors will weigh-in depending on what led us to the current state of affairs. Nevertheless, the CIF is a convenient way to assess our situation, or to compare different situations in a quantitative fashion.

The CIF can be especially useful when we are evaluating forecasts prepared by others. If the CIF is too high, we may be suspicious of the realism associated with their forecast and their ability to actually deliver on their plans.

What is considered to be an acceptable range will vary by organization, situation, and type of project. A common rule of thumb is that a CIF less than 5% may be easily recoverable with the proper attention, a CIF over 10% can be difficult to achieve, and a gray area in between those will require some judgment to assess. This rule of thumb is depicted in Figure 14-1.

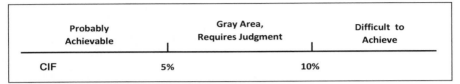

Figure 14-1: CIF Rule of Thumb

For example, if one of our contractors was over budget and their forecast for EAC resulted in a CIF of 3%, we might be inclined to take their word that they could achieve their forecast. If that same contractor made a forecast that resulted in a CIF of 12%, we would like to see more evidence in order to be convinced that they have a credible recovery plan in place.

This does not mean that any CIF over 10% will be impossible to achieve. There may be cases where the problems that occurred to date will not be recurring. In this case it might be entirely possible to have a TCPI significantly above the CPI. Like any rule of thumb, these ranges can be modified to suit the organization, the type of project, and the record of the performers involved.

Let's look at some scenarios as examples where we can apply these ideas.

14-4 SCENARIO #1: FINISHING THE PROJECT ON BUDGET FROM WEEK 2 (EAC = BAC)

In this sample situation, we'll use the status given in Table 14-1 where we are 2 weeks into a 40 week project. This is the same project we used in the last chapter.

BAC	$120,000
EV	$5,450
AC	$6,000
CV	−$550
CPI	0.908

Table 14-1: Project Status at Week 2

Here we want to determine the cost efficiency that will be needed for all future work in order to finish the project on budget. In this case we can use

Equation 14-4 to calculate the result.

$$TCPI \ (BAC \ ) = \frac{\$120,000 - \$5,450}{\$120,000 - \$6,000} = \frac{\$114,550}{\$114,000} = 1.005$$

This means that in order to deliver the project on budget, all future work will need to be performed with a cost efficiency that is one half of one percent greater than planned. Notice that our current cost efficiency (CPI) is almost 10% less than planned.

Why is the TCPI so close to 100% when the CPI is so far away from 100%? The reason has to do with time. Notice that the Actual % Complete, is only 4.5%. This means that we have 95.5% of the project remaining in which to amortize the cost overrun of $550.

The TCPI is a work-dependent indicator. The more work we accomplish in the project, the more we'll see the TCPI increase in value and reach a level that may be impossible to achieve. So the earlier we can address a cost overrun, the easier it will be for us to be successful in managing our costs.

Achieving this TCPI of 1.005 may not be as easy as it seems. In order to make this happen, we must first raise the current CPI from 0.908 to 1, then add another 0.5%, and turn it on a dime!

To be more precise about this, we are going to use the Cost Efficiency Improvement Factor from Equation 14-5.

$$CIF = \frac{1.005 - 0.908}{0.908} = \frac{0.097}{0.908} = 0.1068 = 10.7\%$$

This means that we need a 10.7% cost efficiency improvement from the average of the past in order to meet our target of delivering our project on budget. This is fairly significant, but we are very early in the project. If we can find the cause of our cost overruns, address them quickly, and monitor them closely, we may be able to be successful.

14-5 SCENARIO #2: INCREASING AVAILABLE FUNDING FROM WEEK 2 (EAC > BAC)

In this scenario, we're going to look at the same situation as Scenario #1, but will assume that we obtained an additional $5,000 in funding to perform this project. We probably would not normally be looking for additional funds this early in the project, but let's consider this as a "what if" exercise. This will give us a chance to see what effect this would have on the TCPI and the CIF.

With this additional funding, our EAC is now $125,000. Since it is different than the BAC, we must now use the general formula given in Equation 14-3.

$$TCPI = \frac{\$120,000 - \$5,450}{\$125,000 - \$6,000} = \frac{\$114,550}{\$119,000} = 0.963$$

This is less than 100%, so we may feel that this is going to be easy to accomplish. Just like in the previous scenario, the project is currently operating at a lower efficiency than this. The efficiency must rise to this level and be maintained for the remainder of the project in order for the objective to be achieved.

To put this in perspective, let's calculate the Cost Efficiency Improvement Factor using Equation 14-5.

$$CIF = \frac{0.963 - 0.908}{0.908} = \frac{0.055}{0.908} = 0.0606 = 6.1\%$$

We can see that this is a noticeable improvement from the last scenario.

14-6 SCENARIO #3: FINISHING THE PROJECT ON BUDGET FROM WEEK 8 (EAC = BAC)

Again, using the same project from the last chapter, we are going to look at the status at week 8, which is summarized in Table 14-2.

BAC	$120,000
EV	$28,740
AC	$30,850
CV	–$2,110
CPI	0.932
Actual % Complete	24%

Table 14-2: Project Status for Week 8

We can compute the TCPI(BAC) needed to get back to the original budget.

$$TCPI(BAC) = \frac{\$120,000 - \$28,740}{\$120,000 - \$30,850} = \frac{\$91,260}{\$89,150} = 1.023$$

This is going to be quite a significant challenge. To see how significant, we need to calculate the CIF.

$$CIF = \frac{1.023 - 0.932}{0.932} = \frac{0.091}{0.932} = 0.0976 = 9.8\%$$

In this calculation we used the CPI representing all of the project activity to-date. What we are trying to represent with the CIF is how difficult will it be to achieve our goals from where we are now.

Week	EV ($)	AC ($)	CPI
1	2,200	2,450	0.898
2	3,250	3,550	0.915
3	3,300	3,600	0.917
4	3,500	3,800	0.921
5	3,550	3,900	0.910
6	4,000	4,200	0.952
7	4,500	4,700	0.957
8	4,440	4,650	0.955
Weeks 1 - 8	28,740	30,850	0.932
Weeks 6 - 8	12,940	13,550	0.955

Table 14-3: Project Cost Data through Week 8

Table 14-3 displays the performance of this project over time. Notice that the CPI for the last 3 weeks is 0.955, which is significantly higher than the CPI values from the earlier weeks. If we believe that the problem that contributed to those early low efficiency scores has been remedied, then it might be more realistic to use the recent CPI value in our calculation of CIF, since it is a better reflection of where we are today. If recalculate, we get the following.

$$CIF = \frac{1.023 - 0.955}{0.955} = \frac{0.068}{0.955} = 0.0712 = 7.1\%$$

This may be a better measure of the true challenge facing us at the end of Week 8.

14-7 SCENARIO #4: INCREASING AVAILABLE FUNDING FROM WEEK 8 (EAC > BAC)

Based on the performance so far, and our understanding of the underlying issues, let's assume that we don't believe that we can achieve this level of cost efficiency going forward. Let's also assume that after we have presented our case to Senior Management, they agree to add another $5,000 to the project funding and asked us for an analysis.

With the added funding, the EAC is now $125,000. The BAC has not changed; it remains at $120,000. We can now calculate TCPI using the general formula in Equation 14-3.

$$TCPI = \frac{\$120,000 - \$28,740}{\$125,000 - \$30,850} = \frac{\$91,260}{\$94,150} = 0.969$$

As in Scenario #2 it is less than 100%, which means we can afford to be less efficient than in our baseline plan. It is still above where we are currently, however. Let's calculate the Cost Efficiency Improvement Factor, using the recent CPI of 0.955.

$$CIF = \frac{0.969 - 0.955}{0.955} = \frac{0.014}{0.955} = 0.0147 = 1.5\%$$

This is a significant improvement from our situation in the last scenario. If we start now and implement some aggressive cost improvement actions, we might be able to make up this difference.

14-8 SCENARIO #5: INCREASING AVAILABLE FUNDING FROM WEEK 24 (EAC > BAC)

In this scenario we are going to investigate the effect of time. We will use the same project as in Scenario #4, but at Week 24 into our 40 week project. We'll further assume that we were not able to improve our cost efficiency, but maintained an average CPI of 0.955 from weeks 9 through 24. The status is summarized in Tables 14-4 and 14-5.

BAC	$120,000
EV	$78,020
AC	$82,450
CV	−$4,430
CPI	0.946
Actual % Complete	65%

Table 14-4: Project Status for Week 24

Week	EV ($)	AC ($)	CPI
1	2,200	2,450	0.898
2	3,250	3,550	0.915
3	3,300	3,600	0.917
4	3,500	3,800	0.921
5	3,550	3,900	0.910
6	4,000	4,200	0.952
7	4,500	4,700	0.957
8	4,440	4,650	0.955
9 - 24	49,280	51,600	0.955
Weeks 1 - 8	**28,740**	**30,850**	**0.932**
Weeks 6 - 8	**12,940**	**13,550**	**0.955**
Total	**78,020**	**82,450**	**0.946**

Table 14-5: Project Cost Data through Week 24

Now let's calculate TCPI assuming we still have the extra $5,000.

$$TCPI = \frac{\$120,000 - \$78,020}{\$125,000 - \$82,450} = \frac{\$41,980}{\$42,550} = 0.987$$

$$CIF = \frac{0.987 - 0.955}{0.955} = \frac{0.032}{0.955} = 0.0147 = 3.3\%$$

Notice that the CIF has more than doubled, just because we delayed implementing any cost improvements. As we can see, it would have been much easier to get on track had we addressed the issue earlier.

14-9 SUMMARY

We can use the tools developed in this chapter as aids to help us determine how much of a challenge we face in meeting project cost objectives, as well as a basis for the comparison of different scenarios.

If we are interested in analyzing reports prepared by other parties, we are in a good position to evaluate their forecasts. For example, we may have a contractor performing some of the project work. If we ask them for a forecast of the final actual cost, or EAC, we can determine the cost efficiency that they are assuming for future work. The CIF will help us assess whether their forecast is reasonable and realistic.

The questions that were addressed in this chapter are given in Table 14-6.

Question	Answer
How cost efficient will the project need to be in order to finish on budget?	TCPI(BAC)
What improvement in cost efficiency will be necessary going forward in order to meet the cost objectives?	CIF

Table 14-6: Question Summary

The formulas introduced in this chapter are summarized in Table 14-7.

Modern Convention	Traditional Convention
$TCPI = \dfrac{RV}{ETC}$	$TCPI = \dfrac{BCWR}{ETC}$
$TCPI = \dfrac{BAC - EV}{EAC - AC}$	$TCPI = \dfrac{BAC - BCWP}{EAC - ACWP}$
$TCPI\,(BAC) = \dfrac{BAC - EV}{BAC - AC}$	$TCPI\,(BAC) = \dfrac{BAC - BCWP}{BAC - ACWP}$
$CIF = \dfrac{TCPI - CPI}{CPI}$	

Table 14-7: Equation Summary

EXERCISES

14-1: What is the Cost Efficiency Improvement Factor? How is it used?

14-2: When is it appropriate to use TCPI(BAC)?

14-3: What does it mean if TCPI equals zero?

14-4: In what type of situation would the TCPI(BAC) be less than zero?

14-5: A $300,000 project is 37% complete and $120,000 has been spent so far.

   a) Compute values for the various cost indicators and interpret the status of the project.

   b) What future cost efficiency will the project need to operate at in order to finish on budget?

   c) What Cost Efficiency Improvement Factor will this result in?

14-6: Using the data in Exercise 14-5, what would be the TCPI and CIF if the project was given an extra $20,000 in funding? What do the results indicate?

14-7: The incremental status of a project through the end of Period 10 is given in the following table. The project BAC is $80,000.

Period	inc EV [$]	inc AC [$]
1	1,000	1,125
2	1,500	1,700
3	1,400	1,580
4	1,800	1,980
5	2,000	2,150
6	2,000	2,080
7	2,200	2,250
8	2,400	2,500
9	2,200	2,260
10	2,300	2,380

   a) Determine the incremental CPI for each period.

   b) Calculate the cumulative EV, AC, CV, CPI, Actual % Complete, and Actual % Spent, for all the work performed so far.

   c) Determine TCPI(BAC) and CIF using the cumulative CPI.

   d) What are the pros and cons of using a recent CPI (instead of cumulative CPI) value when calculating CIF?

   e) Calculate CIF using a recent CPI. How significant is the difference between this and the one calculated in c)?

14-8: We have a Contractor that is performing a subproject that is a component of our larger project. A summary of the contractor's latest status report to us is shown in the following table. All figures are in dollars.

Item	Cumulative to Date			At Completion	
	Budgeted Cost		Actual	Budgeted	Estimated
	Work Scheduled	Work Performed	Cost Work Performed		
Task A	15,800	12,600	14,200	30,000	30,100
Task B	8,700	8,500	9,300	42,000	41,600
Task C	4,500	4,300	4,250	35,000	34,800
Task D	0	0	0	20,000	20,000
Total	29,000	25,400	27,750	127,000	126,500

Perform the following analysis for each task and the subproject as a whole.

a) Calculate values for CV, CV%, CPI, SV, SV%, SPI, Planned % Complete, Actual % Complete, and Actual % Spent, VAC, and VAC%. Interpret the cost and schedule results.

b) What TCPI is the Contractor assuming when generating their forecast?

c) What Cost Efficiency Improvement Factor will the Contractor need to achieve in order to meet their projected results?

d) What would be the forecasted EAC and VAC if past performance were to continue? How does this compare with the Contractor's forecast?

e) How should we respond to the Contractor when we meet with them to discuss their report?

Chapter 15

FORECASTING SCHEDULE: DEFINITIONS

15-1 INTRODUCTION

In this chapter we will introduce some schedule forecasting definitions. In the next chapter we'll apply them to several sample scenarios.

Forecasting how our schedule will unfold is inherently more complex than forecasting cost. Cost is relatively simple because it is one-dimensional. If we add up the costs of our individual tasks we'll get the project cost.

If we add up the durations of our tasks we won't usually get the project duration, because normally some of the work can be performed in parallel. This makes forecasting our schedule a little more challenging. To get the full picture for schedule, we need to look at it from multiple perspectives.

This is not to say that our cost forecasts will necessarily be more accurate than our schedule forecasts. It's just that the techniques we use are simpler for cost. In both cases, the quality of the forecast is dependent upon the quality of the assumptions we make about the future.

The project duration is defined by the critical path. If we add up the durations of the tasks along the critical path we will get the project duration. [Note: there are exceptions to this, but we won't address them here.]

This leads us to an interesting approach. Instead of using all of the tasks to forecast a project finish date, what if we limit our analysis to only the critical tasks? This will be analogous to the approach with cost.

This may work well in many situations, but we still can't ignore the non-critical tasks. If the non-critical tasks are delayed enough, they could turn critical and result in a different critical path or even multiple critical paths. We need to be aware of this.

Another option is to identify every possible path through the project network and do a separate forecast along each path. Whichever forecast results in the latest date will be the one that we will use. While this approach may work in principle, it is not simple to implement in practice.

A common approach is to perform the analysis two different ways—using all of the tasks in aggregate and using the critical tasks. If the aggregate forecast indicates a later finish date than that for the critical tasks, it is likely that the critical path has shifted, although it may not be obvious what that new critical path is.

In this case we need to refer to our precedence diagram. An updated precedence diagram will give us the information we need to identify the current critical path. We can then redo our forecast using the new set of critical tasks.

While detecting shifting critical paths with network diagrams is something that should be done, the process for doing so is beyond the scope of our discussion here.

15-2 REMAINING TIME (RT)

In earlier chapters, we defined the Planned Duration (PD) as the scheduled duration of the project as it appears in the baseline plan. The Actual Time (AT), or Actual Time for Work Performed (ATWP), represents how much time has elapsed from the start of the project through the data date, which we usually represent on the graphs as "today."

In the Modern Convention, the Remaining Time, or RT, represents the amount of time from today to the planned project completion date (Planned Duration), or the amount of time we have remaining if we want to finish the project on time. The Remaining Time is also known as the Time Remaining to Complete (TRTC) in the Traditional Convention.

$$\frac{Remaining}{Time} = \frac{Time\ Remaining}{to\ Complete}$$

We can see from the graph in Figure 15-1 that the Actual Time plus the Remaining Time add up to the Planned Duration.

$$\frac{Planned}{Duration} = \frac{Actual}{Time} + \frac{Remaining}{Time}$$

This can also be expressed using the initials in Equations 15-1a and 15-1b.

Modern: $PD = AT + RT$ (15-1a)

Traditional: $PD = ATWP + TRTC$ (15-1b)

In order to determine the Remaining Time, it is more convenient to rewrite this relationship in the form of Equation 15-2a or 15-2b.

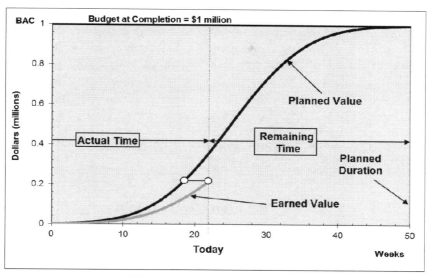

Figure 15-1: PD = AT + RT

Modern: $RT = PD - AT$ (15-2a)

Traditional: $TRTC = PD - ATWP$ (15-2b)

As an example of how to apply this, let's look at the data from Figure 15-1. We can see that the project was planned to be complete at Week 50 and today we are at Week 22.

$PD = 50$ weeks

$AT = 22$ weeks

Now we can compute the Remaining Time.

$RT = 50$ weeks $- 22$ weeks $= 28$ weeks

This means that there are 28 weeks from today to the planned project completion date. So, if we want to finish the project on schedule, we must complete all of the remaining work within the next 28 weeks.

15-3 REMAINING SCHEDULE (RS)

In Chapter 11 we defined the Earned Schedule (ES), or Planned Time for Work Performed (PTWP), as the amount of time that was scheduled in our baseline plan to perform the work that was actually accomplished. The Earned Schedule is obtained by constructing a horizontal line from the end of the Earned Value Curve, i.e. at the Actual Time. The time where this horizontal line intersects the Planned Value curve represents the Earned Schedule. See Figure 15-2.

In the Modern Convention, the Remaining Schedule, or RS, represents the amount of time that was originally planned to perform the remaining work. It is also known as the Planned Time for Work Remaining (PTWR) in the Traditional Convention.

$$\text{Remaining Schedule} = \text{Planned Time for Work Remaining}$$

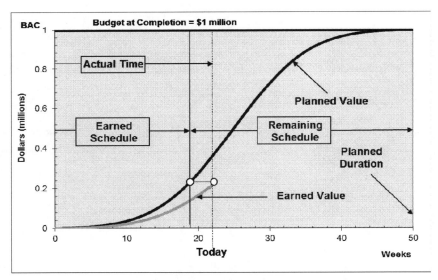

Figure 15-2: PD = ES + RS

From Figure 15-2 we can see how the Remaining Schedule is related to the Planned Duration and the Earned Schedule. The Planned Duration is simply the sum of the Earned Schedule and the Remaining Schedule. This can be expressed mathematically in the following equation.

$$\frac{Planned}{Duration} = \frac{Earned}{Schedule} + \frac{Remaining}{Schedule}$$

We can express this relationship using the initials both in the Modern Convention (Equation 15-3a) and in the Traditional Convention (Equation 15-3b).

Modern: $PD = ES + RS$ (15-3a)

Traditional: $PD = PTWP + PTWR$ (15-3b)

At this point the Planned Duration and the Earned Schedule are known quantities. We can use this relationship to compute the Remaining Schedule from the other terms. It may be more convenient to express this relationship as Equation 15-4a or 15-4b.

Modern: $RS = PD - ES$ (15-4a)

Traditional: $PTWR = PD - PTWP$ (15-4b)

The Remaining Schedule tells us how much time was originally planned for the work yet to be performed. Let's look at an example using the data from Figure 15-2. Then we can use Equation 15-4a to calculate the Remaining Schedule.

$PD = 50$ weeks

$ES = 19$ weeks

$RS = 50$ weeks $- 19$ weeks $= 31$ weeks

This means that the amount of work remaining to finish the project was scheduled to take 31 weeks to perform in the baseline plan.

We saw from Chapter 11 that we can compute the Time-Based Schedule Variance, or SV(t), as the difference between the Earned Schedule and the Actual Time. This was given in a formula repeated here as Equation 15-5a or 15-5b.

Modern: $SV(t) = ES - AT$ (15-5a)

Traditional: $SV(t) = PTWP - ATWP$ (15-5b)

Using the data in Figure 15-2 we can compute its value in this case.

$$SV(t) = 19 \text{ weeks} - 22 \text{ weeks} = -3 \text{ weeks}$$

The negative result indicates that the project is currently 3 weeks behind schedule.

There is another way to calculate SV(t) using the Remaining Time and the Remaining Schedule. This can be seen in Equation 15-6a or 15-6b.

Modern: $SV(t) = RT - RS$ (15-6a)

Traditional: $SV(t) = TRTC - PTWR$ (15-6b)

If we use the data from Figure 15-2 again we should get the same result for SV(t).

$$RT = 28 \text{ weeks}$$

$$RS = 31 \text{ weeks}$$

$$SV(t) = 28 \text{ weeks} - 31 \text{ weeks} = -3 \text{ weeks}$$

Basically, this is telling us that there are 31 weeks worth of work to do, but only 28 weeks left in the schedule if we want to finish on time. Therefore, we are 3 weeks behind schedule.

15-4 TIME ESTIMATE AT COMPLETION [EAC(t)]

We are going to define the Time Estimate at Completion, or EAC(t), to be our forecast for the actual duration of the project. This represents how much total time we believe it will take from the beginning of the project until the project is complete. This will occur when all the value has been delivered, i.e. when EV equals BAC.

In Figure 15-3 we can see that the project was planned to be completed at Week 50. Our forecast, represented by the dashed portion of the Earned Value curve, indicates that the project is now expected to be complete at Week 60, or EAC(t) equals 60 weeks.

Here we have been given the forecast. In the next chapter we will look at several scenarios that will allow us to make forecasts based upon current conditions and some assumptions about the future.

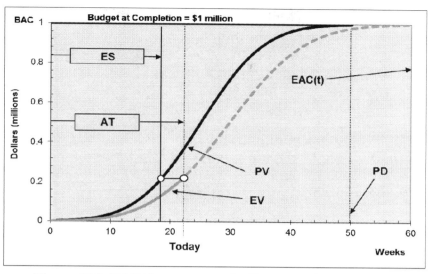

Figure 15-3: EAC(t) represents the Forecasted Finish Date

15-5 TIME ESTIMATE TO COMPLETE [ETC(t)]

The Time Estimate to Complete, or ETC(t), is our forecast for how much time it will actually take to perform the remaining work of the project. This will depend on how we expect the future to unfold.

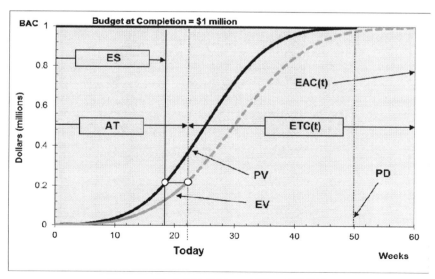

Figure 15-4: EAC(t) = AT + ETC(t)

We can see from Figure 15-4 that ETC(t) is related to both AT and EAC(t). This relationship is given In Equations 15-7a and 15-7b.

Modern: $EAC(t) = AT + ETC(t)$ (15-7a)

Traditional: $EAC(t) = ATWP + ETC(t)$ (15-7b)

Sometimes we are able to generate a forecast for EAC(t) first. We can then use this relationship to back-calculate ETC(t). In this case it would be more convenient to use Equation 15-8a or 15-8b.

Modern: $ETC(t) = EAC(t) - AT$ (15-8a)

Traditional: $ETC(t) = EAC(t) - ATWP$ (15-8b)

Using the data in Figure 15-4, we can see that EAC(t) is 60 weeks while the Actual Time is 22 weeks. We can now calculate ETC(t).

$ETC(t) = 60$ weeks $- 22$ weeks $= 38$ weeks.

This means that if the forecast is correct, it will take another 38 weeks to complete the remaining work of the project.

15-6 TIME VARIANCE AT COMPLETION [VAC(t)]

The Time Variance at Completion, or VAC(t), indicates how much less (or more) time the project will take than originally planned. Its negative is sometimes known as the *Schedule Extension*. We can see it depicted in Figure 15-5.

It is simply the difference between the planned project completion date, or PD, and the current forecasted completion date, or EAC(t). This relationship is shown in Equation 15-9.

$VAC(t) = PD - EAC(t)$ (15-9)

This is keeping with the sign convention of our other variances where positive is good and negative is bad. In this case a positive result for VAC(t) indicates the project is expected to be completed ahead of schedule by that amount. If the VAC(t) is negative, then the project is forecasted to be completed behind schedule by that amount.

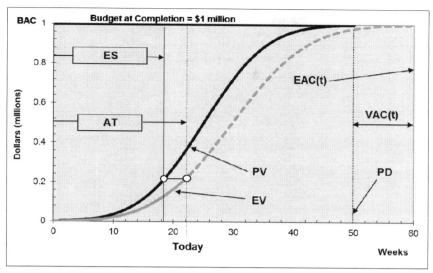

Figure 15-5: VAC(t) = PD − EAC(t)

As an example, we can use the data in Figure 15-5. The Planned Duration is 50 weeks and the Time Estimate at Completion is 60 weeks.

$$VAC(t) = 50 \text{ weeks} - 60 \text{ weeks} = -10 \text{ weeks.}$$

If this forecast is correct, the project will finish 10 weeks behind schedule. It may also be said that the schedule is projected to have an extension of 10 weeks.

At the end of the project, the Earned Schedule will equal the Planned Duration and the Actual Time will equal the Time Estimate at Completion. The Time Variance at Completion is our forecast of what the Time-Based Schedule Variance will be at the end of the project.

Today:

$$SV(t) = ES - AT$$

At the conclusion of the project:

$$SV(t) = PD - EAC(t) = VAC(t)$$

Notice the advantage SV(t) has over SV($) at the end of the project. Since SV($) always goes to zero eventually, it loses memory over time. SV(t), on the other hand, preserves any schedule slippage that may occur.

15-7 TIME VARIANCE AT COMPLETION PERCENTAGE [VAC(t)%]

While the VAC(t) tells us how much the project is expected to finish early (or late) in absolute terms, it does not put things into perspective relative to the size of the project. This is where the Time Variance at Completion Percentage, or VAC(t)%, comes in. It will normalize the VAC(t) to the size of the project.

To get VAC(t)% we simply divide VAC(t) by the Planned Duration and express the result as a percentage. The formula is given in Equation 15-10.

$$VAC(t)\% = \frac{VAC(t)}{PD} \qquad (15\text{-}10)$$

Let's look at a numeric example using the data in Figure 15-5.

$$PD = 50 \text{ weeks}$$

$$EAC(t) = 60 \text{ weeks}$$

$$VAC(t) = -10 \text{ weeks}$$

From these we can calculate a value for VAC(t)%.

$$VAC(t)\% = \frac{-10 \ weeks}{50 \ weeks} = -0.2 = -20\%$$

This indicates that we are forecasting that this project will be completed 20% behind schedule.

The same equation for VAC(t)% can be expressed in a different form, but of course yielding the same results.

$$VAC(t)\% = 1 - \frac{EAC(t)}{PD} \qquad (15\text{-}11)$$

By using this equation, the VAC(t)% can be computed directly in terms of the basic elements without first needing to calculate VAC(t). Using the same data as above, let's calculate VAC(t)% using the alternate method.

$$VAC(t)\% = 1 - \frac{60 \ weeks}{50 \ weeks} = 1 - 1.2 = -0.2 = -20\%$$

We can set acceptable tolerance levels for schedule using VAC(t)%. By calculating VAC(t)% on a regular basis, we can get early warning when our projected finish date is expected to be out of tolerance.

One final note, using an argument similar to the one between VAC(t) and SV(t) discussed earlier, VAC(t)% is simply our forecast of what the SV(t)% will be at the end of the project.

15-8 SUMMARY

Forecasting our schedule is inherently more complex than forecasting cost. To get a better perspective on projected outcomes, the analyses performed here for the whole project should be repeated for the critical path. Whichever approach predicts the later date should be used as the forecast.

If possible, near-critical paths should be considered as well. Ideally, we should update our network diagrams to determine if our critical path has already shifted. If so, we would then be interested in performing a forecast on that new critical path.

Since SV($) and SV($)% will both eventually go to zero, they don't give us any insight about when the work ended. The time-based indicators, on the other hand, do not lose memory over time. This is a great improvement over using value-based schedule indicators for forecasting.

The questions that were addressed in this chapter are summarized in Table 15-1. Table 15-2 is a summary of the schedule forecasting formulas that were introduced in this chapter. All of these formulas are true all of the time, i.e. they are independent of any assumptions we make about the future.

Question	Answer
How much time is remaining from today until the planned project completion date?	RT
How much time was planned to perform the remaining work?	RS
When is the project expected to be completed?	EAC(t)
How much time is it expected to take in order to perform the remaining work?	ETC(t)
How much earlier (or later) than planned is the project expected to finish?	VAC(t)
By what percentage is the project expected to be completed earlier (or later)?	VAC(t)%

Table 15-1: Question Summary

Modern Convention	Traditional Convention
$PD = AT + RT$	$PD = ATWP + TRTC$
$RT = PD - AT$	$TRTC = PD - ATWP$
$PD = ES + RS$	$PD = PTWP + PTWR$
$RS = PD - ES$	$PTWR = PD - PTWP$
$SV(t) = ES - AT$	$SV(t) = PTWP - ATWP$
$SV(t) = RT - RS$	$SV(t) = TRTC - PTWR$
$EAC(t) = AT + ETC(t)$	$EAC(t) = ATWP + ETC(t)$
$ETC(t) = EAC(t) - AT$	$ETC(t) = EAC(t) - ATWP$
$VAC(t) = PD - EAC(t)$	
$VAC(t)\% = \dfrac{VAC(t)}{PD}$	
$VAC(t)\% = 1 - \dfrac{EAC(t)}{PD}$	

Table 15-2 Schedule Forecasting Equations by Convention (Always True)

EXERCISES

15-1: What is the difference between EAC(t) and ETC(t)?

15-2: Why should schedule forecasting take the critical path into account?

15-3: What is VAC(t)? How does VAC(t) relate to SV(t)?

15-4: What would it mean if VAC(t) is negative for the project as a whole, but positive for the critical path? What if they were both positive? What if they were both negative? What approach should be taken in each of these cases?

15-5: Why are time-based indicators preferred over value-based indicators for schedule forecasting? What are the advantages of using value-based indicators?

15-6: It is 12 weeks into a 52 week project. The remaining work is expected to take 45 weeks. Determine the following indicators and interpret the meaning of each.

a) RT

b) EAC(t)

c) VAC(t)

d) VAC(t)%

15-7: It is the end of the fifteenth week of a 52 week project. The latest schedule report is summarized in the table below. Determine the following indicators and interpret the results.

a) TRTC

b) EAC(t)

c) PTWP

d) PTWR

e) SV(t)%

f) VAC(t)

g) VAC(t)%

	Critical Path	**Total Project**
Forecasted time to perform remaining work	38 weeks	40 weeks
Time-Based Schedule Variance	−1 week	−1.5 weeks

Is the schedule performance expected to improve or worsen in the future? What does this suggest about the critical path? What steps should be taken from here?

Chapter 16

FORECASTING SCHEDULE: SCENARIOS

16-1 INTRODUCTION

In the last chapter we defined some terms used in forecasting schedules. The Time Estimate at Completion, or EAC(t), is our estimate for the actual project duration at project completion. The Time Estimate to Complete, or ETC(t), is the amount of time we believe the project needs after today in order to complete all remaining work. The Time Variance at Completion, or VAC(t), indicates how much earlier (or later) the project will actually finish than the Planned Duration.

In the examples that we used in the last chapter, the forecast was already provided to us. Our job there was to interpret the results of that forecast.

In this chapter we'll explore how to arrive at values for ETC(t) or EAC(t) based upon assumptions we'll make about how the future of the project unfolds. Once we generate a figure for one of these variables the other is easy to calculate using one of the formulas that was developed in the last chapter, and displayed here as Equations 16-1 and 16-2 using the Modern Convention.

$$EAC(t) = AT + ETC(t) \qquad\qquad (16\text{-}1)$$

$$ETC(t) = EAC(t) - AT \qquad\qquad (16\text{-}2)$$

16-2 THE CRITICAL PATH

Several times we discussed the importance that the critical path plays in generating and forecasting schedules. Since it is the critical path that defines the project duration, our forecast must predict when the tasks along the critical path will finish.

This can be done relatively simply. In addition to constructing our tables and graphs with all of the project tasks, we can construct a second set which only includes the critical tasks. We can then perform our analyses on that critical path and forecast when it, and thus the project will finish.

An important concern, however, is that in any project, the critical path can change. If there is enough of a delay on a non-critical path, it can turn critical and result in being the new driver of the project duration. Therefore we must be on the lookout for the possibility that the critical path has shifted to a new path.

One common approach to deal with this is to generate a forecast two ways—once for the critical path and then again for the project as a whole. We can then use the forecast that predicts the later finish date.

This is not foolproof, however. If the aggregate forecast results in a finish date earlier than that for the original critical path, it is not a guarantee that the critical path has remained the same.

On the other hand, if the aggregate forecast results in a finish date later than that of the original critical path, then the critical path has likely shifted, however, the duration of this new critical path could even be longer than the aggregate prediction.

Ideally, we would be keeping our precedence diagrams up to date by replacing the planned dates with the actual dates. We could then use the updated diagrams to guide us in our EVM analysis. If we found that our network diagrams have alerted us to a shift in the critical path, we would then perform our EVM schedule analysis on that newly identified path.

While we recognize that precedence diagrams are an important adjunct to EVM for schedule analysis, the processes involved in their maintenance is out of scope for our discussion here. The focus of this chapter will be on EVM forecasting, assuming that the current critical path is known.

16-3 ESTIMATING FROM SCRATCH

One way to determine ETC(t) is to re-estimate the durations of each uncompleted task from scratch, taking into account any lessons-learned from the previously performed work. We can then update our precedence diagrams, determine the new critical path, if necessary, and add up the durations of the critical tasks yet to be performed to give us the ETC(t). This may well be the most accurate way of determining ETC(t) but generating detailed estimates can take a significant amount of time and effort.

In this chapter we'll investigate some simpler ways of utilizing our baseline schedules in order to generate forecasts. We'll look at some of the different assumptions we can make and how those translate into formulas, and finally, specific numbers.

16-4 ESTIMATING USING INDEXES

Another approach to forecasting is to use schedule efficiency factors, or indexes, much like we did earlier with cost. Before we begin, however, let's discuss one potential point of confusion.

There are two different Schedule Performance Indexes. One is time-based, SPI(t), and the other is value-based, SPI($). These were introduced in earlier chapters and their formulas are repeated here using the Modern Convention as Equations 16-3 and 16-4.

$$SPI(\$) = \frac{EV}{PV} \qquad (16\text{-}3)$$

$$SPI(t) = \frac{ES}{AT} \qquad (16\text{-}4)$$

Since we are forecasting time, it is more appropriate to use the time-based index, although there are situations where SPI($) is nearly equal to SPI(t), and may be an acceptable substitute. A discussion of this topic can be found in Appendix E.

16-5 TO-COMPLETE SCHEDULE PERFORMANCE INDEX (TSPI)

Before we begin with the scenarios, we need to define one more term known as the To-Complete Schedule Performance Index, or TSPI. The TSPI is a schedule efficiency factor, much like the SPI(t). The main difference is that it represents the schedule efficiency for work yet to be performed. The TSPI is also sometimes known as the Target SPI.

If we assume that the future work will take the same amount of time as originally planned, then the TSPI equals 1, indicating a 100% schedule efficiency going forward. If we assume that the future work will take more time than planned, the TSPI will be less than 1. If we assume that the future work will take less time than planned, the TSPI will be greater than 1.

A little later we will discuss how we can go about determining a value of TSPI for our forecast. First, however, let us see how the TSPI relates to ETC(t).

Equation 16-5 gives us a simple way to estimate the amount of time necessary to perform the remaining work. It is based on the amount of time budgeted to perform that work, along with the future cost efficiency.

$$ETC(t) = \frac{Planned\ Time\ for\ Work\ Remaining}{Future\ Schedule\ Efficiency} \qquad (16\text{-}5)$$

The Planned Time for Work Remaining is the same as the Remaining Schedule. If we can perform the remaining tasks with their scheduled durations, or with a Future Schedule Efficiency of 100%, the denominator will just be 1 and the ETC(t) is just the Planned Time for the Work Remaining. If on the other hand, the remaining tasks cannot be performed with their scheduled durations, then we must adjust the Future Schedule Efficiency accordingly.

To take a simple, but extreme example, let's assume that the Future Schedule Efficiency will only be 50%. This means that all future work will take twice as long as what was in the plan. If we put 50% in the denominator of Equation 16-5, we can see that the ETC(t) will be twice the Planned Time for the Work Remaining.

Now, how can we express this formula in terms of items that we already know? First, the Planned Time for the Work Remaining has already been defined for us in the last chapter as the Remaining Schedule, or RS. The Future Schedule Efficiency is nothing more than TSPI. From this we can construct Equations 16-6a and 16-6b.

Modern: $ETC(t) = \dfrac{RS}{TSPI}$ (16-6a)

Traditional: $ETC(t) = \dfrac{PTWR}{TSPI}$ (16-6b)

Using definitions from the previous chapter, ETC(t) can also be expressed in an alternate form as shown in Equations 16-7a and 16-7b.

Modern: $ETC(t) = \dfrac{PD - ES}{TSPI}$ (16-7a)

Traditional: $ETC(t) = \dfrac{PD - PTWP}{TSPI}$ (16-7b)

At this point ETC(t) and TSPI are both unknown. If, however, we can generate a value for TSPI, then we can use these equations to find ETC(t). Let's look at some scenarios.

16-6 SCENARIOS

In these scenarios, we are going to assume that the data we examine will represent the critical path. Remember that the project will only end when all of the tasks are completed, and it's the critical path that defines the project duration. As we discussed, however, it is good practice to repeat these steps using the aggregate project data.

The critical path status data for our sample project for the first six weeks appears in Table 16-1. The Planned Duration is 40 weeks.

Week	cum PV [$]	cum EV [$]
1	2,000	1,900
2	4,500	4,200
3	7,500	6,870
4	10,500	9,540
5	14,000	12,775
6	18,000	16,200

Table 16-1: Project Status for Week 6 (PD = 40 weeks)

We can now expand this by computing the Earned Schedule as well as both Schedule Performance Indexes. Using Week 6 as an example let's review how to do the calculations.

$$SPI\,(\$) = \frac{EV}{PV} = \frac{\$16,200}{\$18,000} = 0.90$$

$$ES = Date_1 + (Date_2 - Date_1) \times \frac{(EV - PV_1)}{(PV_2 - PV_1)}$$

$$ES = 5\ weeks + (6\ weeks - 5\ weeks)\frac{\$16,200 - \$14,000}{\$18,000 - \$14,000}$$

$$ES = 5\ weeks + (1\ week)\frac{\$2200}{\$4000} = 5.55\ weeks$$

$$SPI(t) = \frac{ES}{AT} = \frac{5.55\ weeks}{6\ weeks} = 0.925$$

These results, along with the variances for the remaining weeks, appear in Table 16-2. Notice that for Week 1, the two indexes equal each other as we would expect, but after that they diverge (see Appendix E). From the Time-Based Schedule Variance, we are about a half week behind schedule at Week 6.

Note: In Table 16-2, SV($) refers to the Value-Based Schedule Variance, while the [$] indicates that the units are in dollars. Likewise, SPI($) refers to the Value-Based Schedule Performance Index, which has no units.

AT [weeks]	SV($) [$]	SPI($)	ES [weeks]	SV(t) [weeks]	SPI(t)	SV(t)%
1	− 100	0.95	0.95	− 0.05	0.95	− 5.3%
2	− 300	0.93	1.88	− 0.12	0.94	− 6.4%
3	− 630	0.92	2.79	− 0.21	0.93	− 7.5%
4	− 960	0.91	3.68	− 0.32	0.92	− 8.7%
5	− 1225	0.91	4.65	− 0.35	0.93	− 7.5%
6	− 1800	0.90	5.55	− 0.45	0.925	− 8.1%

Table 16-2: Expanded Project Status for Week 6 (PD = 40 weeks)

16-7 SCENARIO #1: FUTURE PERFORMANCE EQUALS PAST PERFORMANCE (TSPI = SPI)

A common assumption is that past performance will continue. This scenario is valid if we believe that there is a systemic issue built into our planned schedule that cannot be resolved. For example, we may have made some incorrect assumptions when estimating the durations of our tasks, and we don't have an expectation of making a recovery.

We will use Equation 16-7a to compute ETC(t), substituting SPI(t) for TSPI.

$$ETC(t) = \frac{40\ weeks - 5.55\ weeks}{0.925} = 37.2\ weeks$$

This means that if past performance were to continue, we are going to need 37.2 weeks to complete the remaining work of the project. Now that we have a number for ETC(t), we can use Equation 16-1 to compute EAC(t).

$$EAC(t) = 6\ weeks + 37.2\ weeks = 43.2\ weeks$$

If our assumption that past performance will continue is correct, the project will end up taking a total duration of 43.2 weeks when it is complete.

We are now in a position to compute VAC(t).

$$VAC(t) = 40\ weeks - 43.2\ weeks = -3.2\ weeks$$

The negative sign indicates that we will end up finishing the project 3.2 weeks behind schedule. Let's complete the analysis by computing VAC(t)%.

$$VAC(t)\% = \frac{-3.2\ weeks}{40\ weeks} = -8\%$$

This indicates that the project will be completed 8% behind schedule.

With the assumption of this scenario, there is a much simpler formula that we can use to calculate EAC(t) directly. This formula, which is specific to this assumption, is given in Equation 16-8.

$$EAC(t) = \frac{PD}{SPI(t)} \tag{16-8}$$

This equation is **not** true all the time. It is only true when the assumption that TSPI is equal to SPI(t) is true. Using this specialized formula, let's calculate EAC(t).

$$EAC(t) = \frac{40\ weeks}{0.925} = 43.2\ weeks$$

This agrees with the result we calculated earlier using the general formula. Sometimes we may find that each method yields a slightly different result due to rounding. We can get the two to match more closely if we carry out the SPI(t) to more significant figures.

Now that we have generated a number for EAC(t) first, we can use Equation 16-2 to compute ETC(t).

$$ETC(t) = 43.2\ weeks - 6\ weeks = 37.2\ weeks$$

VAC(t) and VAC(t)% will, of course, be the same as we computed earlier.

16-8 SCENARIO #2: ALL FUTURE WORK PERFORMED AS ORIGINALLY PLANNED (TSPI = 1)

Here we are going to use the same sample project summarized in Tables 16-1 and 16-2, but make a different assumption. We will assume that we are able to fix the cause of the schedule slippage so that all future tasks will be performed with their originally planned durations. Our future schedule efficiency will then be 100%, or TSPI is equal to 1.

This scenario is valid if the problems that caused the schedule impact are due to special circumstances that have been addressed, and we don't expect to experience similar problems going forward.

Notice from Table 16-2 that SV(t) is –0.45 weeks which means that the project is currently about a half week behind schedule. If our assumption is correct, our VAC(t) should result in the same −0.45.

We can go back to our general formula in Equation 16-7a and substitute 1 for TSPI. As a result we get the specialized formula given as Equation 16-9.

$$ETC(t) = PD - ES \qquad\qquad (16\text{-}9)$$

This equation is **not** true all the time. It is only true when TSPI equals 1 is true.

Using the data in Table 16-5 we can make the computation as follows.

$$ETC(t) = 40 \; weeks - 5.55 \; weeks = 34.45 \; weeks$$

This means it will take 34.45 weeks to perform the rest of the project if our assumption is correct. Using Equation 16-1, we can compute EAC(t).

$$EAC(t) = 6 \; weeks \; + 34.45 \; weeks \; = 40.45 \; weeks$$

In this scenario, the project will take a total of 40.45 weeks to perform from its beginning.

$$VAC(t) = 40 \; weeks \; - 40.45 \; weeks \; = -0.45 \; weeks$$

The project will finish about a half week behind schedule, which agrees with SV(t) as we expected. To round out the indicators, let's compute VAC(t)%.

$$VAC(t)\% = \frac{-0.45 \; weeks}{40 \; weeks} = -1.1\%$$

The project will finish 1.1% percent behind schedule if this assumption is correct.

16-9 SCENARIO #3: SOME ARBITRARY VALUE FOR TSPI

The sample project, depicted in Table 16-2, is currently 8.1% behind schedule at the end of Week 6. In this case we will naturally want to determine the cause of the schedule slippage so that we can take corrective action and get the project back on track. If this is possible, we might be able to improve upon the forecast made in Scenario #1 where past performance was assumed to continue.

In many cases we will not be able to fix everything and only get part way to Scenario #2. The current SPI(t) is 0.925. Let's assume that, based on our findings, we believe we can perform all future work at a schedule efficiency of

95%. In other words, our TSPI is 0.95. We can now make a forecast.

We start with Equation 16-7a or 16-7b to calculate ETC(t). The result for this, as well as for EAC(t), VAC(t), and VAC(t)% appear below.

$$ETC\,(t) = \frac{40\;weeks\;-\;5.55\;weeks}{0.95} = 36.3\;weeks$$

$$EAC\,(t) = 6\;weeks\;+\;36.3\;weeks\;=\;42.3\;weeks$$

$$VAC\,(t) = 40\;weeks\;-\;42.3\;weeks\;=\;-2.3\;weeks$$

$$VAC\,(t)\% = \frac{-\,2.3\;weeks}{40\;weeks} = -5.75\,\%$$

Notice that this scenario forecasts that the project will finish behind schedule by 2.3 weeks, which is in between Scenarios #1 and #2. This is as we expected.

16-10 SCENARIO# 4: LOOKING AT MOST RECENT PERFORMANCE

We are going to use the same sample project here, but add two more weeks of data. Remember it has a Planned Duration of 40 weeks. Table 16-3 shows cumulative and incremental (weekly) data for project performance. The Actual Time is given as the current week in the first column.

Week	cum ES [weeks]	inc ES [weeks]	cum SPI(t)	inc SPI(t)
1	0.95	0.95	0.95	0.95
2	1.88	0.93	0.94	0.93
3	2.79	0.91	0.93	0.91
4	3.68	0.89	0.92	0.89
5	4.65	0.97	0.93	0.97
6	5.55	0.90	0.925	0.90
7	6.46	0.91	0.92	0.91
8	7.36	0.90	0.92	0.90
Weeks 1 - 8		7.36		0.92
Weeks 6 - 8		2.71		0.90

Table 16-3: Weekly Sample Project Cost Data

Notice that for the first five weeks the incremental SPI(t) was oscillating in a range between 0.89 and 0.97. It has since settled down to a small range between 0.90 and 0.91.

How should we proceed from here to make our forecast? If we believe that the performance in Weeks 6 – 8 is a good representation of how the project will unfold going forward, then that's the data we should use when formulating our TSPI. In this case, our best assessment is to use a TSPI of 0.90 when making our forecast. This value for TSPI is obtained by dividing the sum of the incremental Earned Schedules for Weeks 6-8 (2.71 weeks) by the Actual Time for Weeks 6-8 (3 weeks).

This is preferable to taking the average of the three incremental SPI(t) values because our result will be weighted by the amount of schedule earned each period. In this particular case, however, there isn't much difference either way.

Note: Even though we're using an existing SPI(t) as the basis for TSPI, we **cannot** use Equation 16-8. This only works if the SPI(t) we are using is for the *entire* project and not for a portion as we have here. We must use the general formula.

$$ETC\,(t) = \frac{32\ weeks}{0.90} = 35.6\ weeks$$

$$EAC\,(t) = 8\ weeks + 35.6\ weeks = 43.6\ weeks$$

$$VAC\,(t) = 40\ weeks\ - 43.6\ weeks\ = -3.6\ weeks$$

$$VAC\,(t)\% = \frac{-3.6\ weeks}{40\ weeks} = -9.0\%$$

So in this case, the project is expected to be completed 3.6 weeks (or 9.0%) behind schedule.

16-11 SUMMARY

These are only examples of the types of scenarios we may encounter as we generate our forecasts. They certainly don't represent an exhaustive set. The key for us is to be as realistic as possible when generating our forecasts.

In these examples we have been performing the forecasts assuming the data represents the critical path. These calculations should be repeated for the project as a whole, and we should always be on the lookout for potential shifts in the critical path.

It is important to forecast early and often. The earlier we are in the project, the more likely we are able to alter the outcome if we don't like what we find. As we get closer to the end of the project there is less and less work remaining to influence. As time goes by, we will see the forecasts from our various scenarios converging.

It is more appropriate to use time-based schedule indicators rather than work-based indicators in making our schedule forecasts. See Appendix E for a discussion of this topic.

Some of the formulas we used only apply in certain specific cases. When in doubt, we should always use the general formulas. They work all of the time.

The question that was addressed in this chapter is given in Table 16-4. The formulas introduced in this chapter are summarized in Tables 16-5, 16-6, and 16-7.

Question	Answer
What is the projected average schedule efficiency of all future work?	TSPI

Table 16-4: Question Summary

Modern Convention	Traditional Convention
$ETC(t) = \dfrac{RS}{TSPI}$	$ETC(t) = \dfrac{PTWR}{TSPI}$
$ETC(t) = \dfrac{PD - ES}{TSPI}$	$ETC(t) = \dfrac{PD - PTWP}{TSPI}$

Table 16-5: General Forecasting Equations
[Always True]

Modern	Traditional
$EAC(t) = \dfrac{AT}{\%\ Concluded}$	$EAC(t) = \dfrac{ATWP}{\%\ Concluded}$
$EAC(t) = \dfrac{PD}{SPI(t)}$	
$VAC(t)\% = SV(t)\%$	

Table 16-6: Specific Forecasting Equations
[Only True when TSPI = SPI(t)]

Modern	Traditional
$ETC(t) = RS$	$ETC(t) = PTWR$
$ETC(t) = PD - ES$	$ETC(t) = PD - PTWP$
$EAC(t) = PD - SV(t)$	
$VAC(t) = SV(t)$	

Table 16-7: Specific Forecasting Equations
[Only True when TSPI = 1]

EXERCISES

16-1: What role does the critical path play in schedule forecasting?

16-2: How should forecasts be performed in order to capture a shift in the critical path if one were to occur?

16-3: Explain the difference between time-based schedule indicators and value-based schedule indicators. Is one preferable to use in forecasting? Why?

16-4: Show that if TSPI = SPI(t), Equation 16-8 results from Equations 16-1 and Equation 16-7a.

16-5: When would it be appropriate to do a forecast by re-estimating the durations of each uncompleted task from scratch?

16-6: It is the end of Week 10 in a 40 week project. The Earned Schedule for the critical path has been determined to be 8 weeks and the precedence diagram analysis indicates that the critical path has not shifted. Determine ETC(t), EAC(t), VAC(t), and VAC(t)% for the following cases.

a) Past performance will continue.

b) All future work will be performed as scheduled.

c) The future work will be performed with a 90% schedule efficiency.

16-7: The table below contains the cumulative project Planned Value and Earned Value figures for the end of each two-week reporting period through today, the end of week 10. Assume this is representative of the critical path. This 50 week project has a Budget at Completion of $250,000.

Week	cum PV [$]	cum EV [$]
2	3,000	2,000
4	7,000	5,500
6	13,000	11,000
8	20,500	17,000
10	30,000	26,000

a) Calculate all of the value-based and time-based schedule status indicators for the end of Week 10

b) How significantly do the value-based and time-based indicators differ from each other? What does each set tell us?

c) Determine ETC(t), EAC(t), VAC(t), and VAC(t)% assuming past performance will continue.

d) How would the forecast differ if the value-based indicators were used?

16-8: Use the data in the table below for this exercise. Assume that the tasks are scheduled as soon as possible based upon predecessor relationships and that the budget for each task is evenly distributed over the life of the task.

a) Generate a status report for the end of Week 10 and interpret the results. Perform the analysis using the data for all the tasks, then repeat for only the critical tasks. Include the following project-level indicators in your assessment.

– PV   – % Concluded

– EV   – SV($)

– AT	– SV(t)
– ES	– SPI($)
– Planned % Complete	– SPI(t)
– Actual % Complete	– SV($)%
– % Elapsed	– SV(t)%

b) Assuming past performance will continue, develop a schedule forecast for the remainder of the project that includes ETC(t), EAC(t), VAC(t), and VAC(t)%. Perform the analysis using the data for all the tasks, then repeat for only the critical tasks.

c) Prepare a presentation on schedule status and likely outcome for a key stakeholder who knows nothing about EVM.

Task ID	Duration [weeks]	Budget [$]	Predecessor(s)	Actual % Complete (Week 10)
A	3	3,000	–	100%
B	2	2,200	–	100%
C	4	4,200	–	100%
D	5	4,500	A	80%
E	4	4,000	B	100%
F	5	6,000	B, C	100%
G	6	7,200	D	0%
H	3	2,700	E	90%
I	8	7,200	F	60%
J	2	2,400	G, H	0

Chapter 17

EASE OF MEETING SCHEDULE TARGETS

In the last chapter, we assumed a schedule efficiency for future work. This allowed us to determine how much time would be necessary to finish the project. Here, we are going to do the reverse. Given an amount of time available, we'll determine the schedule efficiency that we need to maintain going forward, in order to meet our target finish date. We can then assess if it is something that can realistically be achieved.

17-1 TO-COMPLETE SCHEDULE PERFORMANCE INDEX (TSPI)

The TSPI is similar to the SPI(t) in that they are both efficiency indexes. The difference is that the SPI(t) represents the actual schedule efficiency for the work already performed, while the TSPI represents a target schedule efficiency for work yet to be performed.

In the last chapter we were given Equation 16-6a relating ETC(t) with TSPI using the Modern Convention. It is repeated here as Equation 17-1. ETC(t) is the Time Estimate to Complete and RS is the Remaining Schedule.

$$ETC\,(t) = \frac{RS}{TSPI} \tag{17-1}$$

Notice that there are two unknowns, ETC(t) and TSPI. In the last chapter we generated a figure for TSPI first and then used this equation to calculate ETC(t). This was our forecast for the actual time to perform the remaining work of the project.

Now we will do the reverse. First we'll generate a figure for ETC(t), which represents the time interval within which we would like to complete the remaining work. Then we will back-calculate the TSPI, which represents the schedule efficiency that we need to achieve in order to reach that target.

If the TSPI is reasonable, then we have a realistic chance of achieving our goal. If not, then we must either negotiate for more time or generate an alternate approach.

234

In order to make the calculations more convenient, we'll rewrite Equation 17-1 by solving for TSPI. This gives us Equation 17-2.

$$TSPI = \frac{RS}{ETC(t)} \tag{17-2}$$

The following expression states this in words.

$$TSPI = \frac{Remaining\ Schedule}{Time\ Estimate\ to\ Complete}$$

This can also be expressed as follows.

$$TSPI = \frac{Planned\ Time\ for\ Work\ Remaining}{Time\ Available}$$

So the TSPI here represents the ratio of the time scheduled to perform the work remaining to the amount of time available to perform that work. This is an expression of how efficient we need to be with our time going forward.

Like the SPI(t), the TSPI is an index or a schedule efficiency factor. Let's recall the equation for SPI(t) in the Modern Convention.

$$SPI(t) = \frac{ES}{AT} = \frac{Earned\ Schedule}{Actual\ Time}$$

SPI(t) is simply the ratio of the portion of the schedule actually performed (or earned) to the actual amount of time it took to perform that work. As we can see, the TSPI is the complement of SPI(t). The SPI(t) represents the actual schedule performance of the past, while TSPI represents the projected performance of future work.

Equation 17-2 can also be written in another form shown in Equations 17-3a and 17-3b, where EAC(t) is the total amount of time we have available to perform the entire project.

$$\textbf{Modern: } TSPI = \frac{PD - ES}{EAC(t) - AT} \tag{17-3a}$$

$$\textbf{Traditional: } TSPI = \frac{PD - PTWP}{EAC(t) - ATWP} \tag{17-3b}$$

This is a general equation for TSPI that is true all the time. It's also the most common form that is cited, and will be the form we'll be using as we investigate several scenarios.

17-2 TSPI(PD)

If our project is not currently on target with respect to schedule, we're often interested in determining what schedule efficiency we need going forward in order to deliver our project on time, i.e. where EAC(t) equals PD. In this case we can rewrite Equation 17-3a or 17-3b as Equation 17-4a or 17-4b.

$$\textbf{Modern: } TSPI\,(PD) = \frac{PD - ES}{PD - AT} \tag{17-4a}$$

$$\textbf{Traditional: } TSPI\,(PD) = \frac{PD - PTWP}{PD - ATWP} \tag{17-4b}$$

We are using the designation TSPI(PD) to indicate that the target duration we are aiming for is PD. Note that this equation is **not** true all the time, but only for this specific case where EAC(t) equals PD.

If the project is exactly on schedule, SPI(t) equals 1 and TSPI(PD) is also equal to 1.

If the Project is behind schedule, SPI(t) is less than 1 and TSPI(PD) must be greater than 1. This is obvious since there has to be a higher efficiency in the future to make up for a lower efficiency in the past.

If the project is currently ahead of schedule, SPI(t) is greater than 1 and TSPI(PD) will be less than 1. This too makes sense. If we've been overly efficient in the past, we can afford to be somewhat less efficient in our future work and still come in on schedule.

17-3 SCHEDULE EFFICIENCY IMPROVEMENT FACTOR (SIF)

Once we obtain a figure for TSPI, we can then gauge how difficult it may be to achieve that level of efficiency. One simple way to quantify the extent of the challenge is by a measure known as the Schedule Efficiency Improvement Factor or SIF. It is calculated using Equation 17-5.

$$SIF = \frac{TSPI - SPI(t)}{SPI(t)} \tag{17-5}$$

The result is usually expressed as a percentage. The higher the factor, the greater the challenge we face.

Like the CIF we discussed in an earlier chapter, we don't want to oversimplify and imply that all of our challenges can be reduced to a single number. Many qualitative factors will weigh-in depending on what led us to the current state of affairs. Nevertheless, the SIF is a convenient way to compare different situations or alternatives in a quantitative fashion.

The SIF can be especially useful when we are evaluating forecasts prepared by others. If the SIF is too large, we may be suspicious of the realism associated with their forecast, and their ability to actually deliver on their plans.

What is considered to be an acceptable range will vary by organization, situation, and type of project. A common rule of thumb is that a SIF less than 5% may be easily recoverable with the proper attention, a SIF over 10% can be difficult to achieve, and a gray area in between those will require some judgment to assess. This rule of thumb is depicted in Figure 17-1.

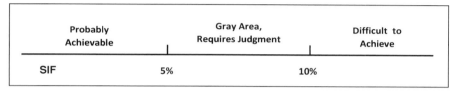

Figure 17-1: SIF Rule of Thumb

For example, if one of our contractors was behind schedule and their forecast for EAC(t) resulted in a SIF of 3%, we might be inclined to take their word that they can achieve their forecast. If that same contractor made a forecast that resulted in a SIF of 12%, we might want to be see more evidence that they have a credible recovery plan in place in order to meet their target.

This does not mean that any SIF over 10% will be impossible to achieve. There may be cases where the problems that occurred to date will not be recurring. In this case it might be entirely possible to have a TSPI significantly above the SPI(t).

Of course, like any rule of thumb, these ranges can be modified to suit the situation, the organization, the type of project, and the record of the performers involved.

Let's look at some scenarios as examples where we can apply these ideas.

17-4 SCENARIO #1: FINISHING THE PROJECT ON SCHEDULE FROM WEEK 2 [EAC(t) = PD]

We are going to use the same project from the last chapter as our example. It is a 40 week project, and the status report for the end of Week 2 is given in Table 17-1. We want to determine what schedule efficiency will be needed going forward in order to deliver the project on schedule. To do this, we must compute TSPI using Equation 17-4a or 17-4b.

$$TSPI\,(PD\,) = \frac{40\ weeks - 1.88\ weeks}{40\ weeks - 2\ weeks} = 1.003 = 100.3\%$$

AT [weeks]	cum PV [$]	cum EV [$]	SPI($)	ES [weeks]	SV(t) [weeks]	SPI(t)	SV(t)%
1	2,000	1,900	0.95	0.95	− 0.05	0.95	− 5.3%
2	4,500	4,200	0.93	1.88	− 0.12	0.94	− 6.4%

Table 17-1: Week 2 report of a 40 week project

This means that in order to deliver the project on schedule, all future work will need to be performed with a schedule efficiency that is about one third of one percent greater than planned. Notice that our current schedule efficiency is almost 6% less than planned.

Why is the TSPI closer to 100% than the SPI(t)? The reason has to do with time. Notice that only 5% of the project time has elapsed (% Elapsed). This means that we have 95% of the project schedule remaining in which to make up the schedule slippage.

The TSPI is a time dependent indicator. The further we get into the project, the more we'll see the TSPI increase in value and reach a level that may be impossible to meet. The earlier we can address a schedule delay, the easier it will be for us to be successful in managing our time.

Achieving this TSPI of 100.3% may not be as easy as it seems. In order to make this happen, we must first raise the current SPI(t) from 0.94 to 1, then add another 0.3%, and turn it on a dime!

To be more precise about this, we are going to use the Schedule Efficiency Improvement Factor from Equation 17-5.

$$SIF = \frac{1.003 - 0.94}{0.94} = 0.067 = 6.7\%$$

This means that we need a 6.7% schedule efficiency improvement from where we are today in order to meet our target of delivering our project on time. This is fairly significant and puts us in the gray area of our rule of thumb, but we are very early in the project. If we can find the cause of our schedule delays, address them quickly, and monitor them closely, we may be able to be successful.

17-5 SCENARIO #2: INCREASING AVAILABLE TIME FROM WEEK 2 [EAC(t) > PD]

In this scenario, we're going to look at the same situation as Scenario #1 (i.e. Table 17-1), but will assume that we obtained an additional week in order to perform this project. Admittedly, we would not normally be looking for additional time this early in the project, but let's consider this as a "what if" exercise. This will give us a chance to see what effect this would have on the TSPI and the SIF.

With this additional week, our EAC(t) is now 41 weeks. Since it is different than the PD, we must now use the general formula given in Equation 17-3a or 17-3b.

$$TSPI = \frac{40\ weeks - 1.88\ weeks}{41\ weeks - 2\ weeks} = 0.977 = 97.7\%$$

This is less than 100%, so we may feel that this is going to be easy to accomplish. Just like in the previous scenario, the project is currently operating at a lower efficiency than this. It must rise to and maintain this level for the remainder of the project in order to be completed within the revised duration of 41 weeks.

To put this in perspective, let's calculate the Schedule Efficiency Improvement Factor using Equation 17-5.

$$SIF = \frac{0.977 - 0.94}{0.94} = 3.9\%$$

We can see that this is a noticeable improvement from the last scenario and puts us into the good range using our rule-of-thumb.

17-6 SCENARIO #3: FINISHING THE PROJECT ON SCHEDULE FROM WEEK 6 [EAC(t) = PD]

Again, using the same project as the earlier scenarios, we are going to look at the status at week 6, which is summarized in Table 17-2.

We can compute the TSPI(PD) needed to get back to the original planned completion date.

$$TSPI\,(PD) = \frac{40\ weeks - 5.55\ weeks}{40\ weeks - 6\ weeks} = 1.013 = 101.3\%$$

This is going to be quite a significant challenge. To see how significant, we need to calculate the SIF.

$$SIF = \frac{1.013 - 0.925}{0.925} = 9.5\%$$

AT [weeks]	cum PV [$]	cum EV [$]	SPI($)	ES [weeks]	SV(t) [weeks]	SPI(t)	SV(t)%
1	2,000	1,900	0.95	0.95	− 0.05	0.95	− 5.3%
2	4,500	4,200	0.93	1.88	− 0.12	0.94	− 6.4%
3	7,500	6,870	0.92	2.79	− 0.21	0.93	− 7.5%
4	10,500	9,540	0.91	3.68	− 0.32	0.92	− 8.7%
5	14,000	12,775	0.91	4.65	− 0.35	0.93	− 7.5%
6	18,000	16,200	0.90	5.55	− 0.45	0.925	− 8.1%

Table 17-2: Project Cost Data through Week 6

Notice that the project has lost ground over the last 4 weeks compared to where it was at the end of Week 2 in Scenario #1. This also puts it very nearly in the bad range using our rule of thumb. It's probably close enough that we might want to treat it as if it were in the bad range.

17-7 SCENARIO #4: INCREASING AVAILABLE TIME FROM WEEK 6 [EAC(t) > PD]

Based on the performance so far, and our understanding of the underlying issues, let's assume that we don't believe that we can achieve this level of schedule efficiency going forward. Let's also assume that after we have presented our case to Senior Management, they agree to add another week to the project duration and asked us for an analysis.

With the added time, the EAC(t) is now 41 weeks. The PD has not changed; it remains at 40 weeks. We can now calculate TSPI using the general form in Equation 17-3a or 17-3b.

$$TSPI = \frac{40 \; weeks - 5.55 \; weeks}{41 \; weeks - 6 \; weeks} = 0.984 = 98.4\%$$

As in Scenario #2 it is less than 100%, which means we can afford to be less efficient than in our baseline plan. It is still above where we are currently, however. Let's calculate the Schedule Efficiency Improvement Factor.

$$SIF = \frac{0.984 - 0.925}{0.925} = 6.4\%$$

This is a noticeable improvement from our situation in the last scenario, but it will still be quite a challenge to accomplish as the project is still solidly in the gray area using our rule of thumb.

17-8 SUMMARY

We can use the tools developed in this chapter in order to evaluate our schedule forecasts and get a sense of how challenging it will be to meet our targets.

If we are in a position to analyze reports prepared by other parties, we can also use these tools to evaluate their forecasts. For example, we may have a contractor performing some of the project work. If we ask them for a forecast of the project completion date, or EAC(t), we can determine what schedule efficiency they are assuming for the future work, and assess whether their forecast is reasonable and realistic.

The questions that were addressed in this chapter are given in Table 17-3. The formulas introduced in this chapter are summarized in Table 17-4.

Question	Answer
What schedule efficiency will need to be achieved in order to finish the work on time?	TSPI(PD)
What improvement in schedule efficiency will be necessary going forward in order to meet the desired finish date?	SIF

Table 17-3: Question Summary

Modern Convention	Traditional Convention
$TSPI = \dfrac{RS}{ETC(t)}$	$TSPI = \dfrac{PTWR}{ETC(t)}$
$TSPI = \dfrac{PD - ES}{EAC(t) - AT}$	$TSPI = \dfrac{PD - PTWP}{EAC(t) - ATWP}$
$TSPI(PD) = \dfrac{PD - ES}{PD - AT}$	$TSPI(PD) = \dfrac{PD - PTWP}{PD - ATWP}$
$SIF = \dfrac{TSPI - SPI(t)}{SPI(t)}$	

Table 17-4: Equation Summary

EXERCISES

17-1: What is the Schedule Efficiency Improvement Factor? How is it used?

17-2: When is it appropriate to use TSPI(PD)?

17-3: What does it mean if TSPI equals zero?

17-4: In what type of situation would the TSPI(PD) be less than zero?

17-5: We have a Contractor that is performing a year-long subproject that is a component of our larger project. They are required to deliver an EVM report of status and forecasts on a monthly basis. In the first report, you notice that their schedule forecast is prepared, using aggregate data, two different ways. The first uses a TSPI equal to SPI($). The second uses TSPI equal to the product of SPI($) and CPI.

    a) What are the implications of using either of these approaches?

    b) What discussions would you have with the Contractor about their forecasts in upcoming reports?

17-6: It is the end of the first week of a 50 week project and we have our first status report available. We find that the BCWS is $2500, the BCWP is $2000, and the ACWP is $2200. The project BAC is $150,000.

a) Compute the indicators below and interpret the results. Assume past performance will continue when computing EAC(t). The SIF should reflect the improvement necessary to finish the project on time.

– PTWP	– % Elapsed
– SV($)	– % Concluded
– SV(t)	– EAC(t)
– SPI($)	– TSPI(PD)
– SPI(t)	– SIF

b) What would be the TSPI and SIF if the project was given an extra 2 weeks in duration? What do the results indicate?

17-7: We have a Contractor performing a 40 week subproject for us under a Time and Materials contract. In the most recent report we have received from them, for the end of Week 8, they indicated that the Earned Schedule for the critical path is 7.8 weeks, the aggregate Earned Schedule is 7 weeks, and the Earned Value equals the Actual Cost.

In the summary of their report, they included the following statement.

"Even though we are slightly behind schedule at the moment, this was due to a problem that we quickly identified and rectified. This problem is not expected to recur in the future. We still plan to complete the project on time, by working weekends if necessary, in order to make up the slippage."

Evaluate the Contractor's report. What are your concerns? What additional information would you like to see? What response would you propose be provided to the Contractor? Include both cost and schedule considerations.

17-8: A 60 week project was planned using 2-week intervals. The cumulative values for PV and EV for the first 8 weeks are given in the table below.

a) Compare the status of the project schedule at the end of Week 4 with the end of Week 8. Did the schedule performance improve or get worse between these two dates? By how much?

b) If past performance were to continue from Week 8, when is the project likely to finish?

c) Assuming that we need to complete the project on schedule, what schedule efficiency will be needed from this point going forward? Is this realistic? What can be done to improve the chances?

Week	PV [$]	EV [$]
2	2,500	2,305
4	6,000	5,550
6	10,000	9,150
8	14,300	12,950

Chapter 18

ODDS AND ENDS

18-1 EVM TOOLS

We are near the end of our investigation of a number of EVM tools. While these belong in every project manager's toolbox, they are also very useful for other stakeholders such as customers and the supervisors of project managers. A common question at this point is, do we really need to use all of the tools that we discussed?

Each situation is unique and imposes a different demand on the participants. Also, different practitioners have different needs. In order for us to make informed decisions, however, we should understand how all the tools work, and understand what each tool provides. It is then up to us to decide which tools are the most appropriate to use in which situations to help us best meet the objectives that we are trying to achieve.

We shouldn't go through the motions of using a tool, just because it was presented to us. If we find that the application of a tool is more trouble than it's worth, then either it's not the right tool or we're not using it properly. Tools exist to make our work easier, not to add additional burdens on us.

Think of it like being a carpenter. A master carpenter has a toolbox filled with a wide array of tools. There's a hammer on the top that's probably used on a daily basis. There are more obscure tools in the bottom of the box that might get used once a year, if that. Even though all the tools are not used with the same frequency, in order for that person to be considered a master carpenter, he or she must know how to use all of the tools in the toolbox. They will then use their professional judgment to determine the best tool to use in each situation.

The same thing applies for EVM tools, or any project management tool for that matter. It is important for us to be familiar enough with each tool in order to have a good understanding of how it can help us and add value. That, coupled with our understanding of the situation at hand, will allow us to identify the right tool and the extent to which we should use it.

18-2 QUALITY

Although we have not spent a lot of time explicitly discussing the quality of work products and deliverables, it is certainly taken into consideration in our analysis. In order for a task to have earned all of its value (i.e., declared to be 100% complete), its work product must be complete and be verified to have met the appropriate standards.

A quality plan should be developed for each work product in order to ensure that there is agreement among the stakeholders on how these quality factors will be measured, and on what constitutes a properly completed work package.

We also use quality information to get an assessment of the actual percent complete of a task in progress. If we are able to identify objective intermediate milestones internal to a task, then meeting those milestones gives us assurance that we are making progress toward the completion of the task. Those milestones rely on quality information in order to be defined and to be tracked.

We set tolerance limits on the "good" side as well as the "bad" side for both our cost and schedule indicators. Being out of tolerance on the bad side indicates obvious problems. Being out of tolerance on the good side is not always a problem, but a prime suspect is the sacrifice of the quality standards in our work products and deliverables.

Contractors cutting corners, producers using a lower grade of material, workers not following proper procedure, or a number of other quality-related issues could be contributors to a tolerance reading of "too good to be true."

18-3 KUDZAL'S RULE OF 5-4-3-2-1

How frequently should we be performing our analyses? This will vary depending on the situation. In a one month project, the Project Manager might be doing an analysis every day or two. In a one year project, once a week might be more appropriate. Every project is unique and requires its own set of guidelines.

A highly constrained project with very limited resources or tight tolerance limits will naturally need to be monitored more closely and frequently than one which is more routine, and which has more flexibility.

There is a rule of thumb, however, that can be useful when planning the monitoring and control schedule. It is called "Kudzal's Rule of 5-4-3-2-1," or simply "Kudzal's Rule." Like any rule of thumb, it is not a strict law—it can be modified to suit the case at hand. First, let's see what it is, and then we'll see why it works.

The 5-4-3-2-1 refers to the suggested timeframes involved; it also makes it easy to remember.

The Project Manager is at Level 5, and should be performing a formal evaluation every 5 days, or once per week. The supervisor of the Project Manager (we'll assume it's a Program Manager) doesn't need to look at status every week. Why duplicate the work of the Project Manager? The Program Manager should be doing a formal evaluation every 4 weeks, or once per month.

The supervisor of the Program Manager (say the Portfolio Manager) again doesn't need to duplicate the efforts of the Program Manager. The Portfolio Manager should be doing a formal evaluation every 3 months, or once per quarter. If there are more levels above, then the next level (e.g., Executive) should be doing a formal evaluation every 2 quarters, or semiannually. The next level (e.g., CEO) should be doing a formal evaluation once per year.

This hierarchy is summarized in Table 18-1.

Level	Frequency	Position
1	1 year or annually	CEO
2	2 quarters or semiannually	Executive
3	3 months or quarterly	Portfolio Manager
4	4 weeks or monthly	Program Manager
5	5 days or weekly	Project Manager

Table 18-1: Kudzal's Rule of 5-4-3-2-1

It is set up this way so that if any person discovers that they have a problem, there is plenty of time to get it fixed before they have to report it up. For example, if the Project Manager discovers that the project is unacceptably over budget the first week, they have 3 whole weeks to get it fixed before they have to report it to the Program Manager.

Likewise, if the Program Manager discovers a problem at the end of the first month, they have 2 whole months to get things turned around before they have to report it to the Portfolio Manager.

If everyone follows this scheme, and a problem is discovered at any level, there is usually enough time to get it fixed before it needs to be reported up to the next level.

Now, what if the Project Manager discovered a problem at the end of a week, and after investigating the root cause, came to the conclusion that he or she didn't have the resources at their disposal to fix the problem before it had to be reported to the Program Manager? What should they do then?

The answer, of course, is to escalate immediately. Don't wait for things to potentially get worse. It is time to bring in bigger guns. The Program Manager normally would have more resources that can be brought to bear.

In order to be successful, Kudzal's Rule should be adopted throughout the organization, and be made the expectation of everyone in the chain of command. As mentioned earlier, the time frames may change from level to level as needed, but the overall idea remains the same.

Adjustments may also be necessary if everyone is not part of the same organization. For example, if part of our project is being performed by a contractor, then they would have a Project Manager at Level 5. Assuming that the contractor is doing what it should be doing, we are at Level 4, and don't need to look at it more than once per month. This is probably the frequency at which we are getting our information from them, anyway.

18-4 CONTRACTING

Speaking of contracting, EVM is a good management tool to evaluate the performance of contractors. Contractors are part of our project team and they should provide enough information to allow us to track their progress and determine how well they are supporting the rest of the project.

EVM reporting can be written into the contract and indicate that the contractor must provide an Earned Value status report and a forecast on a regular basis. This provides several benefits.

If the contractors have suitable EVM systems in place, we can be reassured that they are properly monitoring their own performance. It also provides a vehicle for communication and discussion, since both parties now share a tool that provides early warning if the work is not proceeding as planned.

An important aspect of incorporating EVM into a contract is an agreement on how to apportion value among the tasks and how to measure the value that is earned for tasks in progress. While measuring the value of tasks in progress may not be vital for those that are very short in duration, it does take on an added significance for longer duration tasks. Identifying objective milestones within tasks helps to facilitate an understanding of how to gauge progress.

It is a common belief that EVM doesn't play a role in fixed price contracts. This is certainly not the case. While it is true that the contractor cannot pass along any increases in cost, schedule is still an issue. Also, we may want to structure our payments to the contractor in such a way that they track the value being earned. If, for a given period, the contractor delivered less value than planned, the payments to them would be decreased accordingly.

The most common situation where EVM may not be appropriate is in Level-of-Effort projects. Here the workers perform tasks as they arise, and the work cannot be planned ahead of time. Without the benefit of a plan, there is no way to generate variances, and no way to assess efficiencies. We just do what's necessary at the moment.

18-5 USE OF RESERVES

Reserves are funds that are set aside to cover added expenses for within-scope items. These reserves could be Contingency Reserves to handle known risks that we've chosen to handle with contingency plans, or Management Reserves which are intended for responding to unknown risks.

The contingency plans, which may include small strings of activities, are normally identified in our baseline plan. This is because the risks they are designed to address are known, and we have had time to develop our response. These response plans do not appear in our precedence diagram, however, because we don't know when, or even if, we need to execute them.

Any responses to unknown risks cannot be planned ahead of time. In this case the response plans will be generated as necessary just prior to their execution, and it is obvious that there could have been no mention of them in the baseline plan.

When we set up our initial plan, we ignored the use of reserves when constructing our Planned Value curve, because the activities that might be funded by the reserves were not part of the schedule, and therefore, made no contribution to the spending plan or to the Budget at Completion.

At the moment we realize that we need to react to the presence of a risk event to be funded by the reserves, we need to splice our response plan into the precedence diagram at the appropriate place. Then we proceed as if this had been our intention all along. We update our Gantt charts and other scheduling tools to include these additional activities. We also update our spending plans with the planned cost of these activities, which will require an adjustment of the Budget at Completion and our Planned Value curve.

After the work of the response plan is actually performed, the Actual Cost and Earned Value information will now also include the effect of this additional work. This way, when we measure our variances, we'll have consistency, or as the old saying goes, we'll be comparing apples with apples.

18-6 CHANGE MANAGEMENT

It is not uncommon to have changes or amendments to our baseline plan during project implementation. This requires a formal act in the form of a change order.

If we have a change order that modifies the scope of the project or modifies the approach that the project is taking, we must adjust our schedules, the spending plans, the BAC, and the PV data to reflect the change. At this point we essentially have a new baseline. Any subsequent EV and AC data must also include the appropriate data in accordance with the change.

Some changes may not impact the Planned Value or the Budget at Completion. For example, if we have a project to paint the walls of several rooms in a building, and the change is just to modify the color scheme, chances are there will not be any adjustments necessary to the PV or BAC. If, on the other hand, the change is to add more rooms to the project, then the cost will increase and the schedule will be impacted. In this case we will need to make an adjustment.

Even though it is for a different reason, the effect of a change on our project plan is not unlike that of the use of a reserve. Also, the process that we follow to incorporate a change is very similar to that which we use when integrating the work associated with the reserves that we discussed in the last section.

As we know, there may be a number of changes that a project can experience over its lifetime. It is incumbent on us to stay current with all changes and be aware of the impact of changes on budgets, schedules, and quality. It is also important to communicate these changes to all the relevant stakeholders.

18-7 RESOURCES AND REFERENCES

While this book covers a lot of ground and prepares us to understand and apply the concepts of Earned Value Management, it is not intended to be the final authority on the subject. The mechanics of how to incorporate EVM into the project management process will be governed by stakeholder requirements, organizational policy, data gathering constraints, etc.

Other sources are available and many expand upon the application of EVM. Some address how to apply Earned Value in more depth. Others focus on specific situations, such as how to comply with government regulations or how to incorporate EVM into the contracting process.

Software support is available. General project management applications normally address Earned Value, but usually in a limited capacity. Other applications are more EVM-specific, and they provide more in-depth assistance with the tools.

There are Appendixes in the back of this book that consolidate some of the items that were developed, but scattered among the chapters.

Appendix A contains a list of initials and acronyms that will be helpful, especially to the novice.

Appendix B is a glossary of common terms used in both the Modern and Traditional Conventions.

Appendix C contains a summary of common questions that stakeholders like to ask with the associated EVM indicator that provides the answer to the question.

Appendix F provides a list of all the formulas that were developed in one handy place.

The following links provide more information on the topic of EVM from third party sources.

College of Performance Management   http://www.mycpm.org

Project Management Institute   http://www.pmi.org

Earned Schedule   http://www.earnedschedule.com

Since the Earned Value Management is a dynamic discipline, it is difficult to maintain a current listing of resources in print. The following web site will contain an updated list of resources and references.

http://www.bacorp.com/EVM

18-8 FINAL THOUGHTS

We'll finish with a high level set of reminders for the steps that have proven to be successful. It's not an exhaustive list; feel free to add your own.

1. Establish good relationships with all of the key stakeholders, and discover their requirements and success factors.

2. Develop a good plan, including budget, schedule, and quality elements, with specific costs and measurable milestones.

3. Put systems in place that allow for the timely collection of relevant data.

4. Monitor the project closely by collecting actual data on a regular and frequent basis.

5. Evaluate project performance by routinely analyzing project status and generating forecasts.

6. Provide feedback to the project team on a regular basis and solicit their input for potential improvements.

7. Take corrective action immediately, and escalate when necessary.

8. Continually update the cost, schedule, and other elements of the current plan.

9. Keep all stakeholders informed.

And don't forget to celebrate your project successes!

Appendix A

INITIALS AND ACRONYMS

AC   Actual Cost

ACWP   Actual Cost of Work Performed

AT   Actual Time

ATWP   Actual Time for Work Performed

BAC   Budget at Completion

BCWP   Budgeted Cost of Work Performed

BCWR   Budgeted Cost of Work Remaining

BCWS   Budgeted Cost of Work Scheduled

BR   Budget Remaining

BRTC   Budget Remaining to Complete

CIF   Cost Efficiency Improvement Factor

CPI   Cost Performance Index

CV   Cost Variance

CV%	Cost Variance Percentage
EAC	Estimate at Completion
EAC(t)	Time Estimate at Completion
ES	Earned Schedule
ETC	Estimate to Complete
ETC(t)	Time Estimate to Complete
EV	Earned Value
EVM	Earned Value Management
FPI	Fiscal Performance Index
FV	Fiscal Variance
FV%	Fiscal Variance Percentage
PD	Planned Duration
PTWP	Planned Time for Work Performed
PTWR	Planned Time for Work Remaining
PV	Planned Value
RS	Remaining Schedule
RT	Remaining Time
RV	Remaining Value
SIF	Schedule Efficiency Improvement Factor

SPI	Schedule Performance Index
SPI($)	Value-Based Schedule Performance Index
SPI(t)	Time-Based Schedule Performance Index
SV	Schedule Variance
SV%	Schedule Variance Percentage
SV($)	Value-Based Schedule Variance
SV($)%	Value-Based Schedule Variance Percentage
SV(t)	Time-Based Schedule Variance
SV(t)%	Time-Based Schedule Variance Percentage
TCPI	To-Complete Cost Performance Index
TRTC	Time Remaining to Complete
TSPI	To-Complete Schedule Performance Index
VAC	Variance at Completion
VAC%	Variance at Completion Percentage
VAC(t)	Time Variance at Completion
VAC(t)%	Time Variance at Completion Percentage
WBS	Work Breakdown Structure

Appendix B

GLOSSARY

Actual Cost

The amount of funding required to perform the work actually accomplished. The Actual Cost of Work Performed.

Actual Cost of Work Performed

A synonym for Actual Cost.

Actual Percent Complete

The portion of the total work performed as of the data date expressed as a percentage.

Actual Percent Spent

The portion of the budget actually spent as of the data date expressed as a percentage.

Actual Time

The amount of time elapsed from the start of the project through the data date. The Actual Time for Work Performed.

Actual Time for Work Performed

A synonym for Actual Time.

Baseline Cost

The amount of money budgeted to perform the project work as expressed in the Baseline Plan.

Baseline Plan

The officially approved project plan. The basis from which variances are measured.

Bottom-Up Method	An estimating approach by which the cost of each task is assessed based upon the costs of the individual resources assigned to the task. The costs of each task are then added to provide an estimate of the project cost.
Budget, Project	The amount of money allocated to the project in order to perform the work described in the project plan plus all reserves.
Budget at Completion	The total budget (or value) of the work scheduled to be performed in the baseline plan. Does not include any unused reserves.
Budget Remaining	The amount of money in the budget that is not yet spent and is available to perform future work. The Budget Remaining to Complete.
Budget Remaining to Complete	A synonym for Budget Remaining.
Budgeted Cost of Work Performed	A synonym for Earned Value.
Budgeted Cost of Work Remaining	A synonym for Remaining Value.
Budgeted Cost of Work Scheduled	A synonym for Planned Value.
Change	An official modification to the Baseline Plan.
Change Order	The document that promulgates a change.
Constraint	A limitation on the project team's ability to perform the work of the project.

Contingency Plan	A backup plan used to address a particular known risk. It does not appear in the schedule of the original Baseline Plan, but will be implemented if, and when, its associated risk event occurs.
Control Chart	A graph depicting project performance over time with respect to predetermined tolerance levels. Commonly used with Variance Percentages or Indexes.
Cost Efficiency Improvement Factor	The improvement in cost efficiency that will be necessary in order to achieve the cost objectives.
Cost Performance Index	The average cost efficiency of the work actually performed.
Cost Variance	The difference between the actual cost of the work accomplished and the budgeted cost of the same work. It indicates how much the work was delivered under (or over) budget.
Cost Variance Percentage	The size of the Cost Variance as a percentage of the budgeted cost (EV).
Critical Path	The longest path through a Precedence Diagram; its duration defines the project duration.
Critical Tasks	The collection of tasks that comprise the Critical Path.
Cumulative Data	EVM data generated from the beginning of the project through the data date.

Current Plan	The most recent, unofficial, version of the Project Plan that incorporates "actual" data for work completed and revisions to future work based upon Project Control decisions. Not to be confused with the Baseline Plan.
Customer	The person for whose benefit a project is being performed.
Data Date	The date for which a particular set of EVM data is valid. The Actual Time.
Deliverables	Items produced by the project team that must be formally accepted by the customer.
Duration, Task	The amount of time, on the calendar, it will take to perform a task.
Earned Schedule	The amount of time that was scheduled in order to perform the work that was actually accomplished. The Planned Time for Work Performed.
Earned Value	The amount of money that was budgeted to perform the work actually accomplished. The Budgeted Cost of Work Performed.
Earned Value Management	A project management tool that provides for the evaluation of cost and schedule performance within a single system.
Effort	The number of labor hours required to perform a piece of work.
Estimate	An assessment of the likely quantitative result.
Estimate at Completion	The forecast for what the cumulative Actual Cost will be at the end of the project.

Estimate to Complete	The forecast for how much money will be needed to perform the remaining work.
Fifty-Fifty Rule	A method for estimating the Earned Value of a task in progress. Often used when no other approach is available.
Fiscal Performance Index	The average spending efficiency as of the data date.
Fiscal Variance	The difference between the amount of money planned to be spent and the amount of money actually spent as of a given date. The Spending Variance.
Fiscal Variance Percentage	The size of the Fiscal Variance as a percentage of the budgeted cost (PV).
Float	The amount of time an activity may be delayed without impacting the project finish date. Also known as Slack.
Gantt Chart	A depiction of the project schedule utilizing a time scale. The tasks are listed vertically and the calendar is arranged horizontally. A bar appears next to each task name, under the calendar, indicating when the work is scheduled to be in progress. Can also be used to represent actual dates.
Incremental Data	EVM data generated by activity within a single reporting period.
Mitigation Activities	Tasks that are incorporated into the schedule to address particular known risks. Unlike Contingency Plans, these will be performed whether or not the associated risk event occurs.

Percent Concluded	The point along the project's duration where the work that was actually accomplished was scheduled to take place. It is expressed as a percentage of the Planned Duration.
Percent Elapsed	The percentage of the Planned Duration that has gone by through the data date.
Planned Duration	The amount of time that the project is scheduled to take as expressed in the Baseline Plan.
Planned Percent Complete	The portion of the total work scheduled to be performed as of the data date, expressed as a percentage of the total work.
Planned Percent Spent	The portion of the budget planned to be spent as of the data date, expressed as a percentage of the total budget.
Planned Time for Work Performed	A synonym for Earned Schedule.
Planned Time for Work Remaining	A synonym for Remaining Schedule.
Planned Value	The budgeted cost of the work planned to be performed during a given period. The Budgeted Cost of Work Scheduled.
Precedence Diagram	A type of flow chart or network diagram that explicitly depicts the relationships between the tasks.
Project	A vehicle through which customer needs can be met by performing activities and producing deliverables.

Project Control	The process of making tactical adjustments to the future portion of the Current Plan in order to improve the chances of meeting the Baseline Plan.
Project Execution	The process of performing activities in accordance with the project plan during the implementation phase of a project.
Project Manager	The person responsible for the proper planning and implementation of a project. The leader of the project team.
Project Plan	The entire collection of project requirements, tasks, resources, budgets, schedules, risks, etc. It describes the project objectives, the intended approach, and considerations that need to be addressed in order to meet the needs of the customer.
Project Team	The group of people performing the work of a project.
Quality (of a deliverable)	The degree to which a deliverable meets its intended specifications.
Remaining Schedule	The amount of time that was planned to perform the remaining work. The Planned Time for Work Remaining.
Remaining Time	The amount of time between the data date and the baseline project completion date. The Time Remaining to Complete.
Remaining Value	The amount of money budgeted in the baseline plan for the work yet to be performed. The Budgeted Cost of Work Remaining.

Requirements	The set of deliverables, constraints, and other considerations that must be met by the project team.
Reserve, Contingency	Funding set aside to cover Contingency Plans.
Reserve, Management	Funding set aside to cover unknown risks.
Resource	A person or an item needed in order to perform a task.
Risk	A future event, which may or may not occur, but if it does, will have a positive or negative impact on the project.
Schedule	The collection of planned start and finish dates for all of the project tasks.
Schedule Efficiency Improvement Factor	The improvement in schedule efficiency that will be necessary in order to achieve the schedule objectives.
Schedule Performance Index	The amount of work actually performed as a fraction of the work scheduled to be performed.
Schedule Variance	The difference between the values of the work actually performed and the work planned to be performed. It indicates how much more (or less) value was delivered than planned.
Schedule Variance Percentage	The size of the Schedule Variance as a percentage of the work scheduled (PV).
Slack	A synonym for float.
Specifications (of a deliverable)	The properties and acceptance criteria associated with a deliverable.

Spending Variance	A synonym for Fiscal Variance.
Stakeholder	A person with a role or an interest in a project.
Summary Task	A task that is composed of other tasks.
Task	An activity performed by the project team that is necessary to meet a project requirement.
Time Estimate at Completion	The latest forecast for the total actual duration of the project when it is completed.
Time Estimate to Complete	The forecast for how much time will actually be needed from today to perform the remaining work.
Time Remaining to Complete	A synonym for Remaining Time.
Time Variance at Completion	An indication of how much less (or more) time the project will take than planned.
Time Variance at Completion Percentage	As a percentage of the scheduled duration, the amount of time less (or more) the project is forecasted to take.
Time-Based Schedule Performance Index	The average schedule efficiency of the work actually performed.
Time-Based Schedule Variance	The difference in time between when a piece of work was scheduled to be done and when it was actually done.
Time-Based Schedule Variance Percentage	The size of the Time-Based Schedule Variance as a percentage of the Earned Schedule.

To-Complete Cost Performance Index	The projected average cost efficiency for all future work.
To-Complete Schedule Performance Index	The projected average schedule efficiency for all future work.
Tolerance Limit	The maximum amount of variation from the plan for a given measure that is deemed to be acceptable.
Top-Down Method	An estimating approach that uses analogy or a formula to assess the cost of the project without the benefit of individual task estimates.
Value	The budgeted cost to perform a piece of work.
Variance	The difference between the actual data and the baseline data for a particular measure. Also, the difference between the Current Plan and the Baseline Plan.
Variance at Completion	The forecast for how much under (or over) budget the project is expected to be when it is completed.
Variance at Completion Percentage	The forecast for how much under (or over) budget the project is expected to be when it is completed, expressed as a percentage of the baseline budget (BAC).
WBS Number	A label used to reference a particular element within a Work Breakdown Structure.
Work	The effort expended to produce a deliverable or meet another project requirement.

Work Breakdown Structure	A tool used to identify and organize the work of a project.
Work Package	An activity at the lowest level of the WBS. A task.
Work Product	The output of a task or work package.

Appendix C

QUESTIONS

There are a number of common questions that stakeholders may be interested in asking. Many of them can be answered by the data that are routinely generated by performing our normal EVM analyses. The tables in this appendix organize these questions into four categories. The answers are expressed using terms in the Modern Convention.

- ➲ Funding and Spending
- ➲ Cost
- ➲ Work
- ➲ Time

C-1 FUNDING AND SPENDING QUESTIONS

Question	Answer
How much money was planned to be spent to perform all of the work?	BAC
How much money was actually spent through today?	AC
How much money was planned to be spent through today?	PV
How much less (or more) money was spent than planned through today?	FV
What percentage less (or more) money was spent than planned through today?	FV%

How much money was planned to be spent for each dollar actually spent through today?	FPI
What portion of the budget was planned to be spent through today?	Planned % Spent
What portion of the budget was actually spent through today?	Actual % Spent
How much money in the budget has not yet been spent?	BR
How much money will be required to fund the entire project?	EAC
How much money will be required to perform the remaining work?	ETC
How much less (or more) funding will be required to perform the project than budgeted?	VAC
How much less (or more) funding will be required as a percentage of the budget?	VAC%

Table C-1: Funding and Spending Questions

C-2 COST-RELATED QUESTIONS

Question	Answer
How much money was budgeted to perform all of the work?	BAC
How much money was budgeted to perform the work accomplished so far?	EV
How much money was actually spent to perform the work accomplished so far?	AC
How much under (or over) budget was the work that was actually performed?	CV
What percentage under budget (or over budget) is the work that's been performed?	CV%

How much value was received for each dollar actually spent?	CPI
What portion of the budget was actually spent to perform the work accomplished so far?	Actual % Spent
What is the total project expected to cost when it is complete?	EAC
What is the remaining work expected to cost?	ETC
How much is the project expected to be under (or over) budget when it is complete?	VAC
By what percentage is the project expected to be under (or over) budget when it is complete?	VAC%
How much money was budgeted to perform the remaining work?	RV
What is the projected average cost efficiency of all future work?	TCPI
What future cost efficiency will need to be achieved in order to deliver the project on budget?	TCPI(BAC)
What improvement in cost efficiency will be necessary going forward in order to meet the cost objectives?	CIF

Table C-2: Cost-Related Questions

C-3 WORK-RELATED QUESTIONS

Question	Answer
What is the value of all the work to be performed?	BAC
How much work was planned to be performed through today?	PV
How much work was actually performed through today?	EV

How much more (or less) work was performed than what was planned?	SV
What percentage more work (or less work) was performed than planned?	SV%
What portion of the scheduled work has been actually performed?	SPI
What portion of the total work was planned to be complete through today?	Planned % Complete
What portion of the total work was actually completed through today?	Actual % Complete

Table C-3: Work-Related Questions

C-4 TIME-RELATED QUESTIONS

Question	Answer
How much time was planned to perform all of the work?	PD
How much time has passed since the beginning of the project?	AT
How much time should it have taken to perform the work that was actually accomplished?	ES
How much time is the project ahead of (or behind) schedule?	SV(t)
By what percentage of time is the project ahead of (or behind) schedule?	SV(t)%
How efficiently is the project making use of its time?	SPI(t)
What fraction of the project's time has gone by so far?	% Elapsed
At what fraction of the project's duration was the work performed scheduled to be done?	% Concluded
How much time is remaining from today until the planned project completion date?	RT

How much time was planned to perform the remaining work?	RS
When is the project expected to be completed?	EAC(t)
How much time is it expected to take in order to perform the remaining work?	ETC(t)
How much earlier (or later) than planned is the project expected to finish?	VAC(t)
By what percentage is the project expected to be completed earlier (or later)?	VAC(t)%
What is the projected average schedule efficiency of all future work?	TSPI
What future schedule efficiency will need to be achieved in order to finish the work on time?	TSPI(PD)
What improvement in schedule efficiency will be necessary going forward in order to meet the desired finish date?	SIF

Table C-4: Time-Related Questions

Appendix D

DIVISION WITH ZERO

D-1 INTRODUCTION

Early in the project, most of the task Planned Values, Earned Values, and Actual Costs are zero. This is because, at this time, few tasks have work scheduled to take place, few will actually have work done, and few will actually have money spent.

We have no problem calculating the variances in this situation. With variances, we are dealing with differences, i.e. with the operation of subtraction. Zeros behave very well under subtraction, and with addition and multiplication for that matter. Zeros and division, however, don't always get along.

Since the calculation of variance percentages and indexes involves division, there is always the possibility that we may encounter division by zero. How do we handle these situations when we need to divide with zero?

D-2 ZERO DIVIDED BY ZERO

Let's first look at the case where we have zero divided by zero. Our calculator will give us an "Error" message, but how do we actually deal with this?

Mathematically, zero divided by zero has no definition. We say that it is "undefined." Astute mathematicians can "prove" that zero divided by zero is 2. They can also prove that it is 100, or any other number that we could think of. Since there is no unique answer to this calculation, we say it is undefined or indeterminate.

What does this mean for us poor practitioners of EVM who simply want to calculate the values of some indicators? For us, zero divided by zero means that we have no useful information.

We would experience this in the situation where no work was planned to be done and no work was actually performed. We may also see this when no work was performed and no money spent. Either way, there is just nothing to evaluate.

So, whenever we see zero divided by zero, it's pretty easy to handle. We simply write "Not Applicable" or "NA" for short. Some people prefer to just enter a dash "–" instead. Any of these is OK.

$$\frac{0}{0} = \textit{No Information}$$

D-3 ZERO DIVIDED BY A NON-ZERO NUMBER

What if we see zero divided by some number other than zero? Let's call this non-zero number "N." Zero divided by any non-zero number is simply zero, as we can confirm by keying these numbers into our calculators.

$$\frac{0}{N} = 0 \qquad \text{if} \qquad N \neq 0$$

Here we do have a usable data point. A zero variance percentage means that things are going exactly as planned. It indicates the same situation as a zero variance.

A zero index means something different entirely. Remember that the neutral point for the indexes is 1 and not zero. An index less than 1 is bad. For example if we had a CPI equal to zero, we are definitely over budget because the index is less than 1. Since indexes can never be negative, a zero value for an index is as bad as it can get.

No matter what the tolerance limits are, a zero index means that we are automatically out of tolerance on the bad side. This works equally well for CPI, SPI($), SPI(t), and FPI.

D-4 A NON-ZERO NUMBER DIVIDED BY ZERO

Now let's look at the case where we have our non-zero number, N, divided by zero. Our calculator gives us an error indication. Mathematically, this is also undefined, however, we want to distinguish this situation from the earlier case where we had zero divided by zero. This is because here we do have some usable data to evaluate.

An example of a case where we could see this is if we started a task before its planned start date. Here we would have a positive SV with a zero PV, which obviously means that we are ahead of schedule. How do we describe it?

In this case we are going to define our answer to be "Infinity." For us, we can simply think of infinity as meaning a very large number.

$$\frac{N}{0} = \textit{Infinity} \qquad\qquad \text{if} \qquad\qquad N > 0$$

If N happens to be negative, we define the result as negative infinity.

$$\frac{N}{0} = -\textit{Infinity} \qquad\qquad \text{if} \qquad\qquad N < 0$$

If a variance percentage is at positive infinity, it is on the good side since anything greater than zero is good. This would mean that the indicator is automatically out of tolerance on the good side. We sometimes refer to this as too good to be true. This may or may not actually be a real problem, but we should do our due diligence and investigate just to convince ourselves that things are OK.

If we have an index at infinity, the same applies. We are also out of tolerance on the good side. No matter how large the tolerance limits are, infinity is greater than that.

If we have a variance percentage at negative infinity, this means we are automatically out of tolerance on the bad side. Since indexes can never be negative, we'll never experience negative infinities with them.

D-5 SUMMARY

Table D-1 summarizes the possible range of values for the variance percentages and the indexes. Table D-2 identifies the different situations where we might encounter division with zero. Remember that "Undefined" simply means we have no usable data. Table D-3 summarizes the interpretation of the results of the calculations for the variance percentages and for the indexes.

Note: Some software packages will display a result of zero where it really should be NA or infinity. We now know that this is technically incorrect. Obviously, an infinity means something wildly different than a zero. These software packages do this because it makes it easier to construct the report from their perspective. We should be on the lookout for these situations so that we can interpret our reports properly.

Indicator	Minimum Value	Maximum Value
CV%	– infinity	+ 100%
SV($)%	– 100%	+ infinity
SV(t)%	– infinity	+ 100%
FV%	– infinity	+ 100%
CPI	0	+ infinity
SPI($)	0	+ infinity
SPI(t)	0	+ infinity
FPI	0	+ infinity

Table D-1: Possible range of values

Indicator	−Infinity $\left[\dfrac{N}{0}\right]$ (N < 0)	Zero $\left[\dfrac{0}{N}\right]$ (N ≠ 0)	+Infinity $\left[\dfrac{N}{0}\right]$ (N > 0)	Undefined $\left[\dfrac{0}{0}\right]$
	Conditions required for the following values			
CV%	EV = 0 AC > 0	EV > 0 AC = EV	Not Possible	EV = 0 AC = 0
SV($)%	Not Possible	PV > 0 EV = PV	PV = 0 EV > 0	PV = 0 EV = 0
SV(t)%	ES = 0 AT > 0	ES > 0 AT = ES	Not Possible	ES = 0 AT = 0
FV%	PV = 0 AC > 0	PV > 0 AC = PV	Not Possible	PV = 0 AC = 0
CPI	Not Possible	EV = 0 AC > 0	EV > 0 AC = 0	EV = 0 AC = 0
SPI($)	Not Possible	EV = 0 PV > 0	EV > 0 PV = 0	EV = 0 PV = 0
SPI(t)	Not Possible	ES = 0 AT > 0	ES > 0 AT = 0	ES = 0 AT = 0
FPI	Not Possible	PV = 0 AC > 0	PV > 0 AC = 0	PV = 0 AC = 0

Table D-2: Summary of division with zero results

	−Infinity	Zero	+Infinity	Undefined
Variance Percentage	Automatically out of tolerance on the "bad" side. Not possible with SV($)%	On target	Automatically out of tolerance on the "good" side. Only possible with SV($)%	No usable data
Index	Not possible	Automatically out of tolerance on the "bad" side	Automatically out of tolerance on the "good" side	No usable data

Table D-3: Interpretation of division with zero results

Appendix E

SPI(t) VS SPI($) IN SCHEDULE ANALYSIS

There are two different Schedule Performance Indexes—one is time-based, SPI(t), and the other is value-based, SPI($). When using an index to forecast the time of the actual project completion date, or EAC(t), it would seem to be more appropriate to use the time-based index. As it turns out, this thinking is correct. Instead of just accepting this at face value, however, let's investigate the reasoning behind this assertion.

E-1 LINEAR EXAMPLE

Consider the case where the Planned Value and the Earned Value are both linear with time, i.e. their "curves" both appear as straight lines on the graph. An example of this, where the Earned Value is less than the Planned Value, can be seen in Figure E-1. Here SPI(t) and SPI($) will always equal each other until the Actual Time reaches the Planned Duration (or PD). After the Planned Duration, PV will equal the BAC, so PV turns into a horizontal line at that point.

[Note: If the Earned Value were to be greater than the Planned Value, the two indexes would equal each other until the actual completion date of the project, or at all times throughout the project lifetime.]

In this example, we are intentionally delaying progress so that the project will finish at Week 60 instead of Week 50 as planned. The forecasted EV curve is simply an extension of the Earned Value to date, so we are assuming that past performance will continue.

If we use SPI(t) as our TSPI, we will always get the correct EAC(t) of 60 weeks. If we use SPI($) instead, we will still get the correct result up to Week 50, since SPI($) equals SPI(t) up to that point. After Week 50, SPI($) fails to give the correct forecast.

For example, at Week 55, SPI($) underestimates the ETC(t) by about 11%. Admittedly, this effect is not that great in absolute terms since there is relatively little of the project remaining. The effect would be more significant, however, if this difference occurred earlier in the project.

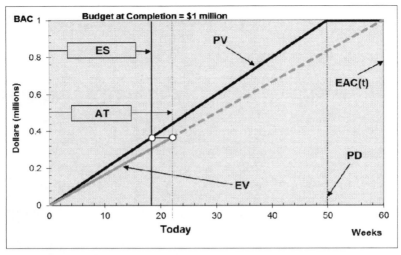

Figure E-1: SPI(t) = SPI($) up to PD for straight line "curves"

In summary, for the unusual case where PV and EV are both linear, using SPI(t) in our forecast will always yield the correct result. We can also confidently use SPI($) in our forecast up to the date of the Planned Duration since, during that period, it will always equal SPI(t) in value. After that, we should use SPI(t).

E-2 COMPARISON OF SPI(t) WITH SPI($) EARLY IN THE PROJECT

Of course, the Planned Value and the Earned Value are not, in general, linear. Even if they are not linear, they can often be approximated to be linear for a number of reporting periods very early in the project.

Remember that both the Planned Value and Earned Value curves are generated by connecting a series of straight lines between the data points for each reporting period. The example in Table E-1 shows the first three weeks of the cumulative PV and EV figures for a sample project.

Week	cum PV [$]	cum EV [$]
1	1000	850
2	2500	2150
3	4200	3650

Table E-1: Sample Project Status for Week 3

If we plot these points we get the graph in Figure E-2. The triangles represent the data points for PV and the squares represent the data points for EV. We then connect these data points with straight line segments to give us the "curves." Note that in this case, the EV is less than the PV.

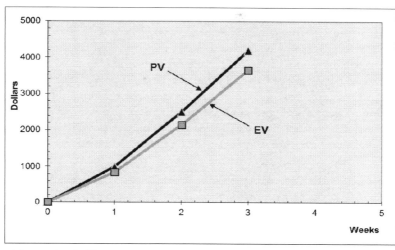

Figure E-2: PV and EV composed of a series of straight lines

Now we want to compute both Schedule Performance Indexes and see how they compare. The formulas, using the Modern Convention, are shown in Equation E-1 and Equation E-2.

$$SPI\ (\$) = \frac{EV}{PV} \tag{E-1}$$

$$SPI\ (t) = \frac{ES}{AT} \tag{E-2}$$

The results of the calculations appear in Table E-2, where AT just represents the current week.

AT [weeks]	cum PV [$]	cum EV [$]	SPI($)	ES [weeks]	SPI(t)	SPI Difference
1	1000	850	0.850	0.85	0.850	0
2	2500	2150	0.860	1.77	0.885	2.9%
3	4200	3650	0.869	2.68	0.893	2.8%

Table E-2: SPI comparison

Notice that in Week 1, both indexes are identical. At the end of the first reporting period, SPI($) will always equal SPI(t) if EV is less than PV. This is because both curves are straight lines from the origin up to that point. In this case we can use SPI($) in our forecast since it is easier to calculate than SPI(t).

For the next two reporting periods the indexes are no longer identical. The difference is still relatively small, however: 2.9% for Week 2 and 2.8% for Week 3. For the first several periods early in the project it may be an acceptable approximation to use SPI($) for forecasting instead of SPI(t).

There is a way to force the two indexes to agree for Weeks 2 and 3. Figure E-3 shows this force for Week 3 using the same data points as in Figure E-2. Here we have drawn straight lines from the origin to the Week 3 data points.

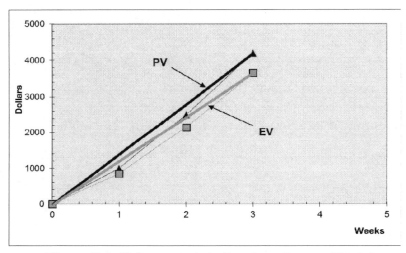

Figure E-3: Using a straight line from Start to Week 3

If we have straight lines from the origin to Week 3, we can do a revised calculation for Earned Schedule and also for SPI(t). The results appear in Table E-3, along with the results for Week 2 using the same approach.

AT [weeks]	cum PV [$]	cum EV [$]	SPI($)	ES [weeks]	SPI(t)	SPI Difference
1	1000	850	0.850	0.85	0.850	0
2	2500	2150	0.860	1.72	0.860	0
3	4200	3650	0.869	2.61	0.869	0

Table E-3: SPI Comparison with straight lines

Notice that the SPI($) figures are the same as before, but the Earned Schedule and the SPI(t) figures are slightly different. For each week, SPI(t) now equals SPI($). This is not surprising because the PV and EV curves are both straight lines from the origin to the current week.

What does this tell us? Since either approach yields the same SPI($), the SPI($) is insensitive to how we arrived at the current status. The SPI(t), however, is sensitive to the path we took to get where we are.

The added precision, by taking the intermediate data points into account, gives us a more accurate view of how the project schedule is unfolding. In other words, using value-based indicators ignores the history of how we arrived at this point. This is why we use time-based indexes for forecasting time.

Note that in our example we used the case where EV is less than PV. If EV were to be greater than PV, then even the first reporting period would not be comprised of two straight lines. We would need to take into account Planned Value data from two non-collinear line segments in order to determine the Earned Schedule. See Figure E-4.

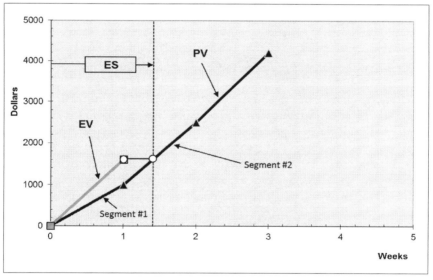

Figure E-4: First Reporting Period where EV > PV

This doesn't alter the assertion that the time-based index is better than the value-based index for forecasting. It does mean that SPI($) won't always equal SPI(t), even for the first reporting period, if EV is greater than PV.

E-3 COMPARISON OF SPI(t) WITH SPI($) LATER IN THE PROJECT

Many projects start with a gradual ramp-up of activity at the beginning, followed by an extended period of high activity, and ending with a gradual tapering at the end as the project winds down. In this case we will get the classical "S" curve for Planned Value shown in Figure E-5. Earned Value is also depicted as a smooth continuous curve.

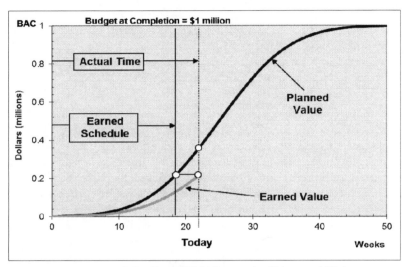

Figure E-5: Idealized "S" Curve for Planned Value

If we were to zoom in on the curves at the very beginning of the project, they may be able to be approximated as nearly straight lines as we saw in the last section. That approach can break down once we get further out into the project.

If we look at the status as of today, Week 22, we can see that PV equals approximately $360,000 and EV is approximately $215,000. We can compute SPI($) and find that it is 0.60. Earned Schedule is about 18.3 weeks so SPI(t) comes out to be about 0.83. This is a difference of 38%, which is significant.

Now instead of following the curves, let's draw straight lines from the origin to today's data for both PV and EV. We can see that depicted in Figure E-6.

Notice that the Earned Schedule has radically decreased to be about 13 weeks. The SPI($) is the same 0.60 since the PV and EV values have not changed. We expect SPI(t) to equal SPI($) using this approach. If we do the calculation, using our approximated values here, we get 0.59 for SPI(t). The difference is just due to rounding.

As we can see, SPI(t) can be forced to agree with SPI($) by ignoring history and only using today's data. The difference between the two approaches is even more striking here than it was very early in the project.

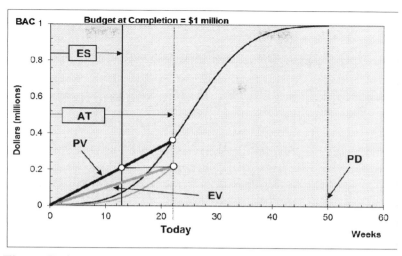

Figure E-6: PV and EV depicted as straight lines through Today

Again, using SPI(t) allows us to take advantage of history by considering how the project unfolded over time to get to the current point. On the other hand, if we believe that straight lines are a good approximation of the PV and EV curves, we can confidently use SPI($) in our forecasts.

E-4 SUMMARY

It is always appropriate to use SPI(t) in time forecasting as opposed to SPI($). There are many situations where SPI($) is sufficiently close to the value of SPI(t) and so its use may be acceptable.

SPI(t) will equal SPI($) if both PV and EV are linear with time. The indexes will be equal to each other during the first period if EV is less than PV. The two indexes will usually be nearly equal to each other during the first reporting period even if EV is greater than PV.

Both indexes will typically be nearly equal to each other very early in the project after the first reporting period. In this case it may be acceptable to use SPI($) in our forecasts, since the calculation is much simpler than that for SPI(t).

As we get further along, the two can disagree significantly. In this case, it would be more appropriate to use SPI(t) in our forecast.

Appendix F

FORMULA SUMMARY

Here we have collected all of the formulas that have been gradually developed through the chapters of this book. They are divided into two groups. The first group represents the Modern Convention. The second group repeats these formulas, but in terms of the Traditional Convention.

As a reminder, the value-based schedule indicators can be written two ways, as can be seen in the following table. The formulas in this appendix are expressed using the implicit forms of these indicators.

Implicit Form	Explicit Form
SV	$SV(\$)$
$SV\%$	$SV(\$)\%$
SPI	$SPI(\$)$

F-1 MODERN CONVENTION

Basic Elements
$PV = BAC \times (\textit{Planned \% Complete})$
$EV = BAC \times (\textit{Actual \% Complete})$
$ES = Date_1 + (Date_2 - Date_1) \times \dfrac{(EV - PV_1)}{(PV_2 - PV_1)}$

Variances
$FV = PV - AC$
$CV = EV - AC$
$SV = EV - PV$
$SV(t) = ES - AT$
$SV(t) = RT - RS$

Variance Relationships
$FV = CV - SV$
$CV = SV + FV$
$SV = CV - FV$

Variance Percentages	
$CV\% = \dfrac{CV}{EV}$	$CV\% = 1 - \dfrac{AC}{EV}$
$SV\% = \dfrac{SV}{PV}$	$SV\% = \dfrac{EV}{PV} - 1$
$FV\% = \dfrac{FV}{PV}$	$FV\% = 1 - \dfrac{AC}{PV}$
$SV(t)\% = \dfrac{SV(t)}{ES}$	$SV(t)\% = 1 - \dfrac{AT}{ES}$

Variance Percentage Relationships
$FV\% = 1 - (1 - CV\%)(1 + SV\%)$
$FV\% = CV\% - SV\% + (CV\%)(SV\%)$
$SV\% = \dfrac{1 - FV\%}{1 - CV\%} - 1$
$CV\% = 1 - \dfrac{1 - FV\%}{1 + SV\%}$

Indexes	
$CPI = \dfrac{EV}{AC}$	$CPI = \dfrac{Actual\ \%\ Complete}{Actual\ \%\ Spent}$
$SPI = \dfrac{EV}{PV}$	$SPI = \dfrac{Actual\ \%\ Complete}{Planned\ \%\ Complete}$
$FPI = \dfrac{PV}{AC}$	$FPI = \dfrac{Planned\ \%\ Spent}{Actual\ \%\ Spent}$
$SPI(t) = \dfrac{ES}{AT}$	$SPI(t) = \dfrac{\%\ Concluded}{\%\ Elapsed}$

Index to Variance% Relationships	
$CV\% = 1 - \dfrac{1}{CPI}$	$CPI = \dfrac{1}{1 - CV\%}$
$SV\% = SPI - 1$	$SPI = SV\% + 1$
$FV\% = 1 - \dfrac{1}{FPI}$	$FPI = \dfrac{1}{1 - FV\%}$
$SV(t)\% = 1 - \dfrac{1}{SPI(t)}$	$SPI(t) = \dfrac{1}{1 - SV(t)\%}$

Proportionate Progress
$Planned \ \% \ Complete = \dfrac{PV}{BAC}$
$Planned \ \% \ Spent = \dfrac{PV}{BAC}$
$Actual \ \% \ Complete = \dfrac{EV}{BAC}$
$Actual \ \% \ Spent = \dfrac{AC}{BAC}$
$\% \ Elapsed = \dfrac{AT}{PD}$
$\% \ Concluded = \dfrac{ES}{PD}$

Cost Forecasting [Always true]	
$BAC = AC + BR$	$BR = BAC - AC$
$BAC = EV + RV$	$RV = BAC - EV$
$EAC = AC + ETC$	$ETC = EAC - AC$
$ETC = \dfrac{RV}{TCPI}$	
$ETC = \dfrac{BAC - EV}{TCPI}$	
$VAC = BAC - EAC$	
$VAC \% = \dfrac{VAC}{BAC}$	
$VAC \% = 1 - \dfrac{EAC}{BAC}$	

Cost Forecasting [Only true when TCPI = CPI]
$EAC = \dfrac{AC}{Actual\ \%\ Complete}$
$EAC = \dfrac{BAC}{CPI}$
$VAC\% = CV\%$

Cost Forecasting [Only true when TCPI = 1]
$ETC = RV$
$ETC = BAC - EV$
$EAC = BAC - CV$
$VAC = CV$

Meeting Cost Targets
$TCPI = \dfrac{RV}{ETC}$
$TCPI = \dfrac{BAC - EV}{EAC - AC}$
$TCPI\,(BAC) = \dfrac{BAC - EV}{BAC - AC}$
$CIF = \dfrac{TCPI - CPI}{CPI}$

Schedule Forecasting [Always true]	
$PD = AT + RT$	$RT = PD - AT$
$PD = ES + RS$	$RS = PD - ES$
$EAC(t) = AT + ETC(t)$	$ETC(t) = EAC(t) - AT$
$ETC(t) = \dfrac{RS}{TSPI}$	
$ETC(t) = \dfrac{PD - ES}{TSPI}$	
$VAC(t) = PD - EAC(t)$	
$VAC(t)\% = \dfrac{VAC(t)}{PD}$	
$VAC(t)\% = 1 - \dfrac{EAC(t)}{PD}$	

Schedule Forecasting [Only true when TSPI = SPI(t)]
$EAC(t) = \dfrac{AT}{\% \ Concluded}$
$EAC(t) = \dfrac{PD}{SPI(t)}$
$VAC(t)\% = SV(t)\%$

Schedule Forecasting [Only true when TSPI = 1]
$ETC(t) = RS$
$ETC(t) = PD - ES$
$EAC(t) = PD - SV(t)$
$VAC(t) = SV(t)$

Meeting Schedule Targets
$TSPI = \dfrac{RS}{ETC\,(t)}$
$TSPI = \dfrac{PD - ES}{EAC\,(t) - AT}$
$TSPI\,(PD) = \dfrac{PD - ES}{PD - AT}$
$SIF = \dfrac{TSPI - SPI\,(t)}{SPI\,(t)}$

F-2 TRADITIONAL CONVENTION

Basic Elements
$BCWS = BAC \times (Planned~\%~Complete)$
$BCWP = BAC \times (Actual~\%~Complete)$
$PTWP = Date_1 + (Date_2 - Date_1) \times \dfrac{(BCWP - BCWS_1)}{(BCWS_2 - BCWS_1)}$

Variances
$FV = BCWS - ACWP$
$CV = BCWP - ACWP$
$SV = BCWP - BCWS$
$SV(t) = PTWP - ATWP$
$SV(t) = TRTC - PTWR$

Variance Relationships
$FV = CV - SV$
$CV = SV + FV$
$SV = CV - FV$

Variance Percentages	
$CV\% = \dfrac{CV}{BCWP}$	$CV\% = 1 - \dfrac{ACWP}{BCWP}$
$SV\% = \dfrac{SV}{BCWS}$	$SV\% = \dfrac{BCWP}{BCWS} - 1$
$FV\% = \dfrac{FV}{BCWS}$	$FV\% = 1 - \dfrac{ACWP}{BCWS}$
$SV(t)\% = \dfrac{SV(t)}{PTWP}$	$SV(t)\% = 1 - \dfrac{ATWP}{PTWP}$

Variance Percentage Relationships
$FV\% = 1 - (1 - CV\%)(1 + SV\%)$
$FV\% = CV\% - SV\% + (CV\%)(SV\%)$
$SV\% = \dfrac{1 - FV\%}{1 - CV\%} - 1$
$CV\% = 1 - \dfrac{1 - FV\%}{1 + SV\%}$

Indexes	
$CPI = \dfrac{BCWP}{ACWP}$	$CPI = \dfrac{Actual\ \%\ Complete}{Actual\ \%\ Spent}$
$SPI = \dfrac{BCWP}{BCWS}$	$SPI = \dfrac{Actual\ \%\ Complete}{Planned\ \%\ Complete}$
$FPI = \dfrac{BCWS}{ACWP}$	$FPI = \dfrac{Planned\ \%\ Spent}{Actual\ \%\ Spent}$
$SPI(t) = \dfrac{PTWP}{ATWP}$	$SPI(t) = \dfrac{\%\ Concluded}{\%\ Elapsed}$

Index to Variance% Relationships

$CV\% = 1 - \dfrac{1}{CPI}$	$CPI = \dfrac{1}{1 - CV\%}$
$SV\% = SPI - 1$	$SPI = SV\% + 1$
$FV\% = 1 - \dfrac{1}{FPI}$	$FPI = \dfrac{1}{1 - FV\%}$
$SV(t)\% = 1 - \dfrac{1}{SPI(t)}$	$SPI(t) = \dfrac{1}{1 - SV(t)\%}$

Proportionate Progress

$$Planned\ \%\ Complete = \frac{BCWS}{BAC}$$

$$Planned\ \%\ Spent = \frac{BCWS}{BAC}$$

$$Actual\ \%\ Complete = \frac{BCWP}{BAC}$$

$$Actual\ \%\ Spent = \frac{ACWP}{BAC}$$

$$\%\ Elapsed = \frac{ATWP}{PD}$$

$$\%\ Concluded = \frac{PTWP}{PD}$$

Cost Forecasting [Always True]	
$BAC = ACWP + BRTC$	$BRTC = BAC - ACWP$
$BAC = BCWP + BCWR$	$BCWR = BAC - BCWP$
$EAC = ACWP + ETC$	$ETC = EAC - ACWP$
$ETC = \dfrac{BCWR}{TCPI}$	
$ETC = \dfrac{BAC - BCWP}{TCPI}$	
$VAC = BAC - EAC$	
$VAC\% = \dfrac{VAC}{BAC}$	
$VAC\% = 1 - \dfrac{EAC}{BAC}$	

Cost Forecasting [Only true when TCPI = CPI]
$EAC = \dfrac{ACWP}{Actual \ \% \ Complete}$
$EAC = \dfrac{BAC}{CPI}$
$VAC\% = CV\%$

Cost Forecasting
[Only true when TCPI = 1]
$ETC = BCWR$
$ETC = BAC - BCWP$
$EAC = BAC - CV$
$VAC = CV$

Meeting Cost Targets
$TCPI = \dfrac{BCWR}{ETC}$
$TCPI = \dfrac{BAC - BCWP}{EAC - ACWP}$
$TCPI\,(BAC) = \dfrac{BAC - BCWP}{BAC - ACWP}$
$CIF = \dfrac{TCPI - CPI}{CPI}$

Schedule Forecasting [Always true]	
$PD = ATWP + TRTC$	$TRTC = PD - ATWP$
$PD = PTWP + PTWR$	$PTWR = PD - PTWP$
$EAC(t) = ATWP + ETC(t)$	$ETC(t) = EAC(t) - ATWP$
$$ETC(t) = \frac{PTWR}{TSPI}$$	
$$ETC(t) = \frac{PD - PTWP}{TSPI}$$	
$$VAC(t) = PD - EAC(t)$$	
$$VAC(t)\% = \frac{VAC(t)}{PD}$$	
$$VAC(t)\% = 1 - \frac{EAC(t)}{PD}$$	

Schedule Forecasting [Only true when TSPI = SPI(t)]
$$EAC(t) = \frac{ATWP}{\% \ Concluded}$$
$$EAC(t) = \frac{PD}{SPI(t)}$$
$$VAC(t)\% = SV(t)\%$$

Schedule Forecasting [Only true when TSPI = 1]
$ETC(t) = PTWR$
$ETC(t) = PD - PTWP$
$EAC(t) = PD - SV(t)$
$VAC(t) = SV(t)$

Meeting Schedule Targets
$TSPI = \dfrac{PTWR}{ETC(t)}$
$TSPI = \dfrac{PD - PTWP}{EAC(t) - ATWP}$
$TSPI(PD) = \dfrac{PD - PTWP}{PD - ATWP}$
$SIF = \dfrac{TSPI - SPI(t)}{SPI(t)}$

INDEX

E

F

G

K

M

P

Q